From Lt. Richard E. Miller's observation of the trail, he had decided that the NVA rarely moved in the area before 0800 so he requested the extractions for 0600. As the team carefully crossed the trail and moved toward the bomb craters, they discovered just how precarious their position had been. According to Miller, "This is when we got a real shock. It turned out we had picked the only wooded area on the hill. When we moved we found the rest of the area looked like Golden State Park—a tree here, a tree ten meters away, but all the underbrush, all the secondary canopy down around the ground, had been cleared away. There were sleeping hooches all over the area—little lean-tos they had built. We were right in the middle of a base area and they were just waking up."

Miller's team quietly moved on through the NVA base camp. A few minutes later they reached the bomb craters where a helicopter dropped a ladder to them. In seconds the Marines hooked on and were lifted from the jungle leaving the enemy unaware they had been observed. Bomb strikes and artillery soon interrupted their complacency. . . .

Also by Michael Lee Lanning
Published by Ivy Books:

THE ONLY WAR WE HAD:
A Platoon Leader's Journal of Vietnam

VIETNAM 1969–1970:
A Company Commander's Journal

INSIDE THE LRRPS: Rangers in Vietnam

THE BATTLES OF PEACE

INSIDE FORCE RECON: Recon Marines in Vietnam

**Michael Lee Lanning
and
Ray William Stubbe**

IVY BOOKS • NEW YORK

Ivy Books
Published by Ballantine Books
Copyright © 1989 by Michael Lee Lanning and
Ray William Stubbe

Library of Congress Catalog Card Number: 89-91134

ISBN 0-8041-0301-1

Manufactured in the United States of America

First Edition: July 1989
Seventh Printing: June 1992

CONTENTS
❖❖❖❖❖❖❖

FOREWORD
========

General P. X. Kelley
28th Commandant of the Marine Corps

> We must remember that one man is much the same as
> another, and that he is best who is trained in the severest
> school.

> Thucydides: *History of the Peloponnesian War*

During my thirty-seven years of service to my country
as a Marine officer, I was privileged to command at every
echelon from platoon to division, including command of
an infantry battalion and an infantry regiment in combat.
It should go without saying that to command fellow Marines on the battlefield is the greatest honor that can be
bestowed on a Marine, whether he is a noncommissioned
officer, staff noncommissioned officer, or commissioned
officer.

Aside from the command of Marines in combat, my
next most rewarding professional experience during almost four decades of service was the command of a fledg-
ling Force Reconnaissance Company as a young captain.

During February 1958, having just completed seven
weeks as a student in the Army's Pathfinder Course at Fort
Benning, Georgia, I reported to Force Troops, Fleet Marine Force, Atlantic, as the prospective executive officer
of the Second Force Reconnaissance Company, which was

to be activated on 1 April 1958. During the next two and one-half years I served this unique organization both as executive officer and commanding officer. And so, when I read names like Maj J. Z. Taylor, our first commanding officer, and Capt Donald E. Koelper, our first operations officer, they bring back vivid memories of those superb Marines who were there "at the creation."

During the late fifties and early sixties, the Marines of the First and Second Force Reconnaissance Companies pioneered new and dynamic techniques in static-line and free-fall parachuting, scuba diving, buoyant ascent submarine escape, long-range radio communications, Fulton Sky Hook pickups, beach and hydrographic survey, underwater sound communications, etc., not to mention the fact that they were the best damned reconnaissance men in the business. By any standard, they were Marines of extraordinary courage, determination, and professionalism.

From 1962 to 1964, I served as reconnaissance officer at the Marine Corps Landing Force Development Center. It was there that I worked closely with the next generation of Marines assigned to the two Force Reconnaissance companies, and I was extremely impressed by the fact that, if anything, they had improved upon the legacy passed to them by their forebears. These were the Marines who sharpened and honed the reconnaissance skills which would prove to be so effective in Vietnam.

LtCol Lee Lanning and Chaplain Ray Stubbe have done their country and the Marine Corps a great service by their book *Inside Force Recon.* It is the intimate story of a small group of heroic Marines whose contributions to the success of Marine operations in a "tough and dirty" war were of inestimable value. Moreover, it is a story of imaginative and innovative tactics and techniques—the hallmark of the Marine Corps. For a Marine of any generation, it is must reading.

Many who know them would agree that Marines are a

paradox. On the one hand, they find great strength in reflecting back upon their history and traditions. On the other, they constantly look forward to insure that they are fully prepared for the next war. When I look forward, I see conventional warfare, low-intensity conflict in particular, as the most likely battlefield of the future. It is on this battlefield that I further see a preeminent role for our Force Reconnaissance companies. Others may argue that "black boxes" will eventually play the vital intelligence role of such units, but I firmly believe that the obfuscation of combat will always require the well-calibrated eyeballs of a Marine.

Just prior to my retirement, the Force Recon Association asked me to be the guest of honor at their annual reunion. It was an evening of nostalgia, one shared with many of the finest Marines in the history of our Corps. As the evening drew to a close and we paid our respects to our departed comrades, with a tear in my eye I asked the question, "Lord, where do we get such men?"

—General P. X. Kelley
28th Commandant of the Marine Corps

INTRODUCTION

*I*T might seem unusual for a Navy chaplain and an Army infantryman to team together to write about Force Recon Marines. Perhaps it is—and is not—for Ray Stubbe and I were determined to tell their story.

Ray W. Stubbe was both chaplain to and friend of the recon Marines at the Khe Sanh Combat Base from July 1967 to March 1968, and at Dong Ha from April to June 1968. While stationed at Parris Island, South Carolina, after his return to the United States, he performed the unenviable task of accompanying teams that notified the families of recon Marines of their sons' and husbands' deaths in Vietnam.

In 1974, Stubbe was assigned to Camp Pendleton, California, where he regularly participated in physical training with the First Force Reconnaissance Company while assigned as the unit's chaplain under "Additional Duty Orders." When the First Company was deactivated in September of that year, Stubbe presented each of the attendees a brief history, which he had compiled in his off-duty hours, of the unit. Many of the recon Marines at the ceremony expressed interest in adding their personal experiences and recollections to the story. Some of those who were particularly helpful included Bruce H. Norton, Eugene Bliss, Joseph Z. Taylor, James Jones, Ernie DeFazio, Regin Fuller, Kenneth Houghton, L. V. "Reb" Bearce, James Steele, David Whittingham, and Patrick J.

Ryan. (The complete list of those interviewed will be found in the bibliography.)

These interviews, combined with numerous individual award citations and reports retrieved from the First Company's discarded records, resulted in a 200-page history of the unit. A copy of this expanded manuscript was forwarded to the Marine Corps History and Museums Division, where its director, BrigGen Edwin H. Simmons, encouraged Stubbe to journey to Washington, D.C., to peruse the official records. With the assistance of Simmons's staff, including Morris Perry, Joyce Bonnett, H. M. Hart, Russell Tiffany, Benis Frank, Bob Fitzgerald, Mary Edmonds, Ralph Donnelly, and Dale Shedd, Stubbe gathered material to expand the work to over 1,200 manuscript pages. This version of Force Recon history, titled "Paddles, Parachutes, and Patrols," was completed in July 1976.

Continuing to revise and add to the history over the years, Stubbe completed another version in 1981 titled "Aarugha"—a yell of enthusiastic approval by recon Marines which likely originated from the sound made by the klaxon of a submerging submarine. By 1985, various editions of the history were in the hands of former recon Marines as well as many senior Marine officers. One copy eventually made its way to Owen Lock at Ballantine/Ivy in New York. Lock was interested in the manuscript, but found it too lengthy and technical to appeal to a general audience.

My experience with reconnaissance and elite units began with my attending the Army's Ranger School in 1968 and was reinforced by my assignment in Vietnam in 1969–70, where I served as an infantry platoon leader, reconnaissance platoon leader, and infantry company commander in the 199th Light Infantry Brigade. After Vietnam, I was an instructor in the Ranger School Florida Phase during 1970–72. My interest in writing about reconnaissance units followed my first two books, *The Only War We Had: A Platoon Leader's Journal of Vietnam* and *Vietnam 1969-70: A Company Commander's Journal.*

By the summer of 1987, I had just completed the final draft of a history of the U.S. Army's equivalent to the Marines' Force Recon, titled, *Inside the LRRPS: Rangers in Vietnam.* A short time after delivery of the manuscript to Ivy Books, Lock suggested that I contact Stubbe's agent to see if we could collaborate to revise his "Force Recon language" manuscript into a work of interest to the general public and the military professional. I responded that I had written my last book on Vietnam, but to placate Lock (you do that sort of thing when a New York editor asks), I agreed to give Stubbe's manuscript a read.

One reading was enough. The story of Force Recon was one that had to be told. A deal was soon struck, and a Navy chaplain and an Army infantryman began work on the history of the Marine Corps Force Reconnaissance.

Ray Stubbe and I would like to express our thanks to Owen Lock for the idea of our partnership and to Russ Galen of the Scott Meredith Literary Agency for making it happen. Finally, Ray and I are extremely grateful to the men of Force Recon who shared their stories and personal papers, and to the USMC History and Museums Reference Section, which catered to our every request. Without their help, this book would not have been possible.

—M. L. L.

Tempe, Arizona

March 1989

CHAPTER 1

An Elite within an Elite

Even the more routine exploits of the Marine Force Reconnaissance companies in Vietnam are the kind that could provide the inspiration from which movies could have been made, books written, and songs sung. Had Vietnam shared the "good war" status of World War II, the men of Force Recon would have had schools, streets, and possibly even a few babies named after them. Yet Vietnam was neither a "good" nor a "popular" war, and conflicts without that status, particularly those that end in defeat, do not lend themselves to the immortalization of their participants, however outstanding their records.

Regardless of popular sentiment about the war at the time, or however history will ultimately record the performance of those who fought, the accomplishments of the Force Recon Marines in Vietnam matched or exceeded the proud traditions of over two centuries of Corps service to its country. Operating in four- to eight-man teams, the patrols of the Force Reconnaissance companies ventured far from other friendly units into the backyard of the enemy. Using tactics and techniques more often associated with their adversary than with the United States military, recon Marines carried the war into former enemy sanctuaries.

The Force Recon Marines were the eyes and ears of the units they served. Information gathered by the recon teams, often in the midst of enemy defensive complexes and assembly areas, provided senior headquarters with intelligence for the planning of operations and the countering of offensive buildups. Although reconnaissance was the primary mission of the Force Recon companies, the patrols often produced body counts in greater numbers than much larger units. No enemy element, regardless of size, was safe from the small patrols. Large enemy forces were cut to pieces by artillery and air strikes accurately guided onto their targets by Force Recon. Small enemy groups were vulnerable to the small arms carried by patrols that often lay in silent, well-camouflaged ambush for days. If a lone soldier or lightly armed enemy group wandered into the recon team's patrol zone, they were likely to be added to the impressive number of live prisoners that Force Recon accounted for.

Respected by friend and feared by foe, the Marines of Force Recon in Vietnam were known for their professionalism and dedication. Martin Russ, one of the few journalists to accompany a Force Recon patrol on a mission, was impressed by his observations of a team being briefed by their helicopter insertion pilots in 1967. Russ later wrote, "I noticed they stared surreptitiously at the team with something like awe. Force Recon has a semilegendary reputation; they're the Commandos of the Corps."[1]

In reality, the reputation of Force Recon was based not on legend, but on facts. According to statistics kept by Maj James Steele during 1967, while he served in the Intelligence Section of the senior Marine headquarters in Vietnam—the III Marine Amphibious Force—the kill ratio for infantry was 7.6 enemy for one Marine.[2] By contrast, Force Recon accounted for 34 dead for each of their own killed in battle. This equated to a mortality rate of 20 percent for a one-year tour in the Marine infantry as opposed to 6 percent for Force Recon.

Infantry troops required about seven tons of supporting-fire ordnance to produce a body count, but the recon Marine required only two tons for the same results. Comparisons of field time were equally impressive, with the infantry requiring 480 man-days per kill and Force Recon only 171.

Steele's study produced one statistic that is perhaps even more impressive than all the others combined: in infantry units, 80 percent of the contacts were initiated by the enemy; Force Recon, which prided itself on stealth, deliberation, camouflage, and patience, was first engaged by the enemy in only 5 percent of its contacts. In 95 percent of their engagements, the recon men determined that it was to their advantage and not the enemy's to begin a fight.

Despite the proficiency of the Force Recon units in Vietnam, little was written about them then, and even less has appeared since. Much of this lack of recognition was not just the nature of the Vietnam War, but is based on the personality and traditions of Force Recon itself. Recon Marines were extremely well prepared, fiercely aggressive, and supremely confident. At the same time, the success of their missions depended on secrecy, silence, and remaining undetected. Habitual clandestine behavior carried over into an avoidance of news coverage and public recognition. Not to be overlooked, however, is the Force Recon Marines' self-awareness: they knew they were good and sought no recognition other than that from their own.

A final insight on the behavior of Force Recon members is that they were first and foremost Marines—any additional indication of superior status was superfluous. A lesson plan for the indoctrination of volunteers for Force Recon summarized this attitude by stating: ''The Recon Marine is no more and no less than an infantryman with special skills. He is not a superman, nor is he really a particularly special kind of Marine. He is simply and proudly a Marine doing a job which has to be done. The reconnaissance unit is a support unit which works for other people. Its mission of reconnaissance is a means to an end, not an end in itself."[3]

While the Vietnam-era Force Recon Marines did not actively seek accolades, they received praise nonetheless. In 1970 LtGen Raymond G. Davis, former deputy commander of XXIV Corps and commanding general of the 3rd Marine Division in Vietnam, addressed a joint service symposium in El Paso, Texas. Davis spoke of the accomplishments by the US and ARVN forces in the northern provinces of Vietnam in finding and destroying enemy safe havens, hospital sites, and logistic bases. According to the general, this success was the result of highly sophisticated intelligence-gathering capabilities. Davis concluded:

> Our most reliable intelligence came from small four- or six-man Marine patrols. Throughout the province, as many as forty of these teams were maintained on the ground in operation at all times—thereby providing a positive and rapid means of checking out indications of enemy activity anywhere. As a result, we knew with some precision where the enemy was located, what he was doing, and, just as important, where he was not.[4]

Maj Bryon A. Norberg, who saw daily the results of the Force Recon patrols as Ground Surveillance Officer in the III MAF Intelligence Section, shared Davis's admiration for the recon Marines. In an oral history interview about Force Recon at the time, Norberg stated:

> We ask a great deal of these men when they go out there. They become very skilled in the use of supporting arms, very knowledgeable about their jobs;

they're well motivated and highly disciplined. They work extraordinarily well together, and one gets the feeling that these are truly professional men. These men are first and foremost good Marines. It becomes very clear that their capability to perform their job is directly related to their first identifying themselves as being some of the very best Marines we have.[5]

The reputation of Force Recon was firmly established even before the United States, involvement in Southeast Asia. This preparation paid benefits not only to the recon units themselves, but also to many Marines who honed their leadership skills and developed their tactical knowledge in peacetime assignments in Force Recon prior to the conflict. William Weise commanded the 2nd Battalion, 4th Marines in 1968–69 in Vietnam and later was promoted to brigadier general before retiring from his last assignment as the Deputy Commander, Marine Corps Recruit Depot, Parris Island, South Carolina. Concerning his time in Force Recon from November 1960 to August 1962, Weise says:

There's no doubt that my tour with First Force had to be the greatest peacetime experience of my career. Working with and learning from so many superb leaders did more to prepare me for combat leadership than anything else I have done, before or since. I could talk on and on about their drive to meet any challenge—the tougher the better, their love of excitement, and their calm, cool competence in times of stress.[6]

Marine Force Reconnaissance in Vietnam was perhaps a near-perfect solution to an imperfect war. Much of its success was predicated on the Marines' willingness to adapt to a new kind of battlefield and to determinedly pursue success with every new challenge. Although this narrative focuses on the war in Southeast Asia, the spirit and professionalism of Force Recon was bred and nurtured during conflicts dating back to the early part of this century. What Force Recon became in Vietnam was directly influenced by the valor and dedication of those recon men that preceded them.

CHAPTER 2

○=○=○=○=○=○=○

The Early Days—Beginnings Through World War II

*A*LTHOUGH the history of the United States Marine Corps since its establishment in 1775 is marked by valorous deeds and magnificent victories, it was not until the twentieth century that reconnaissance played a significant role in the successes of the Corps. Early reconnaissance efforts were generally limited to surveys of uncharted ports, islands, and coastlines. These surveys, usually conducted by the various explorations of the US Navy and directly supervised by a ship's or fleet's intelligence officer, were efforts at mapping rather than war planning. Some nautical charts still in use today of remote sea areas and islands bear annotations that the data was compiled by Marine officers, who traditionally filled the intelligence billets, well over a century ago.

Of the 180 amphibious landings by the Marines prior to World War II, only three—Sumatra in 1832, Drummonds Island in 1841, and Mexico in 1870—were preceded by reconnaissance forces.[1] The reasons for this lack of reconnaissance are many; however, the principal factor was in the overall lack of development of amphibious warfare in general. It was not until the Spanish-American War of 1898 that interest of Naval war planners began to focus on the seizure, preparation for, and defense of forward land bases. Another factor that delayed the formation of Marine recon units, once doctrine began to be formulated on amphibious operations, was that the key to successful beach assaults was surprise. The possibility that detected recon forces might alert the enemy to an impending invasion was of much concern.

The first formal American doctrine for amphibious reconnaissance did not appear until 1906.[2] Maj Dion Williams, USMC, a veteran of the Battle of Manila Bay and commander of the company that raised the war's first US flag on Spanish soil at Cavite, PI, wrote for the Naval War College. He outlined recon requirements and responsibilities ranging from sea to shore and from the beach inland and stressed the need for information on hydrographics, harbors, beaches, built-up areas, and established defenses.

Williams also recommended that only specially talented and experienced men be selected for reconnaissance missions. He listed such qualifications as technical knowledge, an energetic nature to ensure the work was accomplished without unnecessary delay, sufficient resourcefulness to overcome unexpected obstacles, reticence, and above all, exactitude of work. Mastery in surveying and in mapmaking and reading, along with the ability to accurately record observations, were deemed critical.

Williams updated his book in 1917 with significant changes.[3] He added the use of aircraft and submarines, and emphasized acquiring information for long-term planning instead of gathering intelligence strictly for military operations in progress. Williams outlined a more comprehensive mission stating,

> The object of naval reconnaissance of any given locality is to acquire all of the information concerning the sea, land, air, and material resources of that locality, with a view to its use by the Navy in peace

and war, and to record this information that it may
be most readily available for the preparation of plans
for the occupation of the locality as a temporary or
permanent naval base; the preparation of plans for the
sea and land defense of the locality when used as such
a base; or the preparation of plans for the attack of
the locality by sea and land should it be in possession
of an enemy.

While Williams's writings were significant in the development of reconnaissance philosophy, the actual practical
application of the concepts was virtually nonexistent during the first quarter of the twentieth century. This lack of
progress was not merely a manner of complacency but
rather was a result of the historical period itself. The static,
trench conflict of the First World War offered little opportunity for amphibious warfare. One of the few attempts to
conduct an amphibious operation was the ill-fated attack
at Gallipoli in 1915. Its failure dampened further pursuit
of such tactics.

Following the war, the policy of isolationism, combined
with the austerity of the 1920s and 1930s, forced extensive
personnel reductions in the Corps. What few Marines were
available were assigned to such hot spots as China and
Nicaragua, with little time to experiment with new concepts.

While Williams was refining the written doctrine for
amphibious reconnaissance, another Marine major was
leading the way in the practical application of the concepts. Earl H. Ellis[4] was a man lured by the unknown and
attracted to the novel. After being commissioned in 1900,
Ellis served in the Philippines, Japan, Guam, and Saipan,
and he later was awarded the Navy Cross* for actions in
World War I.

*The Navy Cross is the second-highest valor award in the Navy, ranking
only below the Medal of Honor.

The conclusion of the war did not end Ellis's pursuit of adventure. Despite health problems, which included kidney disease and psychological disorders from combat—both compounded by alcohol abuse—Ellis sought additional challenges and responsibilities. On 4 September 1920 he wrote to the Major General Commandant of the Marine Corps* stating, "In order that the Marine Corps may have the necessary information on which to base its plans for future operations in South America and in the Pacific Ocean, I have to request that I be ordered to those areas for the purposes of making the necessary reconnaissance."

Ellis's letter was forwarded to the Director of Naval Intelligence, who immediately approved the request. There is no evidence that Ellis ever focused on South America, but his accomplishments in the Pacific were utterly fantastic.

Before conducting his on-the-ground reconnaissance of the Pacific area, Ellis prepared a report based on extensive study, his previous experiences in the region, and his visions of the future. Ellis's 30,000-word study titled "Advance Base Operations in Micronesia" was approved by the Navy Department on 28 January 1921 and was redesignated *Operations Plan 712*. Perhaps the most amazing report of its type in American military history, it provided a detailed outline of the buildup and aggression by Japan. Ellis wrote, "Japan is a world power, and her army and navy will doubtless be up to date as to training and material. Considering our consistent policy of nonaggression, she will probably initiate the war."

The body of the Ellis study consisted of detailed discussions of the sea, air, and climate, landforms, native populations, economic conditions, and the potential enemy's capabilities. He concluded his study with an outline

---

*The title "Major General Commandant of the Marine Corps" was later changed to "Commandant of the Marine Corps (CMC)."

of strategy for US forces to retake key islands so as to establish bases for the eventual attack on mainland Japan. Included were requirements for airplanes capable of delivering torpedoes against water craft and the development of large, automatic guns for shipboard offense and defense.

OPLAN 712 would later be adapted and renamed the ORANGE War Plan that provided the basic guidelines for the conflict against Japan following Pearl Harbor. Ellis's plan had been so detailed and accurate that despite the fact that it was not executed for more than two decades after it was written, the US efforts in the Pacific closely followed his mobilization projections, timetables, and the predictions of the numbers of troops required to accomplish the victory.

Upon completion of his report, Ellis traveled throughout the Pacific to validate his theories. On 21 May 1923, the Japanese Governor General of the South Sea Islands reported to the American authorities in Yokosuka that Ellis was dead. No official cause of his death was given or ever determined. Some theorize that Ellis was still despondent from his combat experiences and had committed suicide. Others thought the Japanese had murdered him after he had discovered a part of their war preparations. The possibility was also raised that his medical problems and continued alcohol abuse had finally proved fatal. Still another account, presented by a German merchant, Mr. O. Herrman, who had traveled briefly with Ellis in his final days, stated that the major had become seriously ill after consuming a meal of canned eels and beer.

The mystery of Ellis's death deepened when the naval attaché at Yokosuka sent Chief Pharmacist Lawrence Zembsch to recover the remains. When Zembsch returned on 14 August 1923 he was, according to the attaché, "incoherent, his walk was unsteady and he was in a highly nervous condition. He would burst into tears, apparently without any reason, talked of taking his own life, etc."

Zembsch had likely been drugged, tortured, or both. Of particular note was the fact that he cringed in fear at the sight of any Japanese—even those who had been close friends before his mission. Further debriefing of Zembsch was deferred until he regained his health. That never occurred, as both Zembsch and his wife were burned to death in a fire that followed a devastating earthquake that struck Yokohama on 1 September 1923.

The cause of Ellis's death remains a mystery. His foresight and abilities as a true "recon Marine" do not. Although few within or outside the military paid much attention to Ellis's visions of a world war at the time, he had combined experience, analytical reasoning, and reconnaissance to foretell the next war.

Although most of America languished in rampant chauvinism and a belief that World War I was truly the war to end all wars, Marines like Ellis and others continued to prepare for future conflicts. Doctrine concerning amphibious warfare continued to be developed with emphasis on reconnaissance operations for advanced planning, verification of the soundness of established plans, and providing for current intelligence just prior to beach assaults.

This thought process and experimentation crystallized in 1938 with the publication of FTP-167, titled "Landing Operations Doctrine,"[5] which outlined the detailed procedures for Navy-Marine amphibious operations. The publication expanded on previous writings in detailing the role of immediate and long-range reconnaissance activities and emphasized the reliability of ground observation over that conducted from ship, submarine, or aircraft.

Reconnaissance doctrine reflected in FTP-167 was first tested during Fleet Exercise Number 4 (FLEX 4) which was conducted from 13 January to 15 March 1938 in the Caribbean on and near the islands of Culebra, Vieques, and Puerto Rico. Reconnaissance objectives assigned by the Attack Force Commander, Rear Adm A. W. Johnson, included inshore water patrols, location of reserve forces, type and positions of beach defenses, location and suitability of landing beaches and surf, and the extent of inland defenses.[6]

Recon teams for the exercise were formed from the 5th Marine Regiment and attached US Army personnel. Results were mixed, as not all the objectives were accomplished; however, they were encouraging enough to support future experimentation. One major problem that surfaced was the difficulty involved in the recon teams' relaying information to the proper intelligence and operations channels. One notable accomplishment was the first amphibious recon patrol in USMC history being landed from a submarine.[7]

Similar FLEXs were conducted in the same areas for the following two years. By the conclusion of FLEX 6 in 1940, the Marine Corps had developed a comprehensive amphibious reconnaissance doctrine that had been thoroughly tested. The need for this reconnaissance was best summed up by the Chief Umpire for FLEX 6, Maj Gen W. P. Uphsur, when he said, "I do not see how it is possible to issue final, definite orders before we have any knowledge of the location, disposition, and movements of the hostile force."[8]

One of Uphsur's subordinates, Brig Gen H. W. Smith, stated the need for reconnaissance even more concisely: "Without this phase both the Admiral and the land forces would be fighting blind."[9]

Although the need for recon units had been recognized and the doctrine for their employment approved, the prewar Corps was too austere to form the needed units. 7 December 1941 changed that quickly. By January 1942, a small group of two officers and twenty enlisted Marines from various battalion and regimental intelligence sections of the First Marine Division were assembled at Quantico, Virginia. Designated "Observer Group," this unit was the first in Marine Corps history to be organized and trained specifically for amphibious reconnaissance.[10]

The Observer Group was assigned to a joint force composed of the First Marine Division and the US Army 1st Infantry Division under the command of Gen Holland Smith. The mission of the joint force was to prepare for the invasion of North Africa.

Capt James Logan Jones was selected as the first commander of the Observer Group.[11] Considering the focus on North Africa, Jones was a logical selection, because he had visited the area extensively as a sales representative for International Harvester before the war. Jones immediately began to train his unit, fielding patrols and experimenting with landing craft, communications, uniforms, and equipment.

At the same time, the joint force G-2 (intelligence officer) continued to develop recon doctrine in coordination with Jones. Of particular note was the recognition that additional missions incidental to reconnaissance—including diversions, minor night raids, and disruption of enemy communications—were added to the unit's responsibilities.

In September 1942 the War Department, in response to strategic planning and interservice rivalries, redefined theater responsibilities. The Army was to be in charge of the war efforts in the Atlantic region, while the Navy assumed control of the Pacific. As a result, the joint force to which the Observer Group was assigned was disbanded. Jones and his recon Marines were transferred to San Diego as a part of the Amphibious Corps, Pacific Fleet (ACPF).

But the Observer Group continued to train in the same manner as it had on the East Coast. Along with emerging procedures and doctrine, it became more and more apparent to Jones and other advocates of the recon concept that the Marine selected for recon duty was as important as the actual method of operation. This human aspect of personnel selection and training was noted in the ACPF

Intel Order Number 4-42, "Reconnaissance Patrols Landing on Hostile Shores," dated 29 October 1942. The order, which was essentially a SOP for recon operations, stated:

> The elements and principles of scouting and patrolling as well as combat intelligence must be so instilled in them as to be instinctive. The aggressive type of action involved combined with the strain of maintaining secrecy will necessitate, in almost all cases, exceptionally high physical condition and agility. Since the accuracy of the information to be obtained is of an importance which may determine the success or failure of a landing, it is advisable, when possible, to strengthen the patrols by officers who have received the same training.[12]

Training involved the whole person, not simply the ability to scout cunningly or manipulate landing craft. Order Number 4-42 further stated that confidence, perception, and ingenuity in all settings, along with the ability to use a variety of special weapons and equipment, were important characteristics of the recon Marines. Physical and mental conditioning were emphasized as not only important for prolonged patrol actions but also to counteract the stress of long-term surface or submarine transport to the target areas.

The SOP was complete and quite valid as reflected by the fact that it was recopied virtually verbatim in 1944 by the V Amphibious Corps. Its contents were changed little throughout the war, and in 1948 it was again reprinted Corps-wide as MCS 3-1, "Combat Intelligence."

Jones's Observer Group so impressed the commander of the Amphibious Corps that on 7 January 1943 the unit was increased to six officers and ninety-two enlisted men and was redesignated the Amphibious Reconnaissance Company.[13] The Marine recon men continued to train at Camp Pendleton and instructed reconnaissance teams from Army units that were to participate in the battles for the Aleutian Islands.

On 25 August 1943, due to the increasing number of mobilized Marine units, the entire Pacific force was again reorganized. The Amphibious Corps was redesignated the V Amphibious Corps (VAC) and the recon Marines became the Amphibious Reconnaissance Company, VAC.

By the fall of 1943 the tide had turned against the Japanese expansion in the Pacific. It was time for the Marines to lead the way in the island-hopping campaign that would lead to the Land of the Rising Sun. On 10 September, Jones received classified orders to move his unit to Hawaii and report "upon arrival to the Commanding General, Fifth Amphibious Corps, Pacific Fleet, on permanent duty beyond the seas."[14] The recon men were finally going to war.

Jones's stay in Hawaii was brief. Leaving his executive officer, 2ndLt (later LtGen) Merwin H. Silverthorn, Jr., in charge to continue training the company, Jones joined the USS *Nautilus* on her Sixth War Patrol, departing Pearl Harbor on 16 September 1943. The submarine was to conduct photographic reconnaissance off Tarawa, Kuma, Butaritari, Makin, and Apamama islands. Jones was along to lend his expertise in reconnaissance and to have a firsthand look at islands where he and his Marines would soon be landing.

After a month at sea, Jones and the *Nautilus* returned to Hawaii on 16 October. Their stay at Pearl was to be brief, however, as orders were waiting for Jones to reembark the *Nautilus* with three platoons of his recon company and to land on the island of Apamama. The Fourth Platoon of the Recon Company was detached to the Army's 27th Infantry Division for its assault on Makin Island in the same campaign.

On the morning of 8 November the *Nautilus* departed

Pearl with the Marines billeted in the forward and aft torpedo rooms. Attached to the company was an Australian, Lieutenant George Hard, who had lived extensively throughout the Southern Pacific and would act as an interpreter with the local islanders.

Apamama Atoll,[15] located 76 miles south of Tarawa, had been selected as an objective because of its immense lagoon, which would provide a logistic support base west of Pearl Harbor. A Japanese buildup had been reported, and Jones's mission was to determine the size and displacement of the enemy force for a beach assault by follow-on units.

The cruise to the objective was not without incident. On 18 November the *Nautilus* was steaming on the surface to accomplish a secondary mission, rescuing aviators forced down in the aerial bombardment of Helen Island. In her search, the submarine ventured too close to the island and was fired upon by Japanese shore batteries and forced to dive. The next day the *Nautilus* was mistaken for a Japanese sub by the USS *Ringgold* and taken under fire. Fortunately, the only projectile to hit the submarine caused little damage because it failed to explode.

The determination of the submarine crew and its recon Marine passengers remained undaunted despite the difficulties. The *Nautilus*'s skipper later recorded:

> We felt time was running out fast. We had an important date at Apamama and we were going to keep it if we had to surface and fight our way through the horde that was molesting us. The 78 Marines we had aboard were stoic but they were unanimous in the attitude that they would much prefer a rubber boat on the hostile beach to their present predicament. We managed to assure them they would get their boat ride and it was certain none of them would be hesitant about leaving the ship when landing time came.

By the afternoon of 20 November, the *Nautilus* was lying submerged just off Apamama, and Jones and his officers were able to observe the beach through the periscope. Thirty minutes after midnight the submarine surfaced and the recon men paddled through the surf and across a rough coral reef. The Marines landed unopposed.

Shortly after the company reached the beach, two natives were detained by the first platoon. Upon questioning by the Australian, Hard, they proved to be quite friendly and willing to help rid their island of the Japanese. The natives reported that over 300 of the enemy had originally occupied Apamama but that most had withdrawn a month earlier, leaving only about 30 soldiers behind. According to the natives, the Japanese were aware of the Marines' landing and were preparing their defenses.

Although the mission of the recon company had been only to scout for the main assault force due on 26 November, their detection had changed the situation. Jones would later record in his After Action Report that they "had to stay there five days, and there wasn't room for the Japs and us too."

Accompanied by native guides the Marines advanced toward the enemy positions. After several brief skirmishes, one of which resulted in the death of the first recon Marine, PFC William D. Miller, to be killed in combat, they reached the Japanese Command Post on 25 November to find the last defenders had committed suicide rather than face capture.

At 0700, 26 November 1943, the USS *Maryland*, USS *Harris*, and escort ships were sighted closing in on the beachhead by the recon Marines. A message was airdropped to Jones inquiring whether it was safe to land troops. Jones signaled in the affirmative, and soon Marines of the 3rd Battalion, 6th Regiment came ashore without incident.

Apamama was a highly successful first mission for the recon Marines. At the loss of only one life, the atoll became the first island in history to be captured by troops landing from a submarine.

The next target of Jones's reconnaissance was Majuro, an atoll with 56 islets and a lagoon 21 miles long and up to six miles wide. The lagoon was adequate for fleet anchorage, and several areas near the beach were suitable for the construction of airstrips, making Majuro an important stepping stone in the push westward to the home islands of Japan.[16]

On 23 January 1944 the recon company departed Pearl aboard the USS *Kane*.* At 2300 hours on 30 January an advance patrol, under the leadership of 1stLt Harvey C. Weeks, rowed ashore and landed on Luella Island of the Majuro Atoll. They were the first Americans to set foot on territory held by the Japanese prior to their attack on Pearl Harbor.**

Again using friendly natives for intelligence and as guides, the Marines quickly discovered that the Japanese had withdrawn from Luella. According to the natives, only one Japanese warrant officer and four civilian workers remained on the entire chain. The Marines confirmed this information by landing on and patrolling several other islands in the area. Their efforts culminated in the capture of the warrant officer on 1 February.

On the morning of 2 February the company departed, having accomplished its mission of securing the Entrance Islands to safeguard the passage of the remainder of the invasion force. Additionally, the recon men's ascertaining

---

*The *Kane* was a World War I–vintage destroyer that had been remodeled by removing two of its four stacks and one of its firerooms to provide additional bunk space. Classified "Assault Personnel Destroyers," the *Kane* and others of its design were fast, albeit uncomfortable, and were intended to quickly deliver assault forces to landing areas.
**Due to efforts to keep the activities of the recon Marines secret, their operations were classified and were not revealed to the press or public. As a result the first landing on Japanese soil remained unreported until 1945.

that there were no Japanese on the atoll had saved valuable installations, including barracks, hangers, and fortifications, from destruction by naval gunfire and aerial bombardment. Also, the munitions saved could be directed to actual enemy positions, while the captured warrant officer provided useful intelligence for the remainder of the campaign.

The Marines got little rest before their next mission. Continuing to operate from the *Kane*, they next turned their attention to the atoll Eniwetok.[17] On 17–18 February the company systematically landed on 31 of the atoll's islands, finding each deserted. On the next two islands, code named ARBUTUS and FRAGILE, the Marines engaged small groups of enemy and suffered one killed and two wounded before securing their objectives. On 22 February, Jones was ordered to attach his company to the 2nd Battalion of the Regimental Combat Team 22nd Marines to reinforce them in their fierce battle for Perry Island. Before being withdrawn the following day, the recon company had accounted for 15 enemy dead with no friendly casualties.

On return to Pearl Harbor, the Amphibious Reconnaissance Company was recognized for its actions on Apamama, Majuro, and Eniwetok. Jones received the Legion of Merit. The company was given a special commendation by Gen Holland M. Smith, the Commander of the V Amphibious Corps, stating that:

> . . . fully justifying the purpose for which this unit was organized and trained, the Amphibious Reconnaissance Company more than fulfilled its mission. . . . Exhibiting the highest degree of skill, courage, and determination, the officers and men of this unit executed their mission in a most exemplary manner. . . . The high state of efficiency, intrepidity, and resourcefulness displayed by the officers and men of the Amphibious Reconnaissance Company will serve as an inspiration to all ranks of this Corps. . . .[18]

Successes resulted in more than mere commendations for the company and its individuals. On 14 April 1944 the company was expanded to become the Amphibious Reconnaissance Battalion.[19] The unit was now large enough to take on more complex missions and had enough personnel to train replacements for its casualties. The battalion of 20 officers, 270 enlisted Marines, and 13 Navy medical corpsmen was organized into two recon companies and a headquarters company. Although the company had become a battalion, its leadership remained basically the same. Jones was promoted to major and stayed in command, while two of the platoon leaders were named to head the companies—1stLt Leo B. Shinn in A Company and 1stLt Merwin Silverthorn in B Company. Several of the senior NCOs were given field commissions and assumed the duties of platoon leaders.[20]

The first use of the new Amphibious Recon Battalion occurred during the battle for Tinian Island.[21] In planning the operation, Gen Holland Smith supported the proposed landing sites on the western side of the island code-named White 1 and White 2 beaches. Adm Kelly Turner strongly disagreed and insisted the assault take place at Tinian Town, code named Yellow Beach, despite the fact that aerial reconnaissance had revealed that it contained heavy Japanese fortifications. After considerable argument, and no agreement, it was decided to send in the recon Marines to determine which site was the most suitable for the invasion.

The action resulted in the most significant employment of Marine reconnaissance in World War II. Far more important than the reputations of the operation's top planners, which hung in the balance, were the thousands of lives saved as a direct result of the battalion's reconnaissance efforts.

On the night of 9–10 July 1944, the recon men landed near each beach by rubber boat. Although one enemy patrol walked within a few yards of the well-camouflaged

Marines, they were not detected. The Marines got their information. Yellow Beach contained moored mines, potholes, large boulders, barbed wire, pillboxes, and 100-foot cliffs on each flank of the beach. Around-the-clock work was ongoing to strengthen the already formidable defenses. White Beaches 1 and 2 were found to be free of obstacles and lightly defended. The recon Marines accomplished their mission without the loss of a single man and were able to bring back sketches as well as soil and vegetation samples for further study.

The invasion of Tinian was executed with precision. The landing operations officer, Colonel Hogaboom, credited the success directly to the recon Marines: ". . . in the absence of the detailed information which these reconnaissance units gave us on the extremely narrow and restricted beaches it would not have been sound to embark on this very risky operation."

Following Tinian, the recon battalion returned to Hawaii, where on 26 August 1944 it was once again redesignated—this time as the Amphibious Reconnaissance Battalion, Fleet Marine Force. This was a change in name only and had no effect on the unit's organization. Its purpose was to align the battalion's name with the change that had redesignated Fifth Marine Corps to Fleet Marine Force, Pacific.

The Amphibious Recon Battalion continued to play an important role in the remaining battles in the Pacific. Operating in teams as small as three men and occasionally with the entire battalion committed at one time, it participated in the battles for Iwo Jima in February 1945, Okinawa in March, and Ike Shima in April. In each campaign it provided important intelligence and information that conserved the manpower and munitions of the Marines and sailors for whom they served.

Public recognition of the recon Marines remained incommensurate to their accomplishments. Efforts continued to keep the enemy from knowing anything of the battalion's actions. Commendations from senior commanders were frequent but were marked Top Secret. Typical was the classified commendation by MajGen A. D. Bruce, commander of the Army's 77th Infantry Division, who praised the recon men for their assistance on Okinawa and Ike Shima. An endorsement to Brown's praise by the Commander of the Tenth Army, LtGen Simon B. Buckner, also stamped Top Secret, noted: "I personally followed the excellent performance of the battalion with much interest and would add that the part played by this splendid organization materially assisted in the success of our present campaign. The close cooperation of the services, Marine and Army, was here exemplified to the highest degree."[22]

Gen Joseph W. Stilwell, who assumed command of the Tenth Army after Buckner was killed on Okinawa on 18 June, later added his kudos. Stilwell wrote of his appreciation for the recon battalion "for your superior performance under the capable leadership of Maj James Jones in carrying out your assigned missions in the Ryukyus Campaign. The Fleet Marine Force may well be proud of the development of amphibious reconnaissance as exemplified by your activities. Use of your battalion as the only ground reconnaissance agency held under Tenth Army Headquarters expedited the accomplishment of all phases of the present campaign. Your aggressive action made unnecessary the use of large forces in the seizure of the eastern islands of Okinawa, the islands off the Motobu Peninsula, and Kume Shima."[23]

By then the Amphibious Reconnaissance Battalion was not the only Marine recon unit. In the Southwest Pacific the First Marine Amphibious Corps (I MAC), later III MAC, approached its reconnaissance somewhat differently than did the V Amphibious Corps in the Central Pacific.

Prior to the arrival of the Marines in the Southwest Pacific, the Australians had already established a network of deep-reconnaissance agents known as Coast Watchers who operated not only along the coasts but inland as well. Before the formal organization of recon units in the I MAC area, individual Marines were attached to the Coast Watchers.[24]

Amphibious reconnaissance training began in the First Marine Division, which was subordinate to I MAC, in April 1943 when Col E. J. Buckley, the division's Intelligence Officer, foresaw the requirements for amphibious scouts in future operations. Buckley organized a staff to conduct the training in the 5th Marine Regiment's area on Mornington Peninsula, Australia. Each regiment in the division provided two officers and six enlisted men from their intelligence sections. All were seasoned veterans of the campaign for Guadalcanal.

Before the new recon Marines completed their training, a decision was reached by the senior commander in the area, Gen Walter Kruger of the Sixth Army, to form combined service recon units. Marines at the Mornington Peninsula training camp were transferred to Cairns, Australia, where LtCmdr Bill Coultas was in charge of the new training center. Joining the Marines were Australian veterans and soldiers from the US Army 32nd Infantry Division. Twenty natives of New Guinea and New Britain, who had been on the islands during the Japanese occupation and had later escaped, also joined the new recon unit.[25]

Coultas, a scientist who before the war had been a field man for the American Museum of Natural History and had traveled extensively throughout the Pacific, organized the diverse group into four teams, with a Marine in each. He then moved the teams to Ferguson Island, just off the eastern tip of New Guinea, for an intensive training period. At the conclusion of the training, the teams were designated "Special Services Unit Number 1." All operations in the Southwest Pacific thereafter were preceded by reconnaissance from the Special Service Unit or by recon teams that they trained from the subordinate divisions.

The first four patrols employed were landed on New Georgia on 21 March 1943 and remained ashore until 10 April 1943. Reconnaissance of New Georgia was essential since the island was generally unmapped and hydrographic charts were badly out of date. Because aerial photography revealed only thick jungle growth, physical scouting by trained observer teams was the only practical method of gathering accurate information.

Each of the patrols carried out its mission with such skill that at no time was the enemy aware of the recon men's presence. Valuable information, including sketches and pictures of the terrain and enemy dispositions, was obtained. Typical of the patrols was the one under the leadership of 2ndLt H. G. Schrier. Moving almost constantly across jungles by foot and on water in native canoes, the patrol was often in proximity of enemy camps and defensive positions. Another patrol, under the leadership of Capt Clay Allen Boyd, greeted the assault force infantry Marines by leading them to a path they had hacked through the dense vegetation for five miles to within 1500 meters of the enemy positions.[26]

Following the successful invasion of New Georgia, reconnaissance teams continued to lead the way in the remainder of the Allied efforts to retake the Solomon Islands and on into the Treasury Islands and Bougainville. Recon patrols were also employed during the progress through the Empress Bay area and the campaign for New Britain, where an amphibious patrol discovered that the intended assault beach was backed by cliffs and had only one narrow exit. Once again, information gathered by the recon men resulted in an adjusted battle plan and the resulting saving of lives.

The end of the war with Japan after the atomic bombing of Hiroshima and Nagasaki brought a quick end to the reconnaissance units that had served so well. The I MAC recon Marines were returned to their parent units and ceased to exist as a unit. In the V Amphibious Corps, the Amphibious Reconnaissance Battalion was transferred back to Pearl Harbor, where on 24 September 1945 it was disbanded. Many of the former recon Marines remained in uniform after the war and would form the nucleus of future units to be formed when once again the Corps recognized the need for their skills and expertise.

CHAPTER 3

☐☐☐☐☐☐☐

The Challenges of Peace and the Rebirth of Force

*T*HE first few years following the conclusion of World War II were marked by occupation of the defeated nations and demobilization. It was not until the National Security Act of 1947 that postwar missions and organizations for the Armed Services were thoroughly defined. In its study of the assigned missions of the Marine Corps, the senior Marine leadership recognized the need for reconnaissance units at the Force level. Their recommendation was for the formation of a Force Amphibious Reconnaissance Battalion of 21 officers and 308 enlisted men.[1] However, while the need for Force Reconnaissance was apparent, the assets from which to form such a unit in the postwar austerity were not. It would take another war and the passage of nearly a decade before Force Recon became a reality.

That is not to say, however, that continuing efforts to refine recon doctrine and equipment did not take place. One of the most significant developments was the improvement of transportation for recon units. On 20 May 1948 the USS *Perch* was recommissioned after having been mothballed at the end of the war.[2] The *Perch* was redesignated a submarine transport and was remodeled, two of her engines and all of her torpedo tubes being removed to provide troop and cargo space.

A group of Marines of D Company, 5th Marine Regiment, from Camp Pendleton, under the leadership of Capt Kenneth Houghton,* were assigned to develop amphibious recon techniques for the newly configured submarine. Initially training off the California coast, the group sailed in October 1949 aboard the *Perch* for Hawaii to participate in Operation MIKI as the recon company for the Second Army.[3]

Houghton's company continued to train and experiment with the *Perch* over the next six months. Before training could be completed, however, it was terminated because of the onset of the Korean War. The recon company joined its parent 1st Marine Division, and its organization quickly altered from an amphibious unit to one that was "foot mobile." Using jeeps "lent" by the Army, the recon Marines conducted motorized patrols deep behind enemy lines from Wonsan to Hungnam. In one instance, at Hukso-ri, the unit penetrated 40 miles into the midst of the enemy to scout a supply depot.

In addition, the recon Marines conducted seven raids into North Korea in joint attacks with Navy Underwater Demolition Teams (UDT). Operating from the USS *Horace A. Bass*, a team of 16 recon men and 25 UDTs raided the Posung-Myon area, destroying three tunnels and two railway bridges, with the loss of one man. In January 1951, members of the recon company remained hidden for two days in a village in the Andong area where they called in air strikes on North Korean infantry units.[4]

As the war stagnated in the final months before the cease-fire, the recon Marines were used less and less for deep missions and spent much of their time running

---

*Houghton, a veteran of Tarawa, the Marshall Islands, and Saipan, would later command the 5th Marines in Vietnam and the 1st Marine Division after the war. He retired in 1977 at the rank of lieutenant general.

short-range patrols and guarding command posts. While the unit's contributions to the war decreased, the recon company continued to attract the best men in the Corps. As was the case with other elite units, the recon Marines drew a large contingent of displaced persons and immigrants who had fled their countries after defeat or communist takeover after World War II. Peter Kalischer, a writer for *Collier's* magazine in the 25 October 1952 issue called the recon company the "Foreign Legion of the Marine Corps."[5] Kalischer included examples such as PFC Albert Type, a bridge-blowing member of the Polish underground who was captured by the Gestapo in 1943, tortured, then sent as a slave laborer to the coal mines before being liberated by advancing Americans; Cpl Edward S. Chin, Jr., an American-born Chinese who was almost drafted into the Red Army while attending school near Canton; PFC Miguel Alvarez, a refugee from Franco's Spain; PFC Michael Averko Olaff von Hilderbrand, a former member of German Army intelligence who had also been a member of Hitler Youth and was proficient in nine languages; PFC Vytautus Juskus, a refugee from Lithuania; Cpl Saznek Betrosian, an Armenian who had lived all but six of his 22 years in Iran and Russia; Cpl George Feodorovich Homiakoff, a Shanghai-born White Russian; French Rofe, born in Egypt; PFC John Diener, a former German Army tank crewman, who at 15 years of age had fought on the Russian front; Cpl Visvaldis Mangulis, an emigrant from Latvia; and PFC Steven J. Szkupinski, a former member of both the French Foreign Legion and the British Army who could say "which way is the border" in eleven different languages.*

Despite its excellent record, Houghton's company was

---

*The Recon Marines of Vietnam continued to draw similar men who had escaped from such countries as Hungary, Poland, and Cuba who were motivated to fight communism regardless of its locale.

never increased in size. The closest the Corps came to meeting its own objective for recon battalions during the Korean War years was not in the war zone itself but rather back on the East Coast* of the United States. Although a war was raging on the Korean Peninsula, following World War II the United States was a world power with responsibilities around the globe. Marine units on the East Coast provided replacements for the units deployed in the war zone, but at the same time had peacekeeping—and war preparation—requirements in the Atlantic region.

On 1 December 1950 the Second Amphibious Reconnaissance Battalion was formed at Camp Lejeune, North Carolina, under the leadership of Maj Regan Fuller.[6] Many of the early members of the battalion were World War II recon veterans. Over the next two years the battalion participated in training exercises in the Caribbean and the Mediterranean. Due to the continuing requirements for replacements in Korea, the battalion was reduced in strength on 11 August 1952 and was redesignated the Second Amphibious Reconnaissance Company.

Meanwhile, on the West Coast efforts continued to fill the void created by the deployment of Houghton's company to Korea. The First Amphibious Reconnaissance Platoon was formed on 12 March 1951 at Camp Pendleton. Most of the Marines initially assigned to the platoon were straight out of boot camp, but there were some exceptions. TSgts Ernest L. DeFazio and John W. Slagel joined the platoon from Korea, each wearing three Purple Hearts.[7]

---

*Throughout modern history there had been differences far more than geographical between Marines on the East and the West coasts. Each focuses on its ocean area of responsibility, with the conviction that his is the more important—and the better—force. Rivalries often go a bit beyond ''friendly''—more than one barroom brawl has started with an argument over whether Parris Island or San Diego produces the ''best'' Marine.

As the Korean conflict wound down, the platoon was increased to company level on 14 October 1953 and to battalion strength on 11 January 1954. Training included the use of rubber boats and submarines with emphasis on raids (surprise attacks on stationary targets) as well as reconnaissance in areas ranging from Southern California to Adak, Alaska.

At the conclusion of the Korean War, the Marine Corps once again returned to preparing for the next war by applying lessons learned in the past. The proliferation of nuclear weapons produced a tremendous impact on the planning of amphibious operations. Massed assaults by men on tiny objectives were no longer thought to be possible; forces would likely be fighting over areas 200 miles in width and depth. The resulting concept for the "modern battlefield" was one of "dispersion"—attacking an area, not a point, with mobile forces.[8]

Providing the mobility would be helicopters, which had first proven to be a valid means of troop delivery during Operation BUMBLEBEE in Korea on 11 October 1951, when 958 men of the 3rd Battalion, 7th Marines had been airlifted 15 miles to relieve a heavily engaged battalion of the 5th Marine Regiment.[9]

Accordingly, on 1 July 1954, the Commandant of the Marine Corps directed the activation of the Marine Corps Test Unit Number 1 (MCTU #1) with the mission to develop vertical deployment and assault by helicopter. Col Edward N. Rydalch assumed command of the MCTU, which was composed of an infantry battalion, a 4.2-inch mortar platoon, a 75mm pack howitzer battery, and headquarters and support units. In addition to attached aircraft support, the USS *Thetis Bay* was converted to an Assault Helicopter Transport for use by the Marines in testing heliborne amphibious assaults from a carrier.[10]

After only minimal testing of the new concept, it was apparent to the leadership of the MCTU that tactics associated with heliborne assaults—in a nuclear or conventional environment—required a preliminary long-range reconnaissance of proposed landing sites and operational areas. Based on this experience and the predicted direction of future testing of the MCTU, Colonel Rydalch submitted a recommendation to the commandant on 12 May 1955 for a major reorganization of the unit including "provision for a modest reconnaissance element consisting of one reconnaissance officer and thirteen reconnaissance men. It is intended that this element be employed virtually exclusively in training, testing, and exercises designed to validate reconnaissance theories, concepts, methods, and techniques of the all-helicopter assault, not only as they apply to the BLT (Battalion Landing Team), but on higher levels as well."[11]

The request was approved, and the Reconnaissance Platoon, MCTU, was formed. After additional study, its size was increased to one officer and 24 enlisted men, most of whom were senior NCOs. Rydalch described the recon men as "thoroughly screened volunteers of a high degree of intelligence and physical stamina. In addition to intelligence, motivation, and attitude screening, all Marines of this platoon have passed the Submarine Physical Examination, and physical evaluation test equivalent to those required for Army Airborne troops."[12]

Selection criteria for the platoon were stringent in every aspect. Rydalch required that all volunteers below the rank of staff sergeant be unmarried and that "they must be temperamentally and physically suited for rigorous training and operations in the field, and of demonstrated initiative, self-reliance, maturity, and interest in the Marine Corps. It is mandatory that each Marine selected be a non-commissioned officer, who will not require refresher training in basic subjects, and who possesses a sound degree of grounding in weapons, tactics, mapping, and the like. The time available for training members of this platoon is too short to permit for devoting lengthy portions of the training period to basic subjects."[13]

Capt Joseph Z. Taylor was assigned as the platoon's commander and was given great latitude in its development and training. Although the Recon Platoon did train with small rubber/nylon boats, it was soon obvious that under the new concept of amphibious warfare on an expanded battlefield, the recon patrols had to be capable of rapid, undetected introduction into, and recovery from, their reconnaissance objectives by air.

The key to the emerging doctrine was in the concept of "by air." Colonel Rydalch noted that reconnaissance could not be conducted by boat or seaborne patrols because the objectives of future Marine battlefields would reach farther inland from the beaches than those of past wars. Neither could the required reconnaissance be accomplished strictly by or from helicopters. Helicopters were too vulnerable; they were not capable of all-weather flight, were easily detected, were of limited range, and were easily shot down. The only way to deliver the recon patrols to objectives far inland was by parachute from high-performance aircraft. At the same time, it was recognized that recovery of the teams would be difficult. Until better means could be developed, the recon Marines would have to be extremely proficient in escape and evasion if they were to return from their recon zones on foot.

Subsequently, the Commandant of the Marine Corps approved airborne training for the recon Marines as well as Pathfinder training, which was necessary for the selection of drop zones for jump operations and the preparation for heliborne insertions.

In April 1956 the Recon Platoon attended en masse the US Army Airborne School at Fort Benning, Georgia. Selected Marines stayed on at Benning to attend the Army's Jumpmaster Course, which prepared them to rig jumpers and equipment for airdrops. Several members of the platoon also attended the Pathfinder School to refine their knowledge of landing and drop-zone selection and preparation. One of these pioneer Marine Pathfinders was Donald E. Koelper,* who was known to many as "Mr. Pathfinder" for his leadership in that skill.[14]

The transition to the parachute as the basic means of transportation for the recon Marines was prompted by the possibility that in the dispersed modern battlefield "beaches" might well be far inland instead of only along coastlines. A problem that now had to be confronted was the fact that no one had ever parachuted from the principal carrier transport aircraft—the Grumman TF-1. After extensive study, including consultation with Grumman aeronautical engineers and a series of jumps using dummies, on 9 July 1956 the MCTU Recon Marines became the first to parachute from the TF-1.[15]

Less than three weeks later, four recon parachutists launched from the USS *Bennington*, which was 70 miles at sea, and jumped on a desert drop zone near El Centro, California, some 100 miles inland. For the first time in Marine Corps and Naval Aviation history, the technique of introducing recon personnel off a carrier sea base to an inland objective by air had successfully been tested. Recon patrols, inserted by parachute, were thereafter an integral part of amphibious doctrine.

Although the parachute operations were successful in every aspect, they were not without danger. During Ex-

*Koelper, who had enlisted in the Corps in 1952, would eventually become the first Marine killed in Vietnam. While in a Saigon theater with hundreds of servicemen and Vietnamese, including women and children, on 16 February 1964, Koelper detected a terrorist bomb. He immediately shouted a warning and, while assisting in the evacuation, was killed when the bomb exploded. In recognition of his efforts, which saved everyone but himself, Koelper was awarded the Navy Cross and was posthumously promoted from captain to major.

ercise SKI JUMP on 17 January 1957 three Marines from the Recon Platoon—Cpl Benjamin F. Simpson, PFC Matthew J. O'Neill, and 1stLt Kenneth J. Ball—were killed near Camp Springs, California, when sudden winds developed as they landed on the drop zone.[16] The Marines were unable to deflate their canopies and were dragged to death.*

Another airborne operation, conducted on 6 February 1957 to test the possibility of jumping from the F3D aircraft, is a good example of the risks in parachuting as well as the Marines' acceptance of the inherent dangers.[17] Maj Bruce F. Meyers, wearing a standard T-10 parachute and carrying full equipment, rations, and weapons exited an F3D with the airspeed at approximately 150 knots.** Meyers recalls,

> I knew I'd been hurt and the minute I hit the ground I collapsed onto my canopy. Fortunately the drop zone personnel took me to the hospital and it was a simple

---

*Three drop zones at Camp Pendleton were eventually named in honor of the dead recon men. The three Marines were using the standard T-10 parachute. A short time after their death several Army paratroopers suffered the same fate. As a result, quick-release devices known as Capewells were developed, which allowed a jumper to disengage from the canopy once on the ground.

**Jumping from the F3D was no easy matter in itself. The jumper had to squeeze between the pilot's and copilot's seats and take a position in an escape chute. The chute was two and one-half feet wide and seven feet long, sloping at an angle of 45 degrees to the rear of the aircraft, where it ended midway back on the fuselage between the twin jet engines and under the wings. A small hand-hold bar, similar to a chinning bar, was located just above the cockpit entrance to the chute. The jumper grabbed the bar, hung feet down in the chute, and turned to face the pilot. When the pilot gave the thumbs-up signal and tapped the jumper on the helmet, the jumper threw his hands over his head and slid down the chute into the slipstream below the aircraft. With a tight body position and a delay of five seconds, the jumper actually slowed down from 150 to 120 knots, which decreased the opening shock and prevented panels of the chute from literally being "blown out." At least, that was the theory.

line fracture, and five weeks later I was jumping again. I called Colonel Fuller at Camp Pendleton and asked him to call my wife and tell her I wouldn't be home that night, being in the hospital with a fractured pelvis. But it worked out okay. We did learn from this type of thing.[18]

The F3D was limited in that it could only carry one jumper. But the recon Marines soon realized that a four-man team could be jumped into an objective by a tight flying formation of four of the aircraft. Other aircraft were also tested by the platoon with equally successful results. Both the P2V Neptune and the R4D-8 Super Skytrain were put through extensive exercises at El Centro.

Despite the dangers, the recon Marines included parachute drops as a routine part of their testing and training, averaging at least one jump a week, with many drops conducted at night with full equipment. On a recon Marine's fiftieth jump, it became traditional in the platoon for the jumper to wear his full dress-blue uniform in recognition of the milestone.[19]

At the end of over two years of research, field tests, and exercises, the results of the MCTU were declared an unqualified success. The Marine Corps doctrine for vertical assault was firmly established, as was the helicopter's place in combat operations. On 30 June 1957 the 1500 members of the MCTU were transferred to units throughout the 1st Marine Division to assume leadership positions and to teach the new concepts.

The only part of the MCTU to retain its organization and identification was the Recon Platoon. Its accomplishments had convinced the Commandant that reconnaissance was a critical asset at the Force Marine level. On 19 June 1957, the Commandant directed that the MCTU Recon Platoon be merged with the First Amphibious Reconnaissance Company of the Fleet Marine Force, Pacific, to form the First Force Reconnaissance Company.[20] The leadership of the new company, including its commander, Maj Bruce Meyers, were nearly all MCTU Recon Platoon veterans. Furthermore, the Commandant directed that a cadre of the newly formed First Force Recon Company be transferred to the Second Amphibious Reconnaissance Company of the Fleet Marine Force, Atlantic, to reorganize it into the Second Force Reconnaissance Company during the last half of 1958.

Both companies were to provide deep surveillance up to 100 miles inland from the Force beachhead. Based on the experience of the MCTU Recon Platoon, the companies were organized into three platoons: parachute reconnaissance, amphibious reconnaissance, and parachute pathfinders. The patch of the new Force Recon Companies reflected these missions by containing a flame for pathfinder, silver jump wings, and crossed paddles.

Over the next five years the recon Marines of the two Force Recon Companies would participate in nearly every major Marine and Naval exercise around the world. Known nearly as much for their intensive physical-fitness training and unfailing discipline as for their expertise in field environments, the Force Recon Marines quickly became an elite within an elite. While the civilian on the street equated "Marine" with the best of fighting men, the Marines themselves recognized that the recon men were a breed apart within the Corps' own ranks.

The distinction of the Force Recon Marines was not limited to the Corps. Despite the fact that the Army was also well aware of the need for long-range reconnaissance, it did little beyond publish a manual on the concept. It would take the war in Vietnam before the Army finally established its own long-range recon units. From their formation in the late 1950s until 1965, the Force Recon Marines would be the only units in the Department of Defense organized and trained to conduct deep reconnaissance.

Testing new concepts and establishing "firsts" of all kinds became routine in the Force Recon companies. Some ventures became standard procedures, while other experiments proved successful but impractical. Although the Marine paratroopers had experimented with delaying parachute openings for several seconds in order to properly clear their transport aircraft in the MCTU, it was not until 1958 that the recon men learned a new technique of extended delay for thousands of feet and minutes of free-fall known as "skydiving."[21] While free-fall parachuting, or skydiving, is common today in both the military and in civilian sport parachuting, it was unknown until 1957. The developer of the technique was Jacques Andre Istel, who also happened to be a captain in the USMC Reserves. During an active duty period of 20–30 January 1958, Istel taught the free-fall methods to the First Force Recon Company, and it soon became a part of routine operations. The Recon men could parachute from high altitudes, thus avoiding possible detection from the ground as well as insuring more accurate landings. Also, the new method was actually safer than the old short-delay method, which was called "crude and rude" in that the opening shock was much more extreme and produced black-and-blue impact marks and an occasional broken bone or two.

Another reconnaissance benchmark developed at this time involved new methods for amphibious patrols to exit and reenter submerged submarines. Training, once again principally using the USS *Perch*, included use of scuba gear as well as free diving from "lock out, lock in" chambers which would fill with water before the exit door opened. The recon men also developed procedures for reentering a submarine while the craft was still moving (by grasping lines as it passed and pulling themselves to the "lock out, lock in" chamber).

* * *

Recon Marines stepped forward for individual tests as well as for team efforts. The armed forces had long been searching for techniques of recovering downed air crew and recon men from areas out of helicopter range and without landing zones. After extensive study by the Central Intelligence Agency and the Navy, a device known as the Fulton Sky Hook was designed by the Robert Fulton Company of Newtown, Connecticut. The Sky Hook consisted of nylon lines suspended from a balloon 500 feet in the air and leading to a harness on the ground. An aircraft with a yoke on its nose would fly below the balloon, hook the nylon lines, and jerk the man in the harness into the air. The nylon's elasticity—which would allow it to stretch about one-third of its overall length—allowed the man to be propelled vertically up to 200 feet, clearing any trees or vegetation before being towed horizontally behind the plane. A winch would then pull the man aboard.

The Fulton Sky Hook was practical, feasible, and safe—at least on paper.[22] First animals and then dummies were used to test the system. Finally, in the late summer of 1958, volunteers were sought to test the Sky Hook. Sgt Levi Woods, the equipment NCO for the Second Recon Company, stepped forward and was soon strapped into the harness, looking up at the balloon and the sky. On the first pass of the recovery aircraft, the propeller severed the balloon, and it, along with the nylon lines, came tumbling down on Woods's head. The second attempt was satisfactory, and Woods was later awarded the Navy and Marine Corps Medal* for this feat.

The second person to test the Sky Hook was Maj P. X. Kel-

---

*The Navy and Marine Corps Medal, along with its counterpart in the Army, the Soldier's Medal, is the highest award presented for bravery in an action not involving a hostile enemy.

ley, also of the Second Force Recon Company. Kelley, who had recently completed his fiftieth parachute jump in mess whites, received no official recognition for his act. It was not, however, the last success of the young major. He went on to wear the four stars of the Commandant of the Marine Corps before his retirement in 1987.

Despite the success of the test, the Fulton Sky Hook never became an item of general use in any of the services.* The improved ranges of helicopters made the inherent dangers and transport difficulties of the Hook obsolete.

Besides, the helicopter offered more flexibility. Rappeling from hovering helicopters, using ropes and snap links to reach through jungles and other areas of heavy vegetation, was another innovation of the early Force Recon Marines. The recon men become so proficient at the techniques that in the spring of 1962 they were requested to teach rappeling to the US Army Special Forces.[23] It eventually became a standard practice of the Green Berets as well as other Army and Navy recon and infantry units in Vietnam.

The many accomplishments of the Force Recon Marines of the late 1950s and early 1960s were based on two important, closely entwined factors—the intense training and the nature of the men themselves. There were always large numbers of applicants to the Force Reconnaissance companies, but it was difficult to become a member. In 1961 the First Recon Company reported, "The high standards applied have resulted in a consistently high rejec-

*The best-known single use of the Sky Hook was not in training nor on the battlefield but rather on the movie screen. The John Wayne film of 1968, *The Green Berets*, included the extraction of a captured enemy official from a jungle camp using the Sky Hook. Although the movie only showed a "Hollywood" version, of dubious accuracy, of the Hook's use, it was authentic enough to clearly demonstrate why volunteers to test the device were not easy to find.

tion rate. As an example, of 180 Infantry Training Regiment graduates recently screened, 22 volunteered and eight actually were accepted. Only three of these remain in the operational platoons (only two months later).''[24]

New applicants were administered an excruciatingly rigorous physical exercise test, more to ascertain determination and ''guts'' than physical ability. Conditioning could always be developed if the volunteer possessed resolution and self-discipline. Rigorous swimming tests were also administered. Once again, it was more important for the recon candidate to ''go all out'' than to come in first. A man finishing far back in the pack but who ran or swam until he dropped or sank was picked over the man in the lead who, despite his abilities, held back a little. Usually, after the physical tests fewer than 20 percent of the volunteers were selected to pass on to the next phases.

If an enlisted volunteer passed the physical requirements, he was then interviewed by a group of the company's NCO leaders. While a question on weapons was being answered, the recon candidate might suddenly be interrupted with a demand to know why his boots were not shined—after having expended hours shining the rough-surfaced leather boots to a mirror finish. This process, known as the ''scream screening,'' was designed more to see how a man would react under pressure than to test his actual knowledge. Once again, the theory was that knowledge could be taught and that ''attitude'' was the important characteristic. Officer volunteers received similar treatment by a board of company officers.

Those enlisted Marines and officers who passed the physical tests and the scream screening faced one last test. Movies of submarine lock-out and lock-in exercises were shown followed by actual movie footage of a recon Marine whose main parachute failed and who was saved at the last moment by deployment of his reserve. The films served to encourage any candidates with remaining doubts to quit. Usually some did.[25]

Those who remained were accepted into the company on a trial basis. The selection process was only the first step in a volunteer's becoming a full-fledged Force Recon Marine. Pretesting and interviews isolated "raw materials" that with proper training, refinement, and continued motivation could eventually take their places as regular members of the company. Training programs were a continual process and involved the whole person. Areas of emphasis included patrolling tactics, scuba and parachute techniques, pathfinder methods, escape and evasion, first aid, demolitions, and formats for reports.

Each day training began as early as 0530 hours with strenuous exercises followed by lengthy runs and/or swims. Long days of training were often concluded with more physical exercise. In an article about a platoon of the First Recon Company in the Camp Pendleton newspaper of 22 September 1962 a reporter noted, "The week's training found the platoon near San Onofre Beach, only 18 miles from their Camp Del Mar homes, so they decided to run the distance back. The 40 husky Marines, led by 1stLt Jack C. Shopshire and MSgt John A. Echols 'double timed' down US 101 to the Camp Del Mar gate, stopping not once. As they entered the gate, several platoon members pleaded, 'Let's run on down to Tijuana.' "[26]

The proficiency and spirit of the recon Marines was so widely known by March 1961 that the television series *The Twentieth Century* featured members of the Second Company in a show called "The New Marines." Part of the narration stated, "The Force Recon Marines learn to make buoyant ascents at night from submerged submarines, with no breathing apparatus; swim eight-mile surface courses; use scuba gear in pitch darkness; and be plucked bodily from the ground by low-flying 'Sky Hook' planes."[27]

The level of training and the determination of recon Marines of the period are best exemplified by the story of SSgt Donald N. Hamblen.[28] It all began on his 215th parachute jump, which took place on 21 September 1962 at Camp Pendleton. As he descended to the ground from a C-130 aircraft, he drifted onto two levels of high-tension electrical wires. Hamblen's chute collapsed over the top wire, which carried 69,000 volts, swinging him into the lower wires, which were charged with 12,000 volts. There was a big bang, like thunder. Those looking on later said it looked like a ball of flame shot up from his feet to his waist. The flames quickly burned away the canopy and he fell thirty feet to the ground. Fellow Marines quickly unhooked his harness and dragged him away. His boots were so hot that several jackets had to be wrapped around them so they could be removed.

The following weeks and months of Hamblen's recovery would be reported in major newspapers and magazines across the United States and would show the spirit of the recon Marines. *Look* magazine, in an article aptly titled "Toughest Marine," quoted Hamblen. "The doctors tried to save my leg, but gangrene had set in. They decided to take it off below the knee. The thing that hit me was that I'd have to leave the Corps. That was a tear-jerker. I'd been a Marine since I was 17. The idea of leaving the Corps was like suddenly finding out you were no good."

Hamblen was shocked at the air of defeat displayed by others with debilitating injuries in the hospitals. He decided that the mere loss of a leg was not going to defeat him. An article in *Saga* magazine told of those early hospital days. A Veterans Administration official visited him, and thinking he was doing a kindly deed, offered to get him a job "when you return to civilian life." Hamblen replied, "Civilian hell. Get outta here and don't come back. Don't ever talk like that to a Marine."

Hamblen was not going to give up on remaining a Marine and began a long campaign to persuade the Corps to retain him. He wrote letters. He exercised. He persevered. He requested a meeting with the Commanding General of the First Marine Division. On 30 January his injuries had healed sufficiently to allow his transfer to the Navy Hospital in Oakland, where he was fitted with an artificial leg. Finally, on 29 May 1963, the Commandant of the Marine Corps, Gen David M. Shoup, wrote Hamblen pointing out the advantages of accepting medical retirement. More important, Shoup added that if Hamblen wished to remain in the Corps, he could.

Hamblen had succeeded in his desire, but just remaining in the Corps was not enough. His next goal was to prove that he was still as good as the toughest in the Marines, and that meant qualifying for the Force Recon Company. By summer he was ready. As reported by still another magazine, *Male*, "Hamblen was given his chance. The qualifying trial—a series of grueling tests that pushed men to the ultimate—began on a hot day in September. Most of the observers thought Hamblen would give a courageous account—and fail. Men who knew his intense desire and pride hoped that the hawk-faced sergeant wouldn't be humiliated. There was an air of tension in the area when Hamblen began his first test. He ran 100 yards, with only the barest trace of a limp in his powerful stride, and reached the 'casualty'—a 180 pound Marine lying prone in full combat gear. Kneeling swiftly, Hamblen hoisted the man across his shoulders, pushed up on his good leg, and sped to the starting point—40 seconds—within the qualifying time."

Hamblen completed the remaining physical tests, including a three-mile run in less than 28 minutes, with equal success. The final test came on 11 September 1963, when Hamblen made his 216th parachute jump. The Camp Pendleton *Scout* reported, "Courage, determination and what has been described as a barrel full of guts were in a parachute which floated down from 1,250 feet above Lake O'Neill Wednesday morning. The attributes were embodied in SSgt Donald N. Hamblen. . . . Instead of resigning himself to the inevitable medical discharge, the 31-year-old Hamblen launched an attack on tradition. He won. Asked why he would go through the suffering and problems attendant upon his fight to stay in the Corps, when he could accept a lifetime pension more easily, Hamblen answered simply, 'Because I'm a Marine.' " (Not reported was the fact that Hamblen after the jump donned swim fins, one specially made for his prosthesis, and scuba gear and made a dive 100 feet into the Pacific Ocean.)

Hamblen's story would ultimately be told in *Newsweek*, the *New York Times*, and the *Congressional Record*. In an article written for *Family Weekly*, Hamblen would add a postscript by stating, "There's practically nothing a man can't do if he is determined enough to see it through—whatever the odds. But that determination has to come from within. And sometimes it has to be pretty powerful."*

---

*Hamblen continued to serve in the First Force Recon Company until 1966, when he went to Vietnam to instruct Vietnamese paratroopers. He retired in 1968 from the position of First Sergeant of the Fifth Force Recon Company. During his final days in the Corps, as well as today, Hamblen won frequent bets that he could touch the ceiling with one foot while the other remained on the floor. After the bets were made the recon Marine simply detached the artificial leg and stretched it in his arms to the ceiling.

CHAPTER 4
◼◻◼◻◼◻◼

Vietnam—The Curtain Rises

*D*URING the decade following the Korean War, the Marine Corps and the other services focused on the anticipated nuclear battlefield of the future. In the early 1960s, many military planners realized that the armed forces needed to prepare to fight more likely conflicts—particularly counterguerrilla warfare in Southeast Asia.

On 10 May 1960 the CMC announced a series of phased tests known as the Marine Corps Troops Test Program to prepare the Corps for future conflicts.[1] Phase II of the test was begun in September 1960 with the issuing of a high-level program directive.[2] According to the directive, the purpose of Phase II was to provide the basis for determining the organic structure of intelligence, combat support (aviation), and combat service units of the Fleet Marine Force for the Mid-Range Period (1962–1968). The tests were to encompass a variety of tactical and logistical situations with emphasis on the non-nuclear environment. One of the dictates that specifically impacted on the recon Marines was "to determine the requirements, elements, organization and equipment of the

Combat Intelligence Systems within the Fleet Marine Force.''

The initial report by the First Recon Company, dated 10 February 1961, which discussed the validity of the Program Directive's Concept of Employment of the company, began by noting the vast differences between Force Recon and conventional infantry units. Unlike the centrally coordinated operations of infantry units, the recon companies deployed small groups of specialists who operated unprotected in enemy-occupied areas and carried out fairly complex tasks, the teams performing independently once launched. Also noted was that recon operations required personnel who met unusually high and exacting standards.[3]

The report continued with recommendations for maintaining both reconnaissance and pathfinding in the company while at the same time explaining that the two functions were too dissimilar to be integrated into one specialty. Also discussed were the increasing requirements for assigned communications specialists to assist in reporting recon findings and in coordinating pathfinder missions.

One of the results of the Phase II test was the recognition that forward Marine units in the Pacific needed pathfinder assets because of the tension in Southeast Asia. On 12 October 1960, Sub Unit Number 1* of the First Force Recon Company was established at Camp Pendleton. On 19 November it was shipped out to be attached to the 3rd Marine Division on Okinawa.[4]

Sub Unit Number 1 was composed of two pathfinder teams. The first, under the leadership of 1stLt R. J. Rigg and GySgt C. Stacy with ten enlisted men, was under the operational control of the 3rd Marine Division. Also at-

*The ''Sub'' in Sub Unit Number 1 had nothing to do with submarines but was a shortened version of ''subordinate.''

tached to the division was the second pathfinder team led by 1stLt Patrick Duffy and GSgt Wesley L. Fox.*

The largest Southeast Asia Treaty Organization (SEATO) amphibious exercise ever conducted in the Western Pacific, Operation TULUNGUN, was held 2 March to 12 April 1962. It provided an opportunity to evaluate the cumulative result of the training and organization of the First Force Recon Company and its subordinate units that had resulted from the recent studies and tests.[5]

TULUNGUN was conducted off the coast of the island of Mindoro, Philippine Islands, by a joint-task organization composed of a Philippine battalion combat team, elements of the Philippine Air Force and Marine Corps, Australian Air Force elements, and a US Marine division and air wing. The exercise training objectives reflected the growing concern for Southeast Asia—particularly Vietnam. All the objectives were on counterguerrilla operations and included operating in terrain similar to Southeast Asia; support, control, and direction of helicopters in support of ground units; coordination and use of artillery, air, and naval gunfire; and coordination in the rapid collection, evaluation, and dissemination of intelligence.

The operation scenario was even more revealing: "After the fall of Tchepone, Laos, to Pathet Lao and Kong Le forces, aggressor used this route (Route 9 into Khe Sanh) to infiltrate large numbers of guerrilla elements into the northern Republic of Vietnam. By February 1962 these elements had become so strong in this area that by direct attacks on the Republic of Vietnam military posts and subversion and terrorization of the local population aggressor was able to seize control of the area."[6]

The missions assigned the First Force Recon Com-

---

*Fox was later to earn the Medal of Honor for bravery in Vietnam. Duffy was killed in action after being promoted to major.

pany were to evaluate the possibilities for pre-D-Day intelligence gathering within a guerrilla environment using the most advanced methods of insertion and recovery, and to provide pathfinder capabilities for helicopter operations. Another mission was to provide the first actual employment in a field exercise of Navy SEAL Teams that had been organized on 1 January 1962.

Since the SEALs had just completed jump school, there was reluctance in the recon company to employ them in night parachute operations and free-fall insertions. Eventually the SEALs were included in the exercise, but in a limited capacity.

Future exercises also attempted to integrate Force Recon with the SEALs, but with little success. Some of the problems were in the recon Marines' perception that the SEALs' training level was inadequate. Deeper prejudices existed as well. Maj James McAlister and Capt Patrick J. Ryan, both commanders of the First Force Recon Company in the early 1960s, were not supporters of the SEALs in general. McAlister recalled that on a joint Marine Corps, Special Forces, and SEAL operation in July 1963, the SEAL jumpmaster had only seven previous jumps and the other members of his team only six or seven parachute drops each. None of the SEALs had ever jumped at night, and their training in other areas was limited, only one SEAL having attended the Army's Ranger School.[7]

A few months later, after another similar experience, Ryan noted even more specific complaints. To Fleet Marine Force, Pacific, Ryan wrote, "I personally feel SEAL is infringing on USMC missions by moving inland from the high water mark. Representative type USMC corporals and sergeants could, allowing three to six months for scuba/Para training, while polishing patrolling and demolition techniques along the way, arrive at the same degree of proficiency that SEAL Team members currently will take a minimum of 18 months to obtain.''[8]

The SEALs were, of course, in their infancy at the time and would achieve a high level of proficiency in Vietnam. Still, the comments of McAlister and Ryan were valid at the time, and their attitude was difficult, if not impossible, to overcome later. After all, Marines never have had a very high opinion of sailors—regardless of their speciality or claimed ability.

While the Marines were making some progress in preparing for the war that loomed in Vietnam, other crises required their attention on a more immediate basis. During the Cuban missile crisis of 1962, a recon platoon and two pathfinder teams of the First Force Company, under the overall supervision of 1stLt Jack W. Phillips,* were detached to the 5th Marine Expeditionary Brigade (MEB) at Norfolk, Virginia. Their mission was to assist in the preparation and possible execution of OPLAN 314—the invasion of Cuba.[9]

Although the OPLAN was never executed, the preparation for it did reveal many problems in the concept of Force Reconnaissance and the lack of understanding of their mission by the rest of the Corps. In a letter to his company commander, dated 25 October 1963, Phillips explained, ''The majority of our operational problems can be traced back to the fact that we were attached to the 5th MEB. Attempting to employ a force reconnaissance unit on this low of a level is not proper utilization of the unit. There seemed to be a lack of appreciation for the amount of coordination, support, and preparation time needed in the execution of a deep or early reconnaissance mission. They had no knowledge of our communications limitations and expected us to talk directly with the ships at sea whose positions were to be

*Phillips was killed in Vietnam on 14 October 1967 while in command of G Company, 2nd Battalion, 4th Marines.

unknown to us. The major shortcoming of the intelligence annex of OPLAN 314 was the inflexibility of the reconnaissance missions assigned. The missions were assigned in detail nearly a year ago based on the intelligence estimate at that time. There was a great reluctance on the part of the G-2 [Intelligence] section to consider changing the missions in accordance with the vastly different enemy situation existing during the crisis. The reconnaissance missions should not be set forth in such detail until the latest information is available.''[10]

The problems in developing OPLAN 314 were but a prelude to the difficulties that were to come for the Force Recon companies. Although the Marine Corps as a whole was beginning to focus its training and field exercises with Vietnam in mind, the simple fact remained that no one really knew just how to prepare for a guerrilla conflict which was complicated by the fact that the mission had undefined objectives and no cohesive support from the US government or its people.

By 1962, of all the US Armed Forces, the Force Recon companies were the most prepared, best trained units to face the enemy in Vietnam. Unfortunately, over the next two years the recon units would become so fragmented and improperly used that they were all but unable to perform their mission. They would recover to perform great deeds, but their accomplishments would be paid for in unnecessary bloodshed. They would have to regain their training level on the battlefield rather than in the safety of peacetime maneuver areas.

The Marine Corps has always been a small force with multiple responsibilities. Limited assets and changing missions have required constant adjustments and reorganization. Degradation of the Force Recon companies was a result of these changes. In the years prior to US involvement in Vietnam, normal adjustments were compounded by two important factors—the erroneous assumption that information normally gathered by long-range reconnaissance would be available from other sources in a counterguerrilla environment, and the loss of trained recon men to other missions as a result of the country's piecemeal commitment to the war.

The first part of the problem—the assumption that information would be available from other sources—is in retrospect difficult to understand. What must be realized is that Vietnam was a very different kind of war, one in which the US lacked recent experience. Lessons learned in the world wars and in Korea were virtually useless against a guerrilla enemy that formed no lines, had no rear areas the nation was willing to attack, and had no schedule to follow in attaining its objectives. Although experience would change their minds, at the beginning of the war the Marine Corps leadership could not grasp the need for a reconnaissance unit trained to penetrate up to 300 miles behind "enemy lines" and who began their operations as many as 60 days before "D-Day," for in Vietnam there were no lines or "D-Days."

Another blow to the Force Recon capabilities occurred as a result of a series of field exercises in 1963 that concluded with a conference on 23–27 September to determine the missions and manning of future recon units.[11] For years there had been critics against pathfinders being assigned to Force Recon rather than directly to the aviation units.

In the end the critics had their way, and the pathfinder *mission* (not the personnel) was transferred from Force Recon to the Marine Air Base Squadrons (MABS). At the same time, the number of patrol teams assigned to Force Recon was increased by transferring the former pathfinders to the reconnaissance platoons. Not all the pathfinders were pleased with this decision, as many were not proficient enough swimmers to meet recon standards.

As a result, many left the recon companies to join other units.

Long-range impacts were even more disastrous. The transfer of pathfinder responsibilities from Force Recon to MABS was accomplished only on paper. In reality the MABS, due to a lack of personnel, never organized their pathfinder elements—to be called Landing Zone Control Teams—and by the time of US escalation in Vietnam, the Marine Corps was totally without pathfinder capabilities.

While these changes in the organization and missions of the Force Recon companies were detrimental in themselves, there were other factors that further decreased the proficiency of the recon units. In the piecemeal commitment to the growing Vietnam conflict in the early years, large numbers of officers and NCOs who had years of experience in reconnaissance were transferred individually to advisor duties and special assignments in the war zone.

The primary organization that siphoned off qualified men from the recon units was the CIA's Naval Advisory Detachment (NAD) of the Studies and Observation Group (SOG) based in Da Nang. SOG was formed on 16 January 1964 as a result of a visit to Vietnam by Secretary of Defense Robert McNamara. McNamara was dissatisfied with the way the war was being run by the Saigon government and the US Military Assistance Advisory Group (MAAG). He wanted to make it more costly for the North Vietnamese to infiltrate the South. SOG was organized with a joint service staff under the cover mission of "performing an analysis of the lessons learned to that point in the Vietnam war." In actuality, SOG was a special operations group with command decision authority and the mission of conducting cross-border operations into North Vietnam, Laos, and Cambodia to disrupt and destroy enemy units in their home territory. SOG also was responsible for tracking and attempting to recover American missing and POWs, training and dispatching agents into the North to organize resistance movements, and conducting a variety of psychological operations, including kidnappings and assassinations.[12]

SOG obviously needed the very best men available from all the services. Special Forces, SEALs, UDTs, and Force Recon were prime sources. The first operation implemented by SOG was Project TIGER, OPLAN 34A-64, which included a variety of missions to take the war to the enemy on his home ground. To assist in the operation, SOG requested that one officer and four enlisted Marines be assigned from the First Force Recon Company. 1stLt L. V. "Reb" Bearce, Sergeant Giles, Cpl Dennis R. Blankenship, and LCpl James P. Randa soon became the first recon Marines to fight in Vietnam.[13]

The Force Recon Marines attached to NAD were replaced every six months with personnel from the First Company. While working with NAD the recon men usually wore civilian clothes or a mixture of captured enemy uniforms. They never carried any US military identification. Working mostly as individual advisors to teams made up of indigenous and/or mercenary soldiers, the recon Marines were assigned varied and often exotic missions. These missions included blowing up bridges and capturing prisoners in cross-border raids. They also assisted propaganda efforts by distributing leaflets from aircraft and leaving them along trails during ground patrols. One mission included leaving behind a large number of commercial radios for the enemy to find. Each of the radios had been modified to receive only one frequency—the joint US/Vietnamese propaganda station.[14]

Although there were but a handful of recon Marines in Vietnam at the time, they claim to have actually "started the Vietnam War."[15] One of the responsibilities of the first Force Recon detachment assigned to NAD was to plan and conduct harassment raids on North Vietnam ports and fortified beach areas. In July 1964, just before his departure, Lt Bearce coordinated one of these raids scheduled to be conducted on 2 August. The mission was to make a firing run on Han Met and Han Mien from small, swift craft known as NASTY* boats armed with 57mm recoilless rifles. On this particular mission, NVA patrol boats intercepted the NASTYs and gave chase. In the darkness the NVA became confused and fired on the USS *Maddox*, which was in the same area on what was called a De Sota patrol. The brief fight became known as the "Tonkin Gulf Incident" and resulted in a resolution on 10 August by the US Congress that led to the further American involvement in the war.**

Secrecy of the SOG operations was extremely tight at the time (and many of their files remain classified today). The principle of information sharing concerning classified military operations is that only personnel with "a need to know" are briefed or have access to operational documents. Bearce was to demonstrate just how closely the secrets of SOG were held when he arrived in Hawaii on his way back to the States. Intelligence officers at SOG had coordinated with their counterparts in the Pentagon for Bearce to brief LtGen Victor Krulak, the commander of Fleet Marine Force, Pacific. When Bearce arrived in Hawaii to give the briefing, he was told that Krulak was not available and to brief another senior officer. But Bearce would say nothing since he had not

---

*NASTY was not a description of the boats but rather was the name of their Swedish manufacturer. The wooden-hulled craft were 90 feet in length and resembled the torpedo boats of World War II.

**Bearce's account of the Tonkin Gulf Incident is not shared by all of the accounts of the times or the histories written since. However, there is little or no information to refute the Marine's claim, and it is certainly as plausible as other accounts of the incident.

been informed that the officer had "a need to know"—despite the fact that the officer explained to Bearce that he was already informed of the missions and operations of SOG. In his attempt to get Bearce to talk, the officer in exasperation finally stated, "I'm going to have you court-martialed because I'm telling you things no one is suppose to hear!"

Bearce finally received permission to brief the officer, but a new problem surfaced: he was to give the briefing in uniform, and the recon Marine had not worn one for eight months. He was even unsure of his proper rank, although he suspected he had become a captain because he had received a plain government envelope with captain's bars and a note that simply stated, "Congratulations. R. R. Dickey." Bearce used the captain bars on his uniform but needed one more for his hat. Unfortunately the Post Exchange was out of the rank so he purchased two first lieutenant bars and placed them side by side on his hat to approximate captain's insignia. In his makeshift adorned uniform, Bearce gave his briefing on how one of his patrols had "started the Vietnam War."*

*Bearce was awarded the Bronze Star for the period 1 February to 30 July 1964 for his work in training the indigenous and mercenary personnel that transformed them "into skilled military specialists capable of performing specialized and sensitive operations."

CHAPTER 5

Force Recon Arrives

*I*N the early years of the Vietnam conflict, the US Congress pressured the military to limit the number of servicemen assigned to the war zone. As a result, the first Force Recon Marines to serve in-country did so on a temporary-duty basis from their home stations for periods up to six months.

The first Force Recon men to serve in Vietnam as actual reconnaissance teams were from the Sub Unit Number 1 of the First Force Recon Company. Since the Sub Unit's assignment to Okinawa in 1960 as a pathfinder detachment, its members had rotated back and forth to Camp Pendleton. When the pathfinder mission was eliminated from Force Recon, the Sub Unit was restructured into a recon element. The first recon replacements, composed of 11 Marines under the leadership of 1stLt Jack W. Phillips, departed for Okinawa on 5 November 1963. Three of the former pathfinders extended their tours on the island to bring the strength of the Sub Unit to 14.[1]

The newly restructured unit participated in several SEATO exercises in the first quarter of 1964 on Okinawa and in the Philippines with US Special Forces, the Philippine Army, and Australian Special Air Service personnel. Sub Unit Number 1's first mission into Vietnam occurred from 6 July to 6 August 1964 as a part of Mine Flotilla One led by the USS *Epping Forest* and three mine sweepers. Included in the flotilla were members of the Navy's UDT-11.

At Cam Rahn the Navy charted the bay while the UDT conducted hydrographic surveys on the outer beaches. Teams of the Sub Unit conducted a variety of inland missions searching for evidence of Viet Cong (VC) activity. The information gathered by the flotilla was an important factor in the later selection of Cam Rahn Bay as the major port for entry for US supplies into the war zone.*

Following completion of the missions in the bay area, the flotilla conducted similar surveys of selected beaches to the north as far as the Bay of Ben Goi before it returned to Okinawa. No major enemy contacts were made, although the recon teams were subject to frequent but ineffective sniper fire.

When 1stLt David Whittingham led the replacement rotation of 15 Marines from the First Company from Camp Pendleton to Sub Unit Number 1 in November 1964, there was little doubt that they, too, would soon be in Vietnam. Whittingham had carefully selected men who were among the most experienced in the company.

After several false starts, Sub Unit Number 1 sailed for the war zone aboard the USS *Cook* to conduct beach surveys on 23–27 February 1965 as a part of Task Force 76. The targeted area of survey was the beaches near Da Nang where the first regular Marine infantry battalions were due to land. The recon men were to obtain information on beach exits, cross-country trafficability, and engineering data. During their reconnaissance the patrols encountered light sniper fire and made significant findings. The infor-

*The USSR must agree with the assessment, because it has used the port for a major portion of its Southern Pacific fleet since the fall of Saigon in 1975.

mation they collected led to the decision to use Red Beach Number 2 rather than Red Beach Number 1 which had originally been planned. Reconnaissance revealed that Red Beach Number 1 had an extremely flat approach compounded by sandbars which would prohibit use of Navy landing craft, that there were insufficient beach exits to accommodate the anticipated traffic of troops and vehicles, and that a congested hamlet was adjacent to the landing area. Red Beach Number 2 was somewhat better hydrographically and had much better access to the inland as well as providing a less vulnerable route to the Da Nang airfield, which the arriving battalions were to secure.* When the Marine battalions arrived on 8 March, their landing was without mishap largely due to the early recon by the men of Sub Unit Number 1.[2]

After the Red Beach reconnaissance, the Sub Unit operated from 15–20 March in the Hue area to determine the best route for inbound battalions to reach the Phu Bai Airfield. Beginning 25 miles south of Hue City, the patrol teams covered the beaches, the Hue River, and a 12-mile route through the city itself. Reconnaissance revealed that the beaches recommended for the planned amphibious assault did not have deep enough water to accommodate the landing craft and that the beaches were backed by lagoons which were too deep for troop crossing on foot but not deep enough for landing craft. The alternative recommended by the recon Marines, which was ultimately approved and used, was to bring the landing craft up the

---

*A logical question is ''Why if the Marines were coming in-country to secure an airfield did they not fly in?'' Part of the answer is the lack of aircraft and the fact that the Marines were already stationed in Okinawa where ship transport was available. The remainder of the explanation is that ''over the beach'' was the way Marines had been going to war for nearly two centuries, and if nothing else, tradition counts in the Corps. It should also be noted that the first US Army brigades and divisions also deployed to Vietnam by ship. It was only after most units were already in-country that replacements began to arrive by air.

Hue River, debark the troops, and proceed by motor and foot march through the city to the airfield.

Continuing to operate from the *Cook*, the recon Marines conducted beach surveys for the 9th Marine Expeditionary Brigade (MEB)* in the vicinity of Chu Lai on 29–30 March and again on 20–23 April. Only ineffective sniper fire was encountered on the first mission, but on 22 April one recon team drew fire on landing. The recon Marines assaulted, and the enemy withdrew and diffused into a nearby hamlet.

The next day a five-man team was inserted by the captain's gig of the *Cook* near the contact area on the southern side of the Song Tra Bong. Seconds after the landing on a crescent-shaped beach, the team was caught in a cross fire from an estimated 25 VC in dug-in positions. In the initial burst of fire, Lowell H. Merrell was wounded. Under covering fire from the insertion boat, commanded by Lieutenant Whittingham, the team withdrew back to the water with Sgt Herman P. Vialpando carrying the wounded Marine. In the ensuing firefight Merrell was hit again, as were two sailors on the boat. All three died of wounds shortly after the skirmish ended. The Force Recon Marines had lost their first man of the Vietnam War.[3]

Despite the loss of Merrell, the missions revealed beach exits, cross-country trafficability, and obvious evidence of enemy presence. This data contributed to the successful landing by elements of the 1st Marine Division and later establishment of an expeditionary airstrip.

By the end of April most of the Marine units that would fight the Vietnam conflict were in-country and the Force Recon Sub Unit was somewhat overcome in the flux of events that swept the war zone. Battalion Landing Teams

---

*The MEB was later renamed the Marine Amphibious Brigade because the word "expeditionary" reminded Vietnamese of the French colonial forces.

(BLT) arrived on beaches that had been reconned by the men of Sub Unit Number 1. The parent division head-quarters of the BLTs soon followed, accompanied by their organic Division Reconnaissance Battalions.[4]

Battalion and Force Reconnaissance units differed both in mission and method of operations. Force Recon was assigned to the Force level, which was commanded by a lieutenant general (three stars) and was composed of two or more divisions and the various supporting units. Reconnaissance of up to 300 miles inland was the stated mission of the Force Recon companies. The emphasis was always on gathering information that could be used for long-range planning, such as locating rear area assembly and supply areas, determining enemy morale, and analyzing the type and condition of the enemy's equipment. Patrol teams usually had four members.

Battalion Recon units were assigned to the divisions that were commanded by a major general (two stars) and composed of three regiments. The three companies of the Battalion Reconnaissance were detached to the regiments and often further broken down to platoons which were assigned to each of the infantry regiments' battalions. Patrols of Battalion Reconnaissance were conducted to gather immediate tactical information that could impact on present rather than long-range operations. These patrol teams usually had eight or more members because they were more likely to come in contact with an enemy who was alert due to proximity of the field Marine units.*

Force and Battalion were both quite proud of their re-

---

*Marine and Army reconnaissance were somewhat similar in their organization except Army infantry battalions had an organic recon platoon. The equivalent of Force Recon was found at both the division and the corps (in Vietnam called Field Force) levels. It is interesting to note that while the Marine Force Recon units were organized prior to the Vietnam War, their Army counterparts, Long Range Reconnaissance Patrol units (LRRPs, redesignated Ranger companies in 1969) were formed in the midst of the war once the need for such specialists was recognized.

connaissance labels, and many Marines served in both on alternate tours. However, the entrance requirements for Force Recon were more stringent, and its numbers were less than a third of its Battalion Recon counterpart.

One unfortunate similarity shared by Force and Battalion Recon was the lack of understanding by Marine leadership of how to use reconnaissance in a counterguerrilla environment. The misuse of the recon Marines in the early months after their arrival in Vietnam is more easily understood by looking at the backgrounds of the senior commanders. Gen Lewis Walt had been a company commander in a World War II Raider Battalion and three of his regimental commanders had led platoons in the Raiders under him: Wheeler of the 3rd Marines, Dupas of the 4th Marines, and Peatross of the 7th Marines. Walt's principle was "find the enemy *and* kill him." He frequently used the recon units as bait: "You find. We'll bail you out."

Walt's ideas on the use of recon units were shared by MajGen W. R. Collins, commanding general of the 3rd Marine Division, and General Krulak, the commander of Fleet Marine Force, Pacific. Both reflected in correspondence at the time that the recon units should be used for inland raids, attacks against coastal installations, and underwater assaults on enemy shipping and facilities.[5]

LtCol Roy Van Cleve, commander of the 3rd Reconnaissance Battalion, said of the use of his recon teams, "They were being used for any mission that might come up. If you don't have somebody else to do it, why, give it to recon. They ended up on some raider-type missions; they ended up on some infantry-assault-type missions."[6]

Capt Patrick G. Collins, a company commander in the 3rd Recon Battalion, recalls that the early missions were often exotic. According to Collins, many leaders seemed to think in terms of the James Bond movies and television shows such as *Mission Impossible* and *The Man from U.N.C.L.E.* that were popular at the time.[7]

As a result of this thinking, Battalion Recon patrols and

the small Sub Unit detachment of the First Force Recon Company were in the early days frequently assigned missions that were unexpected and even bizarre. One mission involved a recon team's swooping down by helicopter in the midst of an enemy camp to snatch a high-ranking enemy officer. Another proposed rappeling from a hovering chopper and swinging into a cliffside cave to capture an enemy agent suspected of possessing vast quantities of US currency. Most of these operations were aborted en route or before they began because they simply could not be accomplished.[8]

The result of such misuse of recon assets resulted in little—except that neither the division nor the Marine Amphibious Force were receiving the information required for planning and operations. It did not take long for the III Marine Amphibious Force commander to recognize that information that could only be gathered through long-range reconnaissance was needed but was not being delivered. In late May 1965 Sub Unit Number 1 was directed to cease operations with the 3rd Marine Division and return to Marine Amphibious Force (MAF) control. The recon Marines then initiated operations with the Army Special Forces in I Corps* with a twofold mission: gaining experience in the mountain approaches to the Marine tactical area of operations along the Laos border; forwarding useful information directly to the III MAF.

The Force Recon Marines were assigned in teams to Special Forces A-Team camps from Khe Sanh to Chu Lai and served as advisors to Civilian Irregular Defense Group (CIDG) patrols. Teams also occasionally operated in their regular team configuration. The arrangement with the Special Forces was beneficial to all concerned because the Green Berets were happy to have the assistance of the

*South Vietnam was divided into four Corps Zones with I Corps the northernmost, reaching to the DMZ.

experienced senior NCOs and radio operators from Force Recon. III MAF, particularly the intelligence officer, LtCol R. E. Gruenler, found the information gathered by the recon men useful in planning future operations.[9]

On 10 July Sub Unit Number 1 was augmented by a platoon from the First Force Recon Company under the leadership of Lt David L. Grannis. The detachment's strength was then two officers and thirty enlisted men. From the arrival of the reinforcements until the end of August, the Sub Unit conducted patrol operations from the 4th Marine Regiment base at Chu Lai. The patrols, normally lasting three or four days, were limited to about 20 klicks (kilometers) from the base. Most of the patrols were the standard complement of four men with an occasional increase to five or six. Insertion was by helicopter or by deploying with an infantry force and staying behind once the larger unit was extracted. These "stay-behinds" were very successful and often gathered information not available through other sources. On one mission the recon men were able to maintain a hidden position for two days observing a hamlet to see if the suspected VC residents moved out when regular company sweeps came into the village or if they blended in with the local populace.

Although the Force Recon Marines were finally operating more in sync with their doctrine, all of the patrols were well within the support of friendly artillery fire.[10]

CHAPTER 6

●━━●━━●━━●━━●━━●

Force Recon Finds Frustration

In the summer of 1965, the First Force Reconnaissance Company was alerted for deployment to Vietnam. The advance party, consisting of the company commander, Maj Malcolm C. Goffan, the company operations officer, and 14 enlisted men departed Camp Pendleton so quickly that all they carried were their M3A1 submachine guns, called "grease guns" because of their shape, and their packs. Other gear was to be shipped later.[1]

Traveling by air, with an overnight stop on Okinawa, the advance party arrived at Da Nang on 7 August. The unit's first mission was to establish a base camp in an open, sandy field at China Beach just south of the Marble Mountain Air Facility. With the help of Seabees, they built living and working areas within a defensive perimeter with bunkers. They named the base Camp Merrell in honor of the first recon Marine killed in the war.[2]

The advance party was joined at Camp Merrell by Sub Unit Number 1, whose detachment commander became the company executive officer when the two units merged. In the latter part of August, the remainder of the First Company deployed by ship from Pendleton for Vietnam. It was not until November, however, that the company reached its normal strength of 11 officers, 141 enlisted men, and four Navy corpsmen. The delay occurred because two platoons were held briefly on Okinawa and one at Subic Bay, Philippines, for additional training en route.[3]

During the first few months First Force Recon Company was in-country, its members experienced the same problems of misuse and misunderstanding of their capabilities as had the Sub Unit. According to the company intelligence chief, GySgt Gus A. Koch, "It was unknown to all from general on to the private as to actually how to properly employ this unit. No one knew what they should do with Force Reconnaissance."[4]

A good example occurred during Operation STARLIGHT, which took place south of Chu Lai in Quang Ngai Province from 18 to 21 August 1965. The Force Recon Marines, attached to BLT 3/7 operating from the USS *Iwo Jima*, were not informed of the operation's details until the day before the landing, when there was no longer time for a preliminary reconnaissance of the objective area. In fact, the recon teams were left aboard ship on the morning of the assault. According to one recon Marine, Cpl George P. Solovskoy, "They didn't know how to use us, so we spent the first night of STARLIGHT on board ship."[5]

The next day, after many of the amphibious tractors used in the beach assault had become immobilized in mine fields, the recon Marines were ordered to take knives and bayonets to probe for the mines and to mark safe passageways. The recon platoon commander refused the order, and the recon men spent the remainder of the operations as guards for the battalion command post.

Although Operation STARLIGHT was basically successful (over 700 enemy killed despite the misuse of the recon assets) one instance in particular pointed out how the recon men should have been used. An infantry company was air assaulted directly in the midst of an enemy bunker complex despite the fact that trenches and enemy soldiers were spotted from the helicopters. Of the over 100 men in the company, only 12 survived without being killed or wounded. If the recon Marines had had the opportunity to patrol the area, a more satisfactory landing zone might have been located and/or the enemy positions softened up with preparatory fire, saving many American lives. On the day of the abortive air assault, Sgt James B. Schmidt recalls that the recon detachment was still on the *Iwo*, berthed just above the medical treatment area. All Schmidt remembers of STARLIGHT is the dead and injured Marines brought back to the ship.[6]

Solovskoy's recon team was able to play a more appropriate role during Operation DAGGER THRUST from 20 September to 2 October. The four-man patrol's mission on 25–26 September was to recon an area at Vung Mu near Saigon where the enemy was suspected of receiving resupply by boat and caching it in nearby caves. Embarking at night in rubber boats from the USS *Diachenko*, the team was prepared to elude possible detection at sea. The men had wrapped their paddles in aluminum foil so that the *Diachenko* could guide them through the maze of junks and small boats to the shore by radar. Solovskoy remembers, "We'd hear the put-put of a junk and the ship's captain would say, '10 degrees right,' and we'd move and miss the junk. It was a patrol a movie could be made of."[7]

Ashore, the Marines went barefoot because their jungle boots would leave prints indicative of American presence. Once past the sand beach the recon men replaced their boots and moved inland.

On the two-day mission the Marines did not spot any resupply boats but did sight several groups of VC. Of significance was the discovery that many of the enemy were armed with new M-16 rifles and carried PRC-25 radios, both of which were the most current available to US troops and had not yet reached the recon Marines, who still carried M3A1 "grease guns" and PRC-10 radios. It appeared that the VC were receiving weapons and radios from within the South Vietnamese government as well as other supplies by water from the north. After the recon patrol had located the VC, Marines of the 3rd Battalion, 7th Marine Regiment swept the area, killing or capturing the majority of the enemy force.[8]

During the last months of 1965, the First Force Recon Company continued to support various operations with small detachments assigned to battalion and regiment levels. Much of the time the company worked as a part of the 3rd Reconnaissance Battalion with mixed results and no major engagements.

On 27 November the company's 2nd Platoon was detached by III MAV to Special Forces Camp A-106 at Ba To in Quang Ngai Province. The third platoon followed on 7 December, joining Special Forces Camp A-107 at Tra Bong. Both platoons were assigned to assist in Operation BIRDWATCHER with the mission "to gather intelligence about the location of enemy forces through the jungle paths and along the river routes in the interior of the countryside."[9] One of the first actions by the recon platoons was to secure camouflaged "tiger-stripe" utilities so that they would be uniformed like their SF counterparts.

Shortly after the 2nd Platoon, under the leadership of Lt J. C. Lenker and SSgt Maurice Jacques, arrived at Ba To, General Walt personally visited to brief them. According to Walt, the enemy had apparently retreated to the Ba To area to regroup following several battles with the 7th Marine Regiment. A regiment of the 325th Peoples Army of Vietnam (PAVN) along with supply storage areas and a hospital—all connected by high-speed trails—were thought to be in a large bowl-shaped valley.[10]

Initial patrols from Ba To all resulted in contact with

large enemy units armed with automatic weapons. It was decided to increase the size of the four-man Marine patrols by adding three CIDG soldiers (local tribesmen) per team. In addition to more firepower, the CIDG men also brought familiarity with the area of operations.

On 14 December three four-man teams of the second platoon, each reinforced by three CIDG soldiers and accompanied by a 42-man CIDG reaction force, deployed to a patrol base atop a kidney-shaped hill eight kilometers from Ba To.[11] A steep drop-off extended from the concave side of the hill to a river at its base. On the convex side was a gradual slope covered with knee-high grass. Two listening posts (LPs) were placed on the fingers of the hill on the grassy slope.

The hilltop offered the most defendable terrain in the area. From the patrol base the three teams were to recon out from the hilltop during the day and return at night. Despite the standard operating procedure (SOP) never to occupy the same patrol base for more than one night, the platoon planned on using it for two days because of its defendability.

By late afternoon of 16 December a heavy fog had set in, limiting visibility. The fog, combined with one patrol's not returning to the platoon base until 1730 hours, influenced the Marines to remain on the hilltop for a third night. It was a drastic mistake. At 1900 hours, mortar rounds fell on the platoon command post killing a Vietnamese lieutenant, who was in charge of the CIDG soldiers. A brief pause was followed by another mortar barrage which wounded Sergeant West, a Special Forces trooper accompanying the mission. The same rounds also hit Jacques's radio, and the explosions seriously impaired his hearing. During the next two hours the enemy dropped over 100 mortar shells onto the Marines' position. This was accompanied by continuous strafing by automatic weapons and by a ground assault by an estimated 150–200 enemy. An interpreter with the Marines noted that the

shouted orders of the enemy leaders were in a North Vietnamese dialect. The Marines were not up against VC but
rather were fighting well trained and disciplined North
Vietnamese Army Regulars (NVA).

During the initial ground attack by the NVA, many of
the CIDGs scattered into the darkness. The Marines con-
solidated as best they could and formed their own perimeter at the top of the hill. A quick head count by Jacques
revealed that Sergeants Akioka and Baker and Corporals
Woo, Brown, and Sisson were missing. In the next few
minutes more Marines in the newly formed perimeter
were wounded, including the platoon corpsman, Doc
Haskin. The corpsman's wounds were serious but not fatal. But when Haskin pleaded for morphine, Jacques refused permission because under its influence Haskin
might be unable to move on his own, and Jacques knew
that all the Marines would soon be running for their lives.

As the enemy closed on the recon men's positions, the
next Marine to be hit was Cpl Raymond S. Joy, Jr. Jacques
shouted orders for the Marines to withdraw to a rally point
located down the steep side of the hill on the river side
that had been predesignated for just such an emergency.
Jacques, joined by Sergeant Blanton, covered the withdrawal, and they were last off the hill.

As the Marines withdrew, the NVA swept over the hilltop, finding Corporal Brown, who was wounded early in
the fight and was playing dead. The enemy began to strip
the gear from his body. Just as the young Marine thought
that the enemy was about to discover that he was still
alive, Joy's moans a few meters away distracted the NVA.
They immediately turned to Joy, shooting him and searching his body. Brown took advantage of the situation,
crawling and then rolling down the steep drop-off and
luckily running into the main group of Marines in the
vicinity of the rally point.

Just before the Marines reached the rally point, the bold
enemy turned on searchlights and caught the fleeing men

in the bright beams. In an instant, green machine-gun tracer rounds were ripping around the Marines. After checking the rally point for any other survivors, the Marines continued to a small creek bed that blocked the NVAs' observation. Down the creek several hundred meters the Marines reached a grove of banana trees and set up another defensive perimeter. Jacques decided they were well enough hidden to treat the wounded and to wait for daylight when aircraft and reinforcements could be expected.

But sunup brought no relief to the beleaguered Marines. A dense fog still prevented observation or support from the air. Knowing the NVA would soon be on their trail, the Marines began moving overland to the Special Forces camp. Several thousand meters later, the platoon heard rustling in nearby bushes. Jacques recalls that the platoon formed a hasty perimeter and prepared to fight as he thought to himself, " 'This is going to be it.' Deep down I knew I'd never make it out alive.''

Just as Jacques was about to open up, one of the CIDGs that was still with the Marines placed his hand over the sergeant's rifle and whispered for him to hold his fire. Shortly two of the CIDGs who had fled at the beginning of the battle approached the perimeter. A few minutes later more noise was heard and again the perimeter alerted for an attack. This time it was Sergeant Baker and Corporal Young who approached, explaining that they had become separated during the withdrawal from the hilltop and had proceeded in the direction of the SF camp in hopes of linking up with their comrades.

By late afternoon the Marines, assisted by wind and a rainstorm that masked the noise of their movement, reached the SF camp. A few hours later Sergeant Akioka arrived, having used his skills in escape and evasion to make his way back on his own.

It was to be four more days before the last survivor of the hilltop attack walked into the camp. Cpl D. W. Woo, a Chinese-American from the state of Washington, did not do so on his own. He was supported on each side by an NVA with a knife held to each of their throats in Woo's clinched fists. Woo had multiple wounds in his legs and groin and, except for cloth from a parachute flare tied around his waist, was naked. From a hospital bed in Chu Lai, Woo later explained that he had been hit early in the firefight and had been stripped when the NVA overran the hilltop. Playing dead, he had waited until most of the enemy had moved on for his opportunity to escape. He then "recruited" his two "helpers" to assist him in his trek to the base camp.

On 21 December, the same day Woo returned, a joint patrol of Marines, Special Forces, and CIDGs reached the embattled hilltop and recovered 14 bodies—three recon Marines, Sergeant West of the Special Forces, and 10 CIDGs. The three recon men, LCpl R. P. Sisson, LCpl W. R. Moore, and Cpl R. S. Joy, had died of multiple gunshot and fragmentation wounds. A plaque was later erected at the Ba To Special Forces Camp in their honor. Sisson's parents and neighbors from his hometown of Hulberton, New York, eventually sent clothing to the villagers of Ba To as a show of respect and support for the recon Marines.

As a result of the deaths of the three Marines of the second platoon, all the elements of the company that were detached to various units across I Corps were withdrawn. On 27 December the First Force Recon Company was placed under operational control (OPCON) of the 3rd Reconnaissance Battalion.[12]

Not all went well following the company's attachment to battalion recon—especially from the troopers' point of view. Many of the Force Recon men felt that the "good" missions that were more likely to produce intelligence and body count were given to the recon battalion patrols while those of less importance were delegated to Force Recon. There was also resentment on the part of the Force Recon Marines because it seemed that individual awards and decorations were presented much more freely to the battalion recon members.[13]

Not all the problems of the First Force Recon Company, however, were the result of their assigned missions and the lack of understanding of their capabilities by higher commanders. As has been previously noted, most of the company's best-trained personnel had been transferred to other units or assigned individually before the recon unit's arrival in Vietnam. Many of the current members were inexperienced in even the most basic recon tactics and techniques. This was true for officers, noncommissioned officers, and enlisted Marines alike.

The tough physical testing that had been required for acceptance into the unit was waived in the war zone, as was the harassing "scream screening" that revealed how a man would react to pressure. Officers and enlisted men who would have been rejected during the prewar years were now able to join Force Recon.

One officer, Capt Patrick G. Collins, analyzed the officer replacements who joined the Force and Battalion Recon units from February 1965 to February 1966.[14] Collins noted that during the one-year period, 27 officers were relieved of their duties for inefficiency. The primary deficiency was an inability to think or function independently. One of the first lieutenants to arrive as a replacement in the First Company was in excellent physical condition but could not think on his own and had to be told everything by his superiors. Soon after joining the unit, he compounded his exhibited weaknesses with poor navigation, resulting in the insertion of his teams in the wrong locations, causing needless loss of life in the resulting firefights.[15]

Perhaps the greatest impact of the lack of experience and training was in the NCO ranks, where responsibility for the leadership of the patrols lay. Team leaders had to be able to think and operate independently at distances of 10 to 20 kilometers from the company base and other friendly units. In the field, the patrol leader had the absolute final say-so on all matters. His decisions not only affected the mission, but also the safety and welfare of his team.

While insufficient training was often a problem for officers and NCOs, a complete lack of recon instruction was common for many of the enlisted replacements. Cpl R. E. Belinski was typical of the replacements during the first year he reported in as a radioman with no recon training whatsoever.[16] Hospital Mate 3rd Class (HM3)* Harvey E. Messier joined the recon Marines in the way that many replacements did: he had just arrived at the Da Nang Reception Station when volunteers for Force Recon were requested. The Navy corpsman held up his hand and became a recon team member, eventually participating in 22 missions, including two in which his team rappeled into their objective.[17]

For the inexperienced replacement, the only training available was "on the job." Accompanying patrols as observers, they learned as quickly as possible to take their place on the regular teams.[18] This was of course not an efficient—or safe—way to train replacements. The frustration felt by the old-time recon men was best stated by Gunnery Sergeant Koch in an oral history interview shortly after his return to the States in August 1966. Koch said, "Vietnam should not be considered as a training camp. It is not a place for training at first hand, but a place for action. We must be mentally and physically prepared to

*Medical personnel are not a part of the Marine Corps organization. Corpsmen from the Navy are attached to Marine units for medical support.

not only fight a common enemy but to also fight the climate, fatigue, hunger, thirst, disease, leeches, jungles, and mountains—to fight the enemy you must have the will to fight.

"One of the main problems we encountered while we were in Vietnam was personnel strength. At times a platoon consisted of seven to eight men [instead of the 15 authorized]. We received new members directly out of ITR [Infantry Training Regiment]. They just reported into Vietnam; they weren't even acclimatized. Well, we didn't have any personnel to teach them. The only way possible for us to teach them anything about Vietnam and patrol action was to give them on-the-job training by actually going out in the field."[19]

Other than ITR, the primary source of replacements was from the in-country Marine infantry battalions. However, this source added to the problem more often than it offered a solution. Rather than transfer highly motivated, combat experienced Marines, the infantry battalions usually saw the request for Force Recon replacements as an opportunity to unload their "problem" Marines or those who were least qualified.

After several experiences with receiving less than satisfactory recon candidates from the infantry battalions, the Force Recon Company began to rely strictly on the new arrivals in-country straight out of Infantry Training Regiment. Although untrained in reconnaissance, those who volunteered were usually self-disciplined, interested in becoming recon men. With the proper attitude, they at least had a better chance of being molded into assets for the company.

While neglecting reconnaissance and survival training for the Vietnam-bound, the stateside training bases taught recruits some skills which were of little or no use in the war zone. In ITR, amphibious reconnaissance was still taught although it was essentially not used after the first few months of Marine involvement in the conflict. The

helicopter and movement by foot dominated recon insertion methods. Land recon techniques with practical experience in calling for and coordinating air and artillery
support did not receive sufficient emphasis in the training
centers. Simple skills, such as noise discipline and the
proper use of cover and concealment, were covered little
or not at all.

Recon Marine Sgt Joseph R. Crockett noted at the
time, "Every team I've known that has been hit has
been hit due to noise—they cough, they smoke and joke,
they talk, they snore, they sleep. In harbor sites they
don't clear leaves away so when they roll over they
crunch."[20]

One recon Marine noted in an interview near the end
of his tour in Vietnam that stateside training was inadequate and that perceptions of the enemy were incorrect.
According to Cpl John T. Morrissey,

"I know most of the Marines back in the States believe this war is nothing much at all. Well, you actually have to come over yourself and experience it.
The Marines back in the States, a lot of them believe
that the enemy is just 'gooks' and that they're stupid.
The VC aren't good soldiers, but the NVA are—
they're professionals. The enemy is far from being
the 'stupid Oriental' as many believe them to be.
They've been fighting ever since before World War
II—that's a long time. He knows lots of stuff. He can
go on and on. Back in the States it's recon, recon,
recon, all the way, gung ho, and all that kind of stuff.
Running, running, running; pushups, pushups, pushups; deep knee bends, etc. That stuff is all well and
good back in the States where it's mostly "hot dog,"
but over here, it's not going to do you that much
good. The type of conditioning that you should be
getting is to put a 70- or 80-pound pack on your back
and go out humping five days, six days, maybe more,

out in the brush climbing high mountains, down into ravines, crawling on your hands and knees through the brush.[21]

Morrissey was correct: one of the most important characteristics of a successful military organization is its ability to adjust to changing battlefield situations. In every war, doctrine and tactics have had to adapt to the enemy, terrain, and technical advances. This normal process of adjusting to meet the situation had to be accelerated in Vietnam because it was a war like no other that the United States had fought. For the recon Marines this was as true, or more so, than for other combat units.

Some reconnaissance tactics taught before the war had to be "un-learned." Prior to Vietnam, Force Recon doctrine emphasized avoiding compromise. If a team was inserted weeks or months before D-Day, its discovery might jeopardize the entire operation by alerting the enemy to the impending attack. If a pathfinder team was detected, the helicopters and their infantry cargo would be endangered on landing. This conscious avoidance of compromise resulted in less patrolling and intelligence-gathering in the early months of the war. For many Marines, to whom there was only a right way and a wrong way of doing things, it was difficult to "un-learn" years worth of training.

For example, Corporal Solovskoy recalls that a patrol in December 1965 was aborted when a single enemy soldier, who seemed to be looking in their direction, was spotted on a ridge line across a wide valley.[22] Despite the fact that the recon team was unsure if the enemy had observed them—and even if he had they could have moved quickly and undetected to another area—they called for helicopter extraction.

A more reasonable concern by the patrols was compromise either before or during insertion into their recon zones. In a war where there were no "lines" and where the local villager might be a farmer by day and a guerrilla by night, it was difficult for any troop movement to go undetected. This was compounded by many Marine bases being built adjacent to hamlets and towns where enemy agents could report the comings and goings of patrols.

The recon Marines did their best to avoid compromise, but ultimately realized that it was often inevitable and had to be accepted. The recon doctrine quickly changed to "if you find out you are compromised, continue the mission."[23]

Along with the acceptance of compromise came the assumption that the patrols would have to be more willing to engage in direct combat with the enemy. Koch, in an after action tape, stated,

> When we first started out, we traveled light because we were still on our mission to observe and report intelligence. However, as we found out, in Vietnam it is not so. It's almost impossible to complete a mission without a compromise, and it's almost inevitable that contact will be made, and when contact is made, you want all available weapons, grenades, and firepower to your advantage. Therefore, Force Recon adapted themselves as a reconnaissance team but with the ammunition and capability of a combat patrol.[24]

This assumption of combat missions by recon patrols brought on another change in established doctrine. The primary influences on the success and survivability of a recon patrol were stealth, security, and non-detection. Ideally a patrol would gather intelligence and return to report the information to its commander without the enemy ever being aware the team had been in its territory. In the event a patrol was compromised, reporting intelligence already gathered took priority over team integrity. When a patrol was detected standard procedure had the team disperse so at least one member would make it back to friendly lines with the needed information.

This "scatter plan" tactic was as old as reconnaissance itself and was formalized as doctrine in America during the French and Indian Wars of the eighteenth century. Maj Robert Rogers wrote a series of instructions in 1756 for his reconnaissance unit known as Rangers. One of "Rogers' Rules for Rangers"* stated, "If the enemy is so superior that you are in danger of being surrounded by them, let your whole body disperse, and everyone take a different road to the place of rendezvous appointed for that evening."[25]

The scatter philosophy remained a part of recon doctrine into the twentieth century, with Marine Corps officer schools expanding on Rogers' rules by teaching,

All patrol formations must be such that in case of surprise one man is able to escape and carry information back to the commander. If you place your patrol in such a position that all are killed or captured, your commander, lacking information to the contrary, will assume that your patrol is still operating. Whereas if you had a "get-away" man who would have informed the commander of the mishap, the commander could have replaced the patrol.[26]

Despite the advent of radio communications, which allowed immediate reporting of recon findings, the scatter plan remained a part of Marine reconnaissance doctrine

*Rogers' Rules still appear in various forms in many publications for reconnaissance units. Although the US Army LRRPs of Vietnam and the Rangers of today claim Rogers as the "Father of the American Ranger," the Force Recon Marines are certainly just as much his progeny.

in the first months of their involvement in Vietnam. This longevity was based on World War II experience when radio silence was strictly enforced prior to major invasions and offensives. As with many other concepts established in previous wars, the scatter plan proved invalid in Vietnam. Unfortunately, it took the death of another Force Recon Marine to change the policy.

Patrol PRIMNESS I[27] was deployed from Ba To on 26 January 1966 to establish observation posts (OPs) near the village of Tan An. The four-man patrol consisted of 1stLt J. C. Lenker, Corporal Solovskoy, Sergeant Young, and LCpl Jean Pierre Dowling. Solovskoy later reported in an oral history tape that the patrol was apprehensive from the beginning because to reach its recon zone the men had to pass through several villages which likely had VC agents reporting the patrol's movements.

Moving deliberately through thick jungle and across rugged hills after they cleared the villages, the patrol reached their OP site. According to Solovskoy,

> We spent two days on the side of a hill overlooking a village which was in the center of a rice paddy valley. We saw quite a few Cong and NVA that were in the village. My team would take turns with one up in a tree with a spotter scope, one on the radio and the other two on security. We were using the PRC-25 radio. From the tree I would say, "Sir, I see 60 Cong going into the village on bicycles with packs, rain covers, and camouflaged utilities." They had submachine guns and were only 500 yards away and were continually leaving and entering the village.

Solovskoy next remarked on another problem with the early patrols of Force Recon—the lack of trust by their high commands in the intelligence the patrols reported. "I noticed that Lieutenant Lenker wasn't radioing in all the sightings I made so I asked him why. He said, 'Well,

Corporal Solovskoy, they just wouldn't believe it.' That
shook me up because we were risking our lives to call
in sightings. Actually, I saw his point. Other patrols
would be out and they'd make sightings including signs
that they were in imminent danger of being hit. Our CP
group would say, 'Well, just keep on your mission.'
They sort of used our unit like bait; if you get shot,
then they'd believe there're Cong out there and come
pick up what's left. It seemed to me that they wouldn't
believe sightings. They'd only believe actual WIAs or
KIAs of our own unit. Then they'd believe that there
were Cong out there.''

After his turn as the observer in the tree on 29 January,
Solovskoy was replaced by Dowling, a native of France
who had come to the United States and joined the Marine
Corps in order to gain his citizenship. Solovskoy recalls,

> I went down and sat by the radio for a while. Pierre
> was up in the tree about forty feet. There was a lot
> of foliage so he couldn't be spotted. I said, ''Hey,
> Pierre, you better look behind you because if they
> hit us they'll come over the top of the hill.'' He
> turned and answered, ''Yeah, Yeah,'' just as he saw
> six Cong only about 300 yards away. The Cong had
> apparently been following our trail. We had used
> [parachute] rigger tape on our boots to cover up the
> lugged soles on the jungle boots so as not to leave
> an obvious trail, but the Cong had not been fooled.
> As Pierre turned, the tree moved a little bit and the
> Cong noticed and immediately started shooting.
> Rounds were bursting all around. We realized we
> were compromised and the immediate action was to
> ''make our hat'' [withdraw]. The six Cong could be
> a point for a larger unit. With an estimated 1,100
> enemy in the area it was run or likely not make it
> out alive.

The lieutenant and Sergeant Young started run-

ning down the hill as Pierre dropped from the tree
and followed them. I grabbed the radio and called
our CP back at the Special Forces Camp and told
them we had been hit and requested an immediate
chopper to pick us up. As soon as I finished, I got
shot in the leg. The Cong were apparently not good
marksmen because they were only 30 yards away.
The only thing I could think of was getting away, so
I left the radio and my gear. All I took with me was
my rifle. The bullet in my leg had missed the bone
and had just grabbed a little of the meat. It inspired
me to catch up with the others, and in a few seconds
I was leading them down the hill. I was definitely
inspired.

The Cong stopped shooting. Apparently they were
looking over the lieutenant's map, the radio, and other
gear we had left behind. We made a left turn, going
parallel alongside the mountain, trying not to leave a
trail. After about five hundred yards, we ran into a
stream and followed it down to near the valley. We
kept absolutely quiet.

Just before we broke out into the valley, there was
an embankment and a little gulley about five by ten
feet. We got into the gulley and set up our perimeter
with the intent to wait for the choppers to pick us
up. Pierre secured the direction we had come from
the stream and the lieutenant the area toward the
valley. Young took out his bandages and started
wrapping my leg. Pierre turned to watch us and I
said, "Pierre, you better watch your area. They
could come up from the stream." He replied,
"Yeah, yeah, don't sweat it." I was helping Young
wrap the rest of my leg when I looked over my
shoulder and saw a Cong coming up the embankment. He was right on top of us, but he hadn't seen
any of us. He then took another step and almost
stepped on Pierre and started blasting at him with

his sub-Thompson. The lieutenant and sergeant started running. I turned and shot the first Cong and he fell back. I don't take any credit for staying there. I was too afraid to move.

There wasn't anything else I could do. I had nineteen rounds left and that was all. I sat there knowing that in the next ten minutes I'd be dead. There was no way in the world that I'd live to again see Minnesota, my friends back home, or my buddies in Force Recon. Up to that point my knees and hands had been shaking. Then I stopped being scared— once I realized I wasn't going to live, I wasn't scared anymore.

The other five Cong were in the stream bed talking back and forth. I had to find some way out of there. There was no way to crawl through the brush and not make noise so I pulled the pin on a grenade, let the spoon fly and held it a few seconds so that when I threw it, they wouldn't have time to throw it back. I rolled it down the embankment and it went off. Another Cong yelled so I must have gotten another one.

I could hear the other four Cong—two going upstream, two down. The two downstream made a turn to come around and circle me. I realized it was now my only chance to escape. I grabbed Pierre's compass so I could find my way back over the seven kilometers to Ba To. I took a grenade from Pierre's body and crawled over him. At that time I noticed that one of his hands and part of his arm was blown off. There was no way he could live through that. Later when his body was recovered there were 41 bullet holes in him.

When I crawled over the embankment, I found the two dead Cong. One had the lieutenant's map stuffed in his shirt so I took it. I now had a map and compass and knew I could make it back. I crawled through the

brush to the paddy edge and just as I got there I heard
the noise of choppers. I couldn't believe it. I had been
doing all kinds of praying and now two H-34's and
two Army Hueys were overhead.

Between the time we got hit on the hill and when
I heard the choppers was about 50 minutes to an
hour. Those 1,100 NVA had plenty of time to be
looking so I decided to go into the open rice paddy
and flag down the choppers. If I got killed, well
that was it. I ran out into the middle of a rice paddy,
in open view, and waved my jacket up and down.
One of the 34s spotted me and landed three paddies
away. I think I made the fifty yards in two steps. I
grabbed the crew chief's leg and said, "Thank
God."

The crew chief asked me where were the others
and I told him that one was dead and that I didn't
know about the other two. The pilot gained altitude
and we started looking. In about five minutes we
spotted the sergeant. He had crossed the entire valley,
which was a half mile wide, in about ten minutes
from the time of the last contact. We picked him up
and went looking for the lieutenant. About five minutes later we found him across the valley and halfway
up the mountains. We were all flown out to the *Valley
Forge*. [Recovery was completed at 1500 hours, 29
January 1966.]

The actions of Patrol PRIMNESS I and the death of Pierre
Dowling ended the scatter plan technique for breaking
contact with the enemy. In lieu of the "every man for
himself" escape, the doctrine changed to "everybody stays
together, and if necessary they fight their way out."[28]

Along with changes in tactics, the recon Marines made
adjustments to their armament and equipment. The standard recon weapon since the Korean War had been the
M3A1 "grease gun," which was a short-barreled, short-

stock .45-caliber submachine gun. In Vietnam the M3A1 proved to be too limited in effective range and reliability. Originally adopted when it was anticipated that Force Recon would perform only reconnaissance missions, its maximum effective range of 100 meters was satisfactory because the recon men avoided enemy contact and only used their weapons for close combat prior to withdrawal. With the added responsibility of performing combat missions, the recon units needed a weapon with more range. The M3A1 also proved unreliable in the humid jungle of Southeast Asia because the spring in the magazine rusted easily, causing a loss of tension which allowed the weapon to jam. Another fault of the grease gun, especially when used by reconnaissance units that by nature depended on stealth and silence, was that it made a loud "click" just before firing.

The recon men initially secured World War II M-2 carbines and M-1 rifles from the Special Forces and Marine supply channels. These weapons were soon exchanged for M-14s, and the 7.62mm rifles rapidly became the weapon of choice of the recon Marines during the early months of the war. As the fully automatic M-16 rifle—with high velocity, light weight 5.56mm ammunition—became available, it replaced the M-14. A shorter barreled and stock version of the M-16, the CAR-15 was also a popular recon weapon, but was in short supply. The recon Marines usually carried whatever weapons they felt would get the job done. At various times, depending on mission requirements and personal preferences, a patrol might carry a mixture of M-14s, M-16s and CAR-15s with the occasional M-79 grenade launcher, M-60 machine gun, shotgun, and pistol added.

The addition of combat missions to the recon units not only affected weapons but also gradually evolved into the use of recon teams as forward observers (FOs) to capitalize on enemy targets of opportunity. Previous recon operations called for the gathering of intelligence that would be used in planning larger unit operations. In Vietnam this practice simply did not work. By the time an infantry unit could be deployed to respond to a recon finding, the enemy was likely long gone from the area. By using artillery, air, and naval gunnery support, the recon teams could not only find but also destroy as well. 1stSgt Clovis C. Coffman, of the First Force Recon Company, in a 1966 oral history interview stated, ''The concept of reconnaissance in the Republic of Vietnam has changed; all of our units are operationally trained as artillery forward observers, naval gunfire and aircraft controllers, and each reconnaissance patrol leaves our patrol base here in Da Nang loaded for, and acting like, a combat patrol.''[29]

Sergeant Koch added, ''Prior to this, when we had a sighting, all we could do is report and, of course, if a sighting was made at one time, those VC or NVA could be at an entirely different location two hours later. So from then on, we fired artillery on any sighting or target of opportunity.''[30]

Techniques of patrolling, like selection of weapons and the assumption of new missions, could not follow pre-Vietnam doctrine. No manual dictated how to operate in a guerrilla environment. Patrols, either Force or Battalion recon, had to be creative, and they had to choose or invent methods that they felt best fit the particular situation they faced. Unit SOPs were adopted, but were changed or modified when necessary. Often, written doctrine was far behind patrol practice in the field, resulting in individual teams taking great latitude in their methods of operation.

One particular variance was in how teams established their overnight positions, known in Marine language as ''harbor sites.'' Some teams surrounded themselves with Claymore mines while others depended on preplotted artillery fire for their defense. Some teams established a perimeter, with all members in a 360 degree ''wagon wheel," while others preferred to set up in two separate positions to minimize injuries from a single enemy grenade. In the "two-position" harbor sites, a wire or rope was run between the groups to provide silent communications.

Some teams set up at dusk in one location and moved to another under the cover of darkness in case the first site had been observed by the enemy. Capt George "Digger" O'Dell recalled, "It all sounds funny now, but on a number of occasions teams moved and then reported seeing NVA sweeping the area they'd left. It was a good tactic, and I urged teams to use it."[31]

O'Dell also noted lessons learned in communications and noise discipline. According to the captain,

> At night we never talked on the radio. It was all done by keying the handset. Every hour the nearest relay would call and ask if they were "alpha sierra" [all secure]. It would go something like this: "ICE BOAT, if you are alpha sierra, key your handset two times." Naturally if you keyed it once or three times then the relay would start a series of questions, such as "If you have movement around you, key your handset two times," etc. You could even call in artillery this way because all your concentrations were called in before dark, and you received numbers on them. It all sounds complex but it got to be pretty simple.[32]

Another technique that varied from team to team was the practice of "running trails." Patrols that were strictly reconnaissance in nature might set up and observe trails for enemy movement but totally avoided actually moving on them. Other teams with a combat mission might use the trails in the belief that this was the most likely way of making contact.

Those teams that did "run trails" had to be well trained

and extremely careful. 1stLt Russell L. Johnson states, "We found the 3rd NVA Headquarters simply by running trails. It was dangerous; you had to have an excellent point. I had two pointmen, one from Alabama and one from Kentucky. They were excellent trackers and could read trails telling you how many men and how long ago they had passed. They got so they could hear things that others could not. They could pick up smells. It got to be like a sixth sense."[33]

CHAPTER 7

Anatomy of a Patrol

*U*NLIKE regular Marine infantry units, which frequently maintained operations for long periods of time without a break, recon patrols were of short duration, rarely exceeding five or six days. Recon teams were also afforded a period of several days between patrols during which time they were able to train, maintain their gear, prepare for the next mission, and briefly relax.[1]

Patrol leaders were notified as many as three days prior to their deployment on a mission. Immediately upon receiving the order from the company commander or operations officer, the patrol leader assembled his team and related in general terms, known as a Warning Order, the mission and any information immediately available concerning the enemy and friendly situations in the assigned area. If the team had new members or additional men assigned, the patrol leader also used this time to designate specific duties, such as point man, assistant patrol leader, rear security, etc. Instructions on weapons, rations, and special gear were given, along with a detailed schedule of events to take place up to the actual insertion.

Once the Warning Order had been issued, the patrol leader conducted a preinspection of his team to determine if any members were unfit from illness or injury. A minor cold, if accompanied by sneezing or coughing, was enough to scratch a man from a mission where stealth and noise discipline meant survival. Mental attitude received the same emphasis. If a Marine had personal problems that might affect his alertness and concentration, he also was left behind.

At the completion of the preinspection, a Patrol Inspection Check List was prepared containing all the items that would be carried on the patrol. Items were divided into individual and team categories. Some items were carried on every patrol while others might be added or eliminated depending on the mission, enemy, weather, and terrain. Recon teams all carried the same basic weapons and equipment, but great latitude was taken in adding items that the patrol leader or the team felt were needed to accomplish the mission.

Individual items included camouflaged utilities, jungle boots, and "floppy hats" rather than steel helmets. The "floppy" was much better protection from rain and sun and assisted in the Marine's camouflage, as it broke up the outline of the head. Each man carried from ten to twenty magazines of ammunition, a knife of choice, which was usually a K-bar, two snap links, a six-foot nylon rope, two or more canteens depending on the weather and terrain, one bottle of water purification tablets, one small and one large first-aid dressing, weapon cleaning gear, insect repellent, camouflage grease sticks, and dog tags. Varying amounts of fragmentation and smoke grenades, along with Claymore mines, pen flares, and signal mirrors and panels, were packed in accordance with the team's SOP.

Spread out among the team were a PRC-25 radio or its later replacement, the PRC-77, and a PRC-93 or RT-10A survival radio. Whatever the combination, a team tried to always have two means of radio communications. Extra batteries for the radios were packed along with one pair of 7x50 field glasses, two maps, two compasses, and two copies of the radio frequencies, call signs, and code shackles for all units in the area. Additional medical supplies, including serum albumin (a blood expander), morphine Syrettes, malaria pills, and other medicines and bandages, were packed by the team corpsman if one was present or spread out among the team if not.

Planning for the patrol followed similar procedures for either reconnaissance or combat missions. Frequently a patrol deployed initially to gather intelligence and concluded with an ambush to gather more information through documents taken from enemy dead. Throughout the patrol, the recon men were prepared to call in artillery, air, and naval gun support on targets of opportunity. Other missions that might be assigned or included as part of a recon or combat patrol included BDAs (bomb damage assessments—usually of B-52 strikes), implanting electronic sensors, tapping into enemy wire communication lines, or capturing a live prisoner for interrogation.

Many of the same tasks that had been assigned to Force Recon since their earliest formation remained despite the emphasis in Vietnam on combat operations. Whatever the mission, the recon men still gathered intelligence that could assist higher commanders in planning future operations. This included locating enemy infiltration routes, assembly areas, supply bases, and communications sites. Patrol reports noted the adequacy of LZs; trafficability of roads, trails, and streams; map corrections; water sources; and the estimate of enemy morale, logistics, and possible future actions.

One thing common to nearly all patrols, regardless of mission, was that they had total control of their area of responsibility. This recon zone, as it was known, was generally six square kilometers and was totally under the responsibility of the patrol leader. Considered a "no fire, no fly" area by all other friendly units, no one could fire into or fly over the recon zone without permission of the patrol leader. This not only protected the recon team from friendly fire but also gave them the assurance that anyone in their area was enemy and could be treated accordingly.

Once a mission and a recon zone were assigned and the patrol Warning Order issued, the patrol leader's next steps were in the gathering of all available information on the area to be worked. This involved an overflight of the recon zone to check for trails, terrain features, and any signs of enemy activity. The overflight also offered the opportunity to select primary and alternate LZs (landing zones) and PZs (pickup zones) for insertion and extraction.

On return from the overflight, the patrol leader gathered intelligence reports from various higher and lower head-quarters, agent reports, aerial photographs, and any other information available. This information was usually al-ready assembled for the patrol leader by the company in-telligence sergeant, who maintained files of externally secured information as well as intelligence gathered by previous company patrols. When GSgt Gus Koch arrived in-country with the First Force Recon Company as the intelligence sergeant, he realized the fluid nature of enemy sightings and contacts, and developed an incident board to reflect where enemy units were frequently encountered. Using colored grease pencil on clear plastic map overlays to track each enemy spotting, Koch was able after a few months to provide valuable premission intelligence to the patrol leaders. This procedure was later modified to add more overlays to indicate suitable LZs, map corrections, and water sources that had been reported on previous mis-sions.

Intelligence sergeants also provided patrol leaders blank checklists that listed all the areas that he had to prepare for presentation in his formal order to the team once that information had been assembled. Regardless of the num-ber of missions a patrol leader had led, or the number of times he had given similar orders, the blank form insured that nothing would be left out or not be covered in suffi-cient detail.

The patrol members then test-fired their weapons and conducted rehearsals, including immediate-action drills for hasty ambushes, breaking contact, and actions on receiving indirect fire. Regardless of how many times the same team members had been on patrol together, they rehearsed their order of movement, establishment of overnight positions, actions for crossing trails or streams, and security procedures during brief halts.

Once the patrol leader had prepared his detailed operations order, he briefed his team verbally, assisted by sand table mock-ups and aerial photographs and maps of the recon zone. Upon completion of the order, the patrol leader quizzed each of the team members to ensure that all were thoroughly familiar with every aspect of the mission. Each man in the patrol was expected to be knowledgeable enough to take over the leadership in the event of casualties.

During the patrol itself, talking above a whisper was not allowed, and, as much as possible, communication was by arm and hand signals. Many of the signals were standard throughout the recon units, while others were particular to a team. Some of the recon teams developed silent communication to a point of sophistication that rivaled the sign language taught in schools for the hearing impaired.

Once everyone was completely knowledgeable of the mission and well rehearsed in all aspects of it, the team made its final preinsertion preparations: slings were removed from weapons, and loose items that might rattle or shake were taped down; camouflage grease paint was applied to faces, hands, and exposed skin; vegetation or strips of burlap were added to rucksacks and weapons to break up their normal outline and to assist the recon men in blending in with their environment. The final preparations were again followed by an inspection by the patrol leader.

When the patrol leader was satisfied that his men were ready for the mission, the team went into seclusion from the rest of the company to prepare the final asset that made them so proficient—their minds. One recon Marine recalls this "recluse" period: "Just as an actor works on a script for months and months, I knew exactly what I was going to do and how I was going to do it. Nobody would need to tell me what to do."

The actual insertion of the team by helicopter was usually preceded and followed by "false insertions," as the chopper made fake passes at potential LZs to confuse any enemy in the area of the actual destination. When the insertion aircraft actually did touch down, the team moved quickly off the LZ and into the jungle. As soon as cover had been reached, the team halted and listened for any movement that might indicate that they had been detected. Before moving out, the team radio operator conducted a communications check with the company headquarters (or a radio relay point if the distance was too great to the base).

The patrol followed a predetermined route on which every man in the patrol was well briefed. Moving in a file with a point man to the front and a rear security man covering the backtrail, each man in between was assigned responsibility for a sector of the flanks. If the patrol halted briefly, the file expanded into a cigar shape, with all-around security. For halts longer than a few minutes, the team formed a perimeter, set out Claymores, and planned defensive artillery concentrations.

Movement on patrol was slow, with stealth and silence more important than distance covered. Many teams stayed in the thickest of vegetation and navigated the harshest terrain. Doing things "the hard way" was the best—and the safest. At times the point man would move forward for twenty or so meters while the remainder of the team sat and listened. No one ate or drank without permission of the patrol leader. During the monsoon season, teams often deliberately waited for the daily downpour before having chow so the noise of the rain would mask any noise they made. Of course, rations were eaten cold; no fires or heating devices were permitted. Smoking was no problem as it was not allowed in the field. Inspections before insertion insured that no man even carried cigarettes. The same was true for reading material or for anything else not directly needed to accomplish the mission.

Because the patrol teams worked in such small numbers, they did their best to make contact only on their own terms. A smaller force can have an advantage over a larger one if it initiates the fight and does so with complete surprise and overwhelming firepower. The recon Marines preferred to initiate firefights from ambush by exploding Claymore mines and following with hand grenades and small-arms fire. Artillery concentrations could assist by sealing off the enemy's escape or preventing his reinforcement. Strafing runs or low-altitude bomb runs from Marine or Air Force jet aircraft were available, as were Marine and Army helicopter gunships firing machine guns and/or rockets. From offshore, battleships like the *New Jersey* could deliver 16-inch high-explosive shells as far as 24 miles inland. If ground support was needed, other Marine units could be airlifted into the fray. Reaction forces, code named BALD EAGLE or SPARROW HAWK, often were staged at nearby LZs or base camps, ready on minutes' notice to support the recon teams or exploit their findings.*

When the patrol teams encountered enemy units that they could not handle themselves or with the assistance of the various supporting arms, they broke contact and melted

---

*The description of a "typical" patrol is not meant to imply that helicopters were always available or capable of supporting Marine reconnaissance. Helicopter support, despite being one of the key innovations of the war, was an asset always in short supply and much demand. Helicopters were very vulnerable to ground fire and required much routine maintenance. It was not at all unusual for the recon Marines to have to depend on "foot power" to enter and depart their recon zones or to be left dependent on their own firepower in the midst of a battle.

back into the jungle in much the same manner the enemy was prone to do. Using Claymore mines, hand grenades, and charges of TNT or C-4 plastic explosive to cover their retreat, the patrols withdrew by the most expeditious route. Smoke grenades often added to the screen of explosives to mask the withdrawal.

By the fall of 1966 the recon Marines had discovered another means of assisting in breaking contact and adding surprise to ambushes. A section on the First Force Recon Company in an afteraction report for Operation PRAIRIE stated that the extreme vulnerability of recon patrols when detected by the enemy "necessitated the development of a tactic whereby our small units could break contact with a numerically superior force. In the later stages of our participation in Operation PRAIRIE, each individual patrol member carried two CS (tear gas) grenades, M7A2s, with a protective mask. The concept being to use this system to capture prisoners, exploit ambushes, and break contact. It is believed that in at least one ambush the CS was instrumental in the proper and safe exfiltration by our patrol. Subsequent to Operation PRAIRIE the system has been successfully used in breaking contact and exploiting ambushes."[2]

Not included in the report was the added advantage of carrying gas masks. Patrol leaders often required men who snored, coughed, or talked in their sleep to wear the masks. The protective masks and cannisters of CS added to the load of the recon men, but the added influence on their survivability ensured that there were no complaints.

Although the patrol teams did conduct night ambushes on occasion, their general procedure was to withdraw to the thickest jungle possible to await sunrise so they could renew their observations of the enemy. Harbor sites chosen varied with the patrol leader's desires, the size of the team, and the enemy situation. Starlight scopes, which enhance natural light to provide a green-tinted field of observation, were useful in watching avenues of approach to the Marines' position.

Throughout a mission the entire team closely monitored possible extraction PZs in case they came in contact with a superior force. The teams also were briefed on and had memorized possible ground routes back to friendly units in case no helicopters were available.

When a recon team arrived back at the company base by foot or chopper, its mission was not yet complete. The patrol as a whole, and then by individual, was debriefed by the company intelligence sergeant or one of the officers on all that had occurred during the mission. This was a detailed process because in the silence of patrolling or in the heat of a battle men only a few yards apart might observe entirely different items of intelligence value.

Once the debriefing was completed, the team cleaned its weapons, gear, and finally themselves. They then re-packed their packs in case they had to make an emergency insertion to support another team. Finally, after all was ready, the Marines could relax and begin the same process in preparation for the next mission.

After days of complete silence, mixed at times with contact with numerically far superior forces, the Force Recon Marines ''relaxed'' with much the same intensity that they patrolled the jungle. One recon Marine described the men after a patrol as ''howling animals'' as they drank, shouted, wrestled, and enjoyed simply being alive.

CHAPTER 8

●○●○●○●

1966 to STINGRAY

By 1966 the Force Recon Marines had adapted fairly well to the enemy and terrain of Vietnam. Many of the lessons had been learned at the price of sweat and blood, but the recon men were on the right track. There was still much to learn, however, for in the counterguerrilla environment the only constant was change.

Many of the problems still facing the recon Marines were more internal than relating to the enemy. The enemy was crafty, dedicated, and dangerous, but the Marines could fight back. Internal conflicts were more difficult to combat. Higher headquarters still did not totally accept the intelligence gathered by the patrols, and combat missions continued to be emphasized over the traditional reconnaissance role of the First Company. When recon missions were assigned, the company still found itself limited in that it had to remain within the range of friendly artillery support and radio communications. The long-range recon missions that the patrols had been formed to accomplish were put aside for more immediate missions in support of division-level operations rather than at the Force level.

A variety of organizations and attachments were tried with various degrees of success. Platoons of the First

Company were assigned directly to the divisions, attached to other Marine units or to Special Forces camps, in multiple associations with the battalion recon units or to various temporary headquarters for specific operations. During Operation DOUBLE EAGLE I, from 21 January to 16 February, four platoons from the Force Recon company were combined with Company B of the 3rd Recon Battalion to form the "Provisional Reconnaissance Group." The group's mission was to establish observation posts (OPs) and to conduct patrols to find infiltration and exfiltration routes used by regiments of the 325A PAVN Division along the border of Quang Ngai and Binh Dinh provinces. Recon activities by the group were in support of a joint Army and Marine operation that included most of the I and II Corps areas.[1]

During DOUBLE EAGLE I the Provisional Recon Group employed team-size as well as platoon and company OPs and patrols. There were 153 sightings of a total of 919 VC or NVA and 400 VCS (Viet Cong Suspects). On 31 occasions the sightings resulted in contact, with 23 enemy KIA—14 by small arms and the remainder by supporting fires. Along with numerous documents and equipment captured, the recon men destroyed over five tons of rice and rations. The cost to the Provisional Group was two Marines killed, two missing, and five wounded.

Most of the dead, missing, and wounded were involved with platoon-size patrols. It was no surprise to the "old hands" in the First Company that in the business of reconnaissance, small was often better than bigger. Capt J. L. Compton, the commander of the Provisional Group, noted, "It appears obvious that a platoon is too large to move clandestinely and is too small to take care of itself if hit."[2]

Both of the MIAs were from team HATEFUL of Force Recon.[3] The platoon-size patrol paused at 1430 on 21 January 1966 because weather and extremely thick terrain restricted visibility to a few yards. About 1700, four VC approached the patrol base from the southeast and attacked the perimeter's rear security position. After a firefight that lasted only seconds, the enemy scattered amid screams and yells.

Due to the limited visibility, the main body of the platoon was unable to see the contact area and, following SOP, began evading in the opposite direction to break contact. After moving about 40 meters through the dense vegetation, the patrol halted when the men realized the rear security element had not kept up with the platoon. Lt Richard F. Parker immediately led the platoon back to the contact area, where one Marine was still occupying his position. A complete search of the area failed to find any evidence of 1stLt James T. Egan, Jr. A native of Mountainside, New Jersey, Egan was never found and is still listed as missing in action as of this writing in 1988.

HATEFUL continued its mission, and at 0900 the next morning attempted to climb a steep mountain. The grade and a series of cliffs prevented its reaching the top, and they had to backtrack down the slope. At 1015 the platoon was attacked from the high ground by an estimated 30–50 enemy. In a series of hit-and-run engagements down the mountain, the recon men killed at least seven and wounded many more. However, because of the terrain and a determined enemy, control of the withdrawal was lost. Several of the Marines became separated and had to fight their way through the enemy back to the platoon. At the base of the mountain the enemy withdrew. A head count revealed that Cpl Edwin R. Grissett from San Juan, Texas, was missing. Grissett had been spotted several times in the retreat down the mountain by his fellow Marines, but no one could recall seeing him hit. A thorough search of the area produced no sign of Grissett. He also is still listed as MIA.

DOUBLE EAGLE I was followed almost immediately by Operation DOUBLE EAGLE II from 19 to 27 February. Teams from the First Force Recon Company established OPs and conducted patrols in support of the operation, resulting in 29 sightings of 130 VC and NVA and 50 VCS. The recon Marines felt the results were meager because of the restricted size of the tactical area of operations and the high civilian population density in the region. There were also problems in that the recon patrols were often deployed in too close proximity of other Marine and ARVN units.[4]

March of 1966 was slow. Most of the month was spent in the vicinity of the China Beach base camp, training the large number of replacements who had joined the company. It was good that the recon men had the opportunity to train, because April would be one of their most active months.

During April the First Force Recon Company headquarters moved from Da Nang to Hue to Khe Sanh, back to Da Nang, and finally to Chu Lai. Platoons were spread out all over I Corps in support of the 3rd Recon Battalion and the 1st and 4th Marine Regiments. Although most of the patrols were successful, there was tragedy as well.

Patrol HATEFUL started off badly on 21 April and got worse.[5] Minutes before the team's insertion, Lance Corporal Garcia accidentally shot himself in the leg. Three days later, when the team was due for extraction, the mission was extended so that HATEFUL could act as a radio relay for a Battalion Recon team that lacked communications with the rear CP. To compound the team's difficulties, they were out of water and no streams were nearby.

In mid-afternoon of the 24th, the 11-man patrol was in a perimeter two kilometers west of Hue. At 1540 a hard rain began to fall. A few minutes later Corporal Spies detected movement, and then spotted what appeared to be a rifle barrel in the brush 10–15 feet from his position. Before he could react, the perimeter was raked by automatic rifle fire. The Marines returned fire as SSgt K. R. Hall instructed the team to prepare to withdraw. A brief lull in the firefight allowed Hall to move to Spies's position to determine the location and number of enemy. More VC opened up, including at least five with automatic weapons. Hall was struck in the face by several more bullets and fell backward, dead.

Withdrawing toward Hue under control of the assistant patrol leader, the team was only able to break contact because of several sorties of close air support. Unfortunately, the team was unable to retrieve Hall's body. The next day Sgt Johannes Haferkamp, who had been the last man to leave the contested perimeter, led a patrol back into the contact area to recover the remains. They found Hall where he had fallen. After tying a rope to the body and pulling it for several meters to ensure that it wasn't booby-trapped, they wrapped it in a poncho. An H-34 helicopter lowered a basket into a nearby bomb crater and attempted to hoist it aboard. At about 20 feet the basket broke apart, dropping the body back into the jungle. Another line was dropped, and this time the body made it to a height of 50 feet before the hoist broke. The demoralized Marines ended up carrying Hall through the thick jungle and down a steep cliff before finally reaching an LZ where the helicopter could land.

May brought another patrol that ended with the death of a recon Marine.[6] On the 16th, NIGHT STICKER, a patrol of the first platoon, was inserted by helicopter into the same area where Hall had been killed. The patrol's mission was to set up an observation post and radio relay on Hill 679, near Nui Bai Cay Tar. After only six hours in the OP, Cpl R. G. Cotton spotted several VC moving toward his security position. Cotton engaged the enemy, killing at least one before he was cut down by rifle fire. The patrol leader and corpsman who moved to assist Cotton also took fire. When the corpsman, HM2 L. W. Carper, reached the downed recon man, he was mortally wounded.

Other patrols from the First Company were experiencing similar troubles. The area around Hue and Phu Bai was so saturated with enemy that the patrols were badly outnumbered and had difficulty landing at LZs without being detected or ambushed. A few days after Carper was killed, a patrol of the 2nd Platoon landed at an LZ only to be immediately engaged by the enemy. The recon Marines managed to kill three by body count and one more probable before being extracted with four wounded of their own.

As 1966 progressed, the war in the northern part of South Vietnam began to take on more conventional characteristics. The NVA were moving regiments and entire divisions south to test the Marines in I Corps. On 19 May an NVA soldier surrendered to ARVN forces and reported that the 324B Division was preparing to infiltrate across the DMZ and take over Quang Tri Province.

To find out if the information was correct without committing forces that were needed elsewhere, the First Recon Company—along with elements of the 3rd Recon Battalion, E Company of the 2nd Battalion 4th Marines, and a battery of artillery from the 3rd Battalion 12th Marines—was moved to the region just south of the DMZ. Maj Dwain A. Colby, commander of the First Company, was placed in command of the organization called "Recon Group Bravo."

By June, patrols from Recon Group Bravo were finding enemy in platoon-size groups on nearly every mission. To gather as much intelligence as possible, patrols were debriefed and reinserted with only hours between missions rather than days. Enemy contact became so common that one patrol was on the ground for only 18 minutes before it had to be extracted. Another lasted only 43 minutes. Sgt James Donner recalls that on one patrol the recon Marines debarked their helicopters with bayonets fixed because of the previous heavy fighting in the area. Inserted at 1800, they had to be extracted under fire only 30 minutes later.[7]

Oddly, the initial reports by Recon Group Bravo on the large number of enemy sighting and contacts were ignored by higher commands. GySgt Billy M. Donaldson, the company's intelligence chief at the time noted, ''I was caught on one patrol—me and my teams—where the Cong tried all night to rush our position. I turned in a report of about 2,500 Cong being in that particular valley. I was positive that was an accurate figure. In fact, I thought it was conservative. I later heard a joke or two about the report and that many at higher headquarters didn't feel that there were that many out there. They should have listened. If you recall, 'I' Company of the 4th Marines was anni-hilated in that same area only a couple of days later.''[8]

During the period 1–15 July, a total of 18 patrols were conducted, 14 requiring early extraction because of enemy contact. This, combined with the capture of two NVA sol-diers who corroborated the intentions of the 324B Divi-sion, led to a commitment of US and SVN Marines and ARVN forces to counter the division along the DMZ in what was known as Operation HASTINGS.

Operation HASTINGS was officially launched at 0800 on 15 July. Although it was somewhat belated, Recon Group Bravo received credit for the initiation of the operation because of the intelligence it had gathered. The recon men were finally gaining the credibility that they deserved.[9]

Recon Group Bravo remained along the DMZ as the reconnaissance element for Operation HASTINGS. The scheme of maneuver for the US and SVN forces closely followed the findings of the group prior to and during the operation. When HASTINGS concluded on 3 August, there were 882 known enemy casualties. The Recon Group not only assisted the operation by providing intelligence but also contributed directly to the enemy body count. On one occasion a five-man recon team observed approximately 250 NVA only 400 meters from its position. They called in artillery on the enemy formation, killing 50. The artil-lery barrage was followed by a fixed-wing air strike which began with the delivery of a 2,000-pound bomb directly on target, destroying most of the remaining enemy.[10]

Operation HASTINGS was immediately followed by Operation PRAIRIE, which was to continue detecting and destroying elements of 324B Division's attempt to cross the DMZ. The 3rd Marine Division was in charge of the operation; the First Force Recon Company was its reconnaissance element. Several of the company's platoons that had been OPCONed to other units rejoined the company for the operation. It was the first time in the company's combat history that all six platoons had been dedicated to the same mission and under their own chain of command.[11]

The mission of the recon Marines during PRAIRIE was "to determine size, disposition, and location of VC/NVA units and their infiltration routes and to engage targets of opportunity with supporting arms." To accomplish this mission the company was to follow the same method of operations used during HASTINGS. Small patrols of five men were inserted by UH-1 "Huey" helicopters for missions of three to six days.

During the month of August, the company conducted 38 patrols, with 54 sightings of 986 VC/NVA.[12] One of these patrols would lead to the major battle of the operation.

Team 61 of the First Company's 6th Platoon was inserted 13 miles west of Dong Ha and four miles south of the DMZ on 6 August.[13] Over the next two days the four-man team directed artillery onto enemy groups they observed in the valley below their OP. On the morning of 8 August the patrol reported that the enemy were apparently sweeping up the hill on line, in an attempt to find the recon team. By the time the NVA were within 50 meters of the Marines, Major Colby—the company commander— had dispatched helicopter gunships to strafe areas marked by the patrol's white phosphorus rifle grenades. Colby also requested a platoon-size reaction force from E Company,

2nd Battalion, 4th Marines (known as the "Magnificent Bastards"), to fly into an LZ about 150 meters from the patrol's position. The platoon landed without incident and linked up with the besieged patrol.

At the arrival of the reaction platoon, the enemy broke contact. After a search of the area, the helicopters were requested to return for an extraction. At 1600 four choppers landed, and just as the first lifted off, the PZ was raked by heavy automatic-weapons fire. Two birds were damaged but were able to escape. Twenty-one Marines, including the four-man recon team, were stranded on the hilltop and were soon under ground attack by 30–40 enemy. The NVA made it to within hand-grenade range of the perimeter before being repelled. A second attack was made an hour later and again was beaten back.

As darkness fell, the E Company commander, Capt Howard V. Lee, was able to fly into the Marines' position with ten reinforcements and a resupply of ammunition. Lee had no sooner taken command of the small force when the enemy attacked for a third time—this time from three sides. There were now an estimated 250 enemy against the 32 Marines. Despite the numbers, the enemy was once again driven back; however, Lee had been severely wounded by grenade fragments in the body and one eye. The entire perimeter was low on ammunition.

Major Colby was also making efforts to extract or reinforce his recon team and the Marines of E Company. Fighting again flared up after darkness, and Colby knew that an extraction could not take place until first light. A volunteer gunship crew was recruited to fly in ammunition. The chopper reached the Marines but was hit and crash-landed into the perimeter. With assistance from the men on the ground, the aviators were able to dismount their machine guns, unload the additional ammo, and join in the defense. Lee's wounds made him unable to continue in command; the chopper pilot, Maj Vincil W. Hazelbaker, took charge.

The fight continued throughout the night. At one point the commander of the 2nd Battalion, 4th Marines, LtCol Arnold E. Bench, was able to make radio contact with the Marines on the hilltop. Bench's call was answered by Corporal Bacta of the original four-man patrol. When the battalion commander demanded to speak to the "6 actual" (commander) rather than a radio operator, Bacta replied that Lee's wounds prevented his coming to the radio and that while Hazelbaker was in the same hole with him, the major was unconscious from wounds suffered in the crash. Bench then questioned, "Well, then, who is in charge?"

Bacta replied, "I am." During much of the night Bacta was, in fact, in charge of the perimeter. He organized the defenses and coordinated the artillery and air strikes that pounded the enemy.[14]

At daybreak, Bench, along with two of his infantry companies, air-assaulted into the LZ and made their way to the beleaguered perimeter. The enemy had had enough and had melted into the jungle. Around the Marines' position were 37 NVA dead—most within 15 meters of the defenders. Drag marks and blood trails gave evidence of a higher body count. Later in the day an aerial observer spotted an enemy column hurrying from the area carrying 27 more bodies. They were not fast enough, for the artillery fire he called on them added to the body count. Final reports of the battle estimated the enemy dead at over 100.

Captain Lee eventually received the Medal of Honor for his bravery on the hilltop.[15] Corporal Bacta was recommended for the Navy Cross in a citation for his "outstanding and extraordinary work in continuing his communications while at the same time assuming partial command of the troops during a time when persons in charge were unable to function." In what some might consider "the finest traditions of Force Recon," Bacta never received the medal. After being extracted from the hilltop, Bacta and the other recon men were given a brief break in Da Nang. During his celebration of surviving the patrol,

Bacta "misappropriated" a jeep and "in the worst of Force Recon traditions" was caught. Bacta's Navy Cross was downgraded to a Silver Star as part of his punishment.[16]

Major Hazelbaker soon recovered from his injuries and again flew in support of the recon men. On 23 October 1966 a Force Recon team led by SSgt Larry Kester was surrounded by an NVA force. Low clouds, monsoon rains, and the approach of darkness offered a grim outlook for the Marines. Hazelbaker, ignoring the weather, flew at treetop level to stay below the clouds as he searched the valleys, looking for the team. After half an hour he spotted their smoke and amid automatic rifle fire and grenade explosions set down and extracted the team.

The First Force Recon Company's support of Operation PRAIRIE concluded on 17 November. Its patrols had produced 170 sightings of a total of 2,023 enemy. In 41 contacts the company had killed 73 by body count, claimed an additional 57 probables, and had taken two prisoners. The recon men were credited with calling in 144 artillery missions and 27 air strikes that produced 30 more killed and 168 probables. Casualties taken by the recon men were one killed and nine wounded.[17]

By the end of 1966 the First Force Recon Company had become an integral part of Marine operations in Vietnam, proving its worth through battlefield exploits marked with daring and bravery that firmly established its reputation as the superelite of the Corps.*

The evolution of Force Reconnaissance, and its brother

---

*This distinction was well earned but had its negative aspects. While elites are admired and envied in all armed forces, they are also resented by some within them who believe that elite units drain superior leaders and limited assets from the remainder of the forces. Others feel that elites detract from the other uniformed members. In the Marines, where the stance has always been that the Corps itself is an elite, it is reasonable that there were those who did not appreciate an "elite within an elite."

in arms, Battalion Recon, had come a long way from the first landings at Red Beach. Although the First Company and the Recon Battalions still had the mission and name of reconnaissance, they had become reconnaissance with a lethal punch—for by the close of 1966 the recon units were responsible for killing as well as finding.

Employing small groups of men to harass, destroy, and create confusion in the enemy's rear was certainly not novel. What was new was the speed of reaction in destroying enemy units without actually being in contact with them. Recon teams could attack by acting as forward observers (FOs) and eliminate the enemy through artillery and air strikes. A small patrol, which ensured swift, silent movement, no longer implied avoidance of offensive action. The key was to engage the enemy with indirect fire (artillery, for example) while remaining undetected in the process. Action was no longer the same as contact.

Not everyone agreed with this evolving role. Neither did the existing prewar doctrine. Fleet Marine Force Manual (FMFM) 2-2, *Amphibious Reconnaissance*, written in 1963, clearly dictated a supportive, not combative, role for reconnaissance units. FMFM 2-2 specified, "the company has no offensive capability and is not employed as a tactical unit; that is, it is not assigned tactical missions, objectives, or tactical areas of responsibility."[18]

The recon Marines in the field cared little about what the books had to say, as they were more than willing to take on any mission assigned. For those who were concerned about such things as doctrine, there were "loopholes" in the guidance for recon units. FMFM 6-2, *Marine Infantry Regiment*, and FMFM 6-1, *Marine Division*, both include descriptions of a "reconnaissance in force" mission and an important paragraph about the "control and adjustment of long-range fires." FMFM 8-1, *Special Operations*, notes parachute and subsurface entry in connection with raiding. Since these methods were particular to recon companies, 8-1 indirectly sanctioned force recon to be used as raiders. FMFM 8-2, *Counterinsurgency Operations*, while noting that recon units were to gather information of use to commanders in planning larger operations, also stated that recon personnel could be employed for attacking isolated enemy forces.[19]

Despite the apparent conflicts in doctrine, the success of the recon Marines in adapting to the unique situation in Vietnam was obvious. In a war where victories were measured in body count rather than in land taken, the recon men certainly knew how to keep score. The numbers of VC/NVA killed by the recon Marines became so significant that a new reporting system, operational code-named STINGRAY, was developed. Soon the code name became the generic name for all recon patrols that were inserted into OPs with the specific intent of destroying the enemy by artillery and air strikes.

The origins of STINGRAY were recorded by USMC Reserve Capt Francis J. West, Jr., in a report he wrote after being called to active duty and sent to Vietnam. West's tour in the war zone was as a special observer for the Marine Corps Operations Officer, MajGen William R. Collins. Collins's objective was to send officers who were qualified in small-unit tactics and historical research to Vietnam to observe and then write factual narratives of the Marines in combat.

West knew where the action was, as he spent time with both Force and Battalion recon teams and the infantry battalions. His report, *Small Unit Action in Vietnam, Summer 1966*, was used to train replacement leaders for Vietnam and was published in 1967 by Arno Press for general release.

In a subsequent report published in the US Naval Institute's *Proceedings* magazine, West wrote of the beginnings of STINGRAY. On 26 July 1966, West accompanied a First

Force Recon Company patrol led by Sgt Orest Bishko. According to West, the team had been

> given a simple mission: get into the bush, find the enemy, and destroy him. For two days we moved through the thick undergrowth, staying well hidden, occasionally hearing the enemy chopping wood or shouting. By the third morning we knew where their battalion bivouac area was, and called in artillery fire. . . . Chased by a NVA platoon, we left the scene at top speed and before we could be overtaken . . . jet fighters were scrambled. Following the debrief, General Walt and his G-3 (Operations Officer), Col John C. Chaisson, Jr., decided that such missions merited a special section in the reporting system and chose for the teams the operational code name of STINGRAY.[20]

The STINGRAY concept was officially adopted a month after Bishko's patrol.[21] Although the recon Marines would continue to conduct a variety of missions other than the small FO teams, STINGRAY would be the principal use of the First Company for the remainder of the war. By the end of December 1966 the STINGRAY patrols had accounted for a total of 601 enemy dead, with the loss of only nine recon Marines.[22]

During 1967, STINGRAY continued to be prolific in body count. By the end of the year the number of enemy killed was 1,845. Friendly losses were 69, for a ratio of 27 to 1 in favor of the recon Marines.[23] As West recorded in his report of the patrols, "Five men with one radio had the firepower of a regiment at their disposal."[24]

STINGRAY patrols destroyed the enemy in small and large groups alike. On 12 January 1967, Team HONG KONG of the First Company's 2nd Platoon, operating from an OP atop Hill 257, spotted groups of five to ten VC/NVA moving along a valley trail. Previously plotted artillery concentrations were called in, inflicting casualties in each group. Despite their losses, the enemy continued to come down the valley. At twilight another group appeared wearing black uniforms and carrying weapons and heavy packs. Before darkness obscured observation, the recon team had counted 557 enemy. They called for artillery and tactical air strikes, which dropped bombs and napalm and straffed the valley. To pinpoint the team's location for the aircraft, Arnold held a poncho around a man holding a strobe light so that it would only be visible from the air. Secondary explosions followed each air strike and artillery barrage when enemy ammunition and demolitions were hit. The next morning the valley was littered with dead.

Arnold was later asked why he remained on the hilltop and continued to direct the air and artillery when his team was in obvious danger from the large number of VC/NVA. The sergeant modestly replied, "We stayed there at the OP site because we knew we hadn't finished our job. There were still a lot of live VC in the area."[25]

Other STINGRAY patrols encountered smaller groups—with the same results. Team CLASSMATE in support of Operation UNION II on 26 May reported in an oral history tape:

. . . at 0900 we saw five VC step off a trail on the high-ground side. About 50 meters above the trail they set down their packs and weapons and appeared to be observing the trail from which they had just come. We called in artillery, had excellent coverage of the area, and we noted one VC limping away. Again we called artillery and brought it right on top of the man . . . 25 minutes later we observed two VC by a large dike full of water. We called another artillery mission on them and got one confirmed KIA—we could see his body on the dike—and one probable. Only 40 minutes later we observed five VC moving up the hill toward our position carrying packs and weapons. We called a fire mission right on the target.[26]

Team CLASSMATE, on the same patrol, reported spotting one enemy soldier who was approximately six feet tall and weighed about 250 pounds. The man neither looked nor walked like the VC he accompanied, and the patrol thought he was a mainland Chinese advisor.*

STINGRAY patrols protected friendly troops and bases in addition to destroying the enemy. In one instance, a patrol foiled a large-scale attack on Da Nang before the VC/NVA could reach their objectives. 1stLt Robert F. Drake and Team HATEFUL were assigned on 12 June to conduct an area reconnaissance in the Elephant Valley region to find infiltration routes and staging areas along the approach to Da Nang. Drake was briefed by intelligence sources to expect a quiet patrol, as few sightings of the enemy had been made recently in the area. They were wrong.

When the team was inserted at 0900, it immediately received fire. Drake decided to break contact and continue the mission. On their way through the jungle to an OP, a brief engagement resulted in one enemy KIA and one recon Marine wounded by a grenade blast. HATEFUL was still not ready for extraction and, after a med-evac (medical evacuation by helicopter) of the wounded man, moved farther into the jungle as they fired artillery to cover their withdrawal.

That night a group of 10–20 enemy probed the Marines' position. Drake called in artillery "very, very close, in fact, we had shrapnel flying all over us, cutting trees and everything, but it protected us; that was the main thing."[27]

For the next two days HATEFUL had no sightings or contacts except with what the team recalls as extremely dense jungle and multitudes of leeches that assaulted every part

___

*There are far more reports than confirmations of Chinese advisors and advisors from other communist bloc countries being spotted with the enemy. Although there is little doubt that some of these sightings were reliable, it should be understood that ethnic Chinese and other nationalities were native to North Vietnam and were equally subject to the NVA draft.

of the body. In the late afternoon of the 15th, Drake called for their planned extraction. Shortly after he was informed that they would not be pulled out until the next day due to mechanical problems with the helicopters, Drake heard voices on a trail only a few feet from his position. The team soon observed 10 heavily armed enemy moving slowly and carrying shrubs as camouflage. A similar report was made minutes later by Team CONSULATE a few kilometers farther down the valley. Both teams shortly detected larger groups, up to company-size, headed in the direction of Da Nang.

From 2100 until 0400 the next morning, the two recon teams directed air strikes, artillery, and SPOOKY gunships on the enemy formations. SPOOKY, a C-47 twin-engine transport fitted with miniguns, was particularly successful in cutting the columns to shreds. On a nearby river, they were also able to destroy several sampans which were moving rockets to support the attack on Da Nang. After enduring seven hours of fire directed by HATEFUL and CONSULATE, the remaining enemy fled back toward Laos. The expected attack never came. Drake, who could understand some Vietnamese, was close enough to the trail to hear one retreating Cong say to a fellow soldier that he "didn't like this at all and wasn't going to be able to make it."

Successes by the STINGRAY patrols continued. MajGen Raymond G. Davis, commander of the 3rd Marine Division in 1968, credited STINGRAY patrols, coupled with rapid reinforcement and exploitation, with the destruction of enemy units in his area of operations.

Other commanders expressed the same view, and statistics bore them out. By the end of the Corps involvement in Vietnam, 8,317 STINGRAY missions had been completed, with 15,680 sightings of over 138,252 enemy. The recon teams had called in 6,463 artillery-fire missions and 1,328 air strikes, resulting in 9,566 confirmed kills and the capture of 85 prisoners.

CHAPTER 9

□□□□□□□□

The Only Three Combat Jumps in Marine Corps History

*A*LTHOUGH parachuting was a routine event during peacetime, it was a skill that had never been used in combat by the Marines before Vietnam. Marine airborne units had fought in World War II but had never entered battle by way of the sky. No Corps parachute units were assigned to the war zone during the Korean conflict.

Many leaders during the Vietnam era felt that the helicopter had made the parachute obsolete, and except for a battalion-size drop by the Army's 173rd Airborne Brigade in Tay Ninh Province on 22 February 1967, the concept of airborne gave way before the air-assault capability of the helicopter. There were, however, those who still believed that silent entry by parachute had its advantages, and the Force Recon Marines were more than willing to give it a chance. The men of Sub Unit Number 1 conducted low-level parachute-jump rehearsals on secured drop zones in Vietnam in 1965, though no immediate use was made of their practice.[1]

On 12 June 1966, Capt Jerome Paull, platoon commander of First Company's 4th Platoon, was alerted to prepare his platoon to parachute into an area near Hill 555, about 35 miles west of Chu Lai, to establish an OP.

The mission was planned to kick off Operation KANSAS, which sought three enemy regiments suspected to be in the area.[2]

Terrain in the zone favored small-unit movement, and a clandestine airborne insertion might prevent enemy countermovement.* Once the Force Recon team was in its position, other units would be helicoptered into the area of operations.[3]

On the morning of 13 June, Paull made an aerial recon overflight in a UH-1 helicopter to select a suitable drop zone. A hasty return to Chu Lai was required when the Huey was taken under ground fire. Fortunately a satisfactory DZ had already been spotted. Paull returned for another overflight that afternoon in the Army CV-2 Caribou that would be used for the actual drop.

The 13-man patrol departed its base camp for the Chu Lai airfield at 2350 that night. Included in the team were experienced recon veterans SSgt Maurice Jacques, Sgt Johannes Haferkamp, and SSgt Bacta. At 0115 the Caribou lifted off to deliver the first Marine combat parachute jump in history.

Paull, the patrol leader, describes the drop.

We jumped at approximately 0205. We tailgated the Caribou; in other words, we went off the lowered ramp in the rear of the aircraft instead of exiting the side doors. I was the first man to jump, and we all went out on one pass over the DZ. We used the standard T-10 parachute with static line. The jump alti-

---

*Criticism for the jumps by the 173rd and the recon Marines has focused on the belief that the drops were more public-relations stunts than tactical actions. Critics say that more risk was involved than the anticipated results justified. While there is some truth in these charges, the decision to conduct airborne operations was much like other options tried during the war: commanders at all levels constantly tried new techniques, or in the case of airborne, revived old ones, to best fight a war like no other that Americans had faced.

tude was 800 feet, and the DZ was a small hilltop
clearing approximately 500 meters long and covered
in grass. It was bordered on two sides by a river, the
Thong Trong, and the other side by a ridge 550 meters high. We exited the aircraft on the signal of the
pilot, a green light, and he put us right on target,
which was a difficult feat due to poor visibility. It was
a moonless night and there was a lot of ground fog
from the river.[4]

Haferkamp recalls, "You know, you always think in
training that one day you will make a combat jump, and
you look forward to that day. It finally came. I was the
last man in the stick. We all knew that there was a VC
village at the end of the DZ so we would have to stay
close. It was one of the tightest sticks I ever saw in all my
jump experience."[5]

From the harnesses of their parachutes, the only things
the Marines could see on the ground were the glimmers
of numerous campfires along the surrounding ridge lines.
The team maneuvered its chutes to avoid the fires and to
stay as close together as possible. All 13 men landed on
the DZ and within a 150-yard area. Ironically, the only
man injured on the jump was a former member of the
Army Airborne, Sergeant Martin, who suffered a sprained
ankle.

Although the assembly presented no problem, disposal
of the parachutes did. The plan was to make as compact
a bundle as possible and cover it with grass and brush.
During the planning phase the patrol had considered bury-
ing the chutes but had decided that digging the hole would
take too much time and would be too noisy. Also, the
newly turned earth would be easily spotted by the enemy.
Another alternative considered, but judged to be impractical, was to call in an airstrike, drop napalm, and burn
the chutes.

The patrol moved until daylight and established an OP

from which they observed 45 VC in groups varying from three to fifteen during the day. It was apparent from the way the enemy was moving, with little security, that they were unaware that the Marines were in the area.

At 1835 the team spotted two Vietnamese and a dog walking along a trail near the DZ. Suddenly the dog picked up a scent and darted to where a parachute was hidden. When the two men saw the chute, they immediately hurried away. Paull, who was relaying all this information back to the company CP, recommended that the team be extracted. It would only be a matter of time, Paull felt, before the two men returned with a larger search force.

At 1915 a VC force was spotted searching the area where the parachute had been found. Before it could discover the recon team, helicopters swept in and extracted the patrol.

Despite the early extraction of the team, the mission was considered a success. A message from the commander of the 1st Reconnaissance Battalion stated, ''You're the greatest,'' and the commanding general of the 1st Marine Division added his congratulations, saying, "I report with pride that every Recon type, past, present, and future can stand tall in the shadow of the daring exploit of Paull and 12 First Force Recon Marines who made the first successful jump 37 miles deep into Viet Cong territory. I am honored that they served with us.''[6]

Paull's report of the jump stated the enemy now had another threat against which they would have to guard. He also praised the Caribou as an excellent aircraft for dropping parachutists and recommended that the T-10 be modified to make it more steerable to assist a team in landing close together. Paull concluded that problems in parachute disposal after the jump and the chances of having injured jumpers should be considered in the planning process.

Known to few at the time was the impact of the airborne operation on another action going on at the same time.[7] On 13 June, an 18-man team from Company C of the 1st Recon Battalion had been inserted by helicopter about twenty miles southeast of Paull's drop zone to establish an OP atop Hill 488. Under the leadership of SSgt Jimmie E. Howard, the team was scheduled to be extracted two days later but was left in place for an extra day to serve as a radio relay for Paull's team. At 2200 on 15 June, an NVA battalion attacked Howard's team. The battle lasted all night, but despite the tremendous numerical advantage of the enemy, they failed to overrun the hilltop. By sunrise the next morning, six of the team were dead; all the rest, including Howard, were wounded. Dead NVA were literally stacked in front of the Marines' positions. Howard later received the Medal of Honor and two of his men were awarded Navy Crosses. Over time, much has been written about the bravery of Howard and his team. Mixed with the praise has been some criticism for the team's remaining the third night on the hill, mostly by those uninformed of Howard's radio relay support of the first combat jump by Marines.[8] Howard's support of the Force Recon Marines was more than a sense of duty, for he had been one of the first members of the company when it was formed.

Although the first combat jump in the Corps' history was considered a success, no rush to introduce parachute operations in the war zone occurred. The recon men had proven that it could be done; it would be used again only if a mission arose that could not be handled by helicopters and that was worth the risks involved. It would have been much better if the opportunity and requirement for the second jump had never occurred at all.

In early September 1967, intelligence sources revealed that the NVA were moving heavy 300mm rockets into the Happy Valley region southwest of Da Nang. Unfounded reports even added that the rockets might possibly have nuclear warheads. While there were ample LZs in the area, a critical shortage of helicopters existed throughout I Corps due to maintenance problems caused by cracked rotor blades. With no chopper support available and an immediate need for accurate information about the rockets, it was decided to parachute a recon team into the valley.[9]

GySgt Walter M. Webb, Jr., was assigned to prepare his Team CLUB CAR for a drop into Happy Valley at 0400 on 5 September. The nine-man team from the First Company's 5th Platoon consisted of Webb, SSgt Thomas J. Vallario (APL), Sgt James W. Hager, Sgt D. M. Woo, Sgt M. D. McNemar, Cpl C. N. Owens, Cpl R. J. Garcia, LCpl John W. Slowick, and HM2 Michael L. LaPorte (Corpsman).

Webb instructed his team to pack for a four-day mission. Each man carried 300 rounds of M-16 ammunition, four fragmentation grenades, and one grenade each of CS and smoke. In addition to the team's two PRC-25 radios carried by the radio operators, Webb packed an RT-10A survival radio, normally used by pilots who had to eject from their aircraft.

During the planning phase, Webb decided that the team would assemble after the jump using a method common to airborne operations. The assistant patrol leader would jump last and "roll up" the stick by moving in the direction of the drop, picking up each man until they reached the lead jumper's landing point. Each man would recover and carry his parachute, reserve, and harness until all were assembled. Then the gear would be buried in a single hole with a thermite grenade to destroy the chutes. To assist in the night assembly, each jumper carried a "clicker" that had first been used by paratroopers during the Normandy Invasion of World War II. Originally designed as a child's toy, the device produced a metallic click when pressed. One click answered by two would assist the Marines in finding each other on the dark drop zone and was much safer than voice communications.

CLUB CAR departed the company CP at 0230 on the 5th, arrived at the airfield about 0300, and began to suit up. It boarded a Caribou at 0350 and took off within minutes for the DZ in Happy Valley. During the flight the crew chief had trouble lowering the ramp at the rear of the aircraft. Things would not get better.

The Caribou returned to Da Nang, but the crew was able to repair the ramp while the plane circled the airfield. En route back to the DZ on the same flight pattern, a patrol at the other end of the valley reported that there were negative ground winds. As the plane approached the DZ the pilot cut its engines and began to descend to the drop altitude of 700 feet. On the command of "Go," the recon Marines stepped off the ramp into the darkness.

After Webb exited, he immediately checked his canopy to be sure it had deployed correctly. He then glanced around to see if the team had a good tight stick. What he noticed was that they were not at 700 feet above the DZ, but more like 1500–2000 feet. Even worse, the wind was not calm but rather was gusting from 25 to 30 knots. Fighting the winds, the team was still able to maintain a fairly tight stick except for one chute that was last seen rapidly drifting to the northwest.

A minute later the recon men began crashing into the trees on the eastern side of Happy Valley, more than two kilometers from the drop zone. Webb recalls,

I fell through the top of the trees for approximately six or seven feet and felt a sharp pull. My magazine pouch on my belt hit me in the kidney and another branch hit between my legs in the scrotum. I fell another 20 feet or so and the canopy caught and held me there. It was dark. I couldn't tell how high I was, so I took off my jump helmet and dropped it. It took approximately three seconds to hit, and I heard it bounce; it sounded like on rocks and I could hear water running below me. I looked at my watch; it was 0435. I decided to just hang there until daylight. I reached into my pack, pulled out my RT-10A radio, and started calling, "Any station this net, this is CLUB

CAR 6.'' I got no response so I switched on the radio's homing signal.

At about 0500 Webb heard aircraft overhead and was able to make radio contact and report his situation. About an hour later there was enough daylight for him to see that he was hanging about 70 feet above a stream filled with large rocks. By swinging back and forth he was able to grab the tree's trunk and rest for a while to get circulation back in his numbed legs. He then popped his reserve chute and, with his rifle slung over his back, climbed down the risers and canopy and dropped the last six feet to the ground.

Webb immediately put on his pack and began to climb out of the streambed. After climbing 40 feet up the steep incline, he heard movement. Knowing that Hager should have landed closest to him, he took the chance and called the sergeant by name. Hager replied, ''Is that you, gunny?'' Webb answered in the affirmative and began moving toward him. Before Webb and Hager could link up, three VC appeared in the streambed and spotted Webb. The two Marines evaded in different directions, with the enemy in pursuit of Webb.

Gunny Webb never merged with the others of the patrol. Continually moving, he lost his pursuers and about noon was able to briefly halt and analyze his situation. ''Everything I ever learned in survival school was running through my mind. The main thing was not to get panicky. My pack was fairly heavy, so I decided to take an inventory to see what gear that I didn't actually need. I got rid of some of the chow. There seemed to be plenty of water in the area so I emptied three of my canteens.''

A half hour later Webb could again hear helicopters above him but was unable to raise them on his radio. He considered popping his smoke grenade but felt that there was no chance for the smoke to penetrate the dense jungle canopy. At 1300 a monsoon downpour drove the choppers back to their base. When the rains let up two hours later, the birds returned, and this time Webb was able to make contact. Finally, at 1830 with darkness approaching, Webb was winched aboard a Jolly Green Giant helicopter on a jungle penetrator. The patrol leader was anxious to find out what had happened to his team and, except for blood in his urine from the blow to his kidney, and aching testicles, was fit for duty.

The assistant patrol leader, Sgt Thomas Vallario, remembers seeing the jungle as he descended from the Caribou. Although he was prepared for a tree landing, a thick branch striking his head made him see stars before the canopy caught and jerked him to a halt. Hearing splashing and garbled voices below, Vallario decided he had to get out of the tree regardless of the darkness. He popped his reserve, climbed down to the canopy, and dropped his pack. The two seconds it took to reach the ground indicated that he was still at least 50 feet from the ground. Assuming that if he released himself from his main chute the reserve would catch in the lower branches and break his fall a few feet from the ground, Vallario pulled his Capewell quick releases and began to fall. As with the rest of the mission, this particular portion did not go according to plan, for he fell and continued to fall until he struck the ground.

What must have been about an hour later, Vallario regained consciousness and crawled from his landing point to the stream to splash his head in the water to regain his senses. After he hid his harness and chute, he heard movement. Popping his clicker, he received a most welcome two clicks in return from Garcia and McNemar. Both had gone into the trees, with Garcia suffering torn ligaments in a knee and McNemar receiving a deep gash in the back of his head. A few minutes later, Slowick, moving slowly because of a wrenched back, answered another click and joined the team.

Vallario, acting as patrol leader, realized that there was

little chance of accomplishing the team's recon mission. Survival, escape and evasion, and finding the rest of the team were now the priorities. The four men were able to move only a few hundred meters over the next two hours. Garcia was in extreme pain and could hardly walk, while McNemar kept lapsing into unconsciousness because of his head injury. All excess gear, including chow, was discarded to lighten their loads as they continued their search for the rest of the team. Fortunately, Slowick had been carrying one of the PRC-25s on the jump, and when a helicopter flew overhead he was able to make contact. At 1230 Vallario was able to find a small clearing and medevac Garcia and McNemar. Despite the pain from his back injury, Slowick stayed with Vallario to continue the search for the other recon Marines.

With helicopters acting as aerial spotters and relaying their observations, Vallario and Slowick were able to link up with Woo, Owens, and Hager about an hour and a half later. Except for Woo, who had a badly sprained ankle, all were uninjured. At 1830, while Woo was being medevacked, Vallario received word that Webb had also been picked up. The only missing member of the team now was Doc LaPorte.

CLUB CAR's remaining four Marines stayed in the jungle the night of 15 September. At dawn the next morning they continued the search for the missing corpsman. A circling helicopter reported spotting what appeared to be a parachute in the trees to the northwest. After five hours of difficult movement, the team found the wreckage of a Navy observation drone aircraft. The men continued to search the rest of the day, assisted by a plane with a loudspeaker, but failed to find any trace of LaPorte. Just before sundown Team CLUB CAR was extracted and returned to China Beach.

During the debriefing of the reunited team, Webb recommended that on all future jumps each Marine carry an RT-10A survival radio, a signal mirror, pencil flares, and a 50–100-foot length of rope for climbing out of trees. Webb added, "It is my belief that the RT-10A was the only thing that saved me. It got me out of the jam I was in."

Webb also noted that terrain such as Happy Valley did not lend itself to airborne operations. The high ridges surrounding the valley and the many corridors leading into it created sudden winds and updrafts like those that had blown the team off target.

As for Doc LaPorte, no sign of him was ever found, and he is still carried on the rolls of the missing. Vallario notes that LaPorte was an inexperienced parachutist who had only 12 or 13 previous jumps and no tree-landing experience. While all tree landings are dangerous, the trees in Happy Valley were particularly treacherous. Many had been stripped of leaves and small branches by previous air strikes, and they resembled giant punji stakes from the air. LaPorte may have been impaled on one of the trees or he may have landed in the midst of the enemy.

LaPorte, from Los Angeles, was an experienced recon man and was considered to be a "good trooper" by the other members of the company. At times he had even led patrols, which was extremely unusual for a corpsman. One of his ears bore the scars of a wound suffered in an earlier firefight near Dong Ha.

It was rare for anything in Vietnam to be clear-cut or easily explainable. LaPorte's disappearance was no exception. He had eagerly volunteered for the parachute mission and had made an issue of it until he was accepted. Team members recall that he had great empathy for the Vietnamese, and it was later discovered that he had a wife and child in Saigon. A search of his area in the company revealed that he had taken an unusually large quantity of medical supplies on the mission and from the appearance of his personal things did not intend to return. Other members of CLUB CAR remembered the single jumper that seemed to maneuver with the wind instead of against it until he disappeared from sight.[10]

As might be expected, the disastrous outcome of the recon Marines' second combat parachute jump precluded similar operations for several years. The third jump was not undertaken until 17 November 1969—and it was done as much to reestablish the feasibility of parachute insertions as for any tactical necessity.

Along the coast of the South China Sea, near the village of Nui Tran, was a peninsula suspected of containing an enemy supply and logistic staging base for forces operating to the south. Infantry units had swept the area, uncovering numerous caches of food and ammunition, but had been unable to locate the VC responsible. A parachute assault was planned so that a force could enter the region unobserved and catch the enemy unaware. Team 51, NIGHT COVER, a six-man patrol under the leadership of 1stLt Wayne E. Rollings, was assigned the airborne assault mission.[11]

An hour before daylight on the morning of 17 November, NIGHT COVER jumped from a CH-46D Marine helicopter at an altitude of 1000 feet using T-10 parachutes onto a shrub-covered DZ located 200 meters from the beach. Each Marine carried a compass to assist in moving east toward the beach after landing. Once the jumpers reached the water, they proceeded south to the designated assembly point. The drop and assembly were executed exactly as planned, with no problems or injuries.

Once assembled, the team moved out on a four-day patrol covering the peninsula from end to end. Except for three empty caves, the patrol found nothing other than signs that the enemy had not been in the area for at least several days. The patrol's only accomplishment was to reconfirm that the recon Marines could conduct a successful night combat jump.

CHAPTER 10
■□■□■□■□

Third Force Recon Company
Goes to War

*V*IETNAM was a different kind of war not only from the tactical aspect, but also in the length of the combat tour of duty. Rather than going to Vietnam for the duration of the conflict, servicemen were assigned to the combat zone for one year.* While the tour was limited to one year, that did not mean that a man was limited to one tour. Many men, especially career soldiers such as many of the recon Marines, returned to the States only to rotate back to the war zone in a year or two. With America's involvement lasting more than 10 years, many would have the opportunity to serve two or more tours in the war zone.

To support this rotation cycle of the First Force Recon Company, the Second Company remained at its Camp Lejeune base to provide assignment billets for returning veterans and to train replacements.[1] Another mission of the

*A normal tour of duty in Vietnam was 12 months—except for the Marines, whose tours were 12 months and 20 days. The original reason for the extra 20 days was to allow for transportation to and from Vietnam aboard ship. The later shift to flying in replacements did not affect the ''12 and 20'' policy.

Second Company was to be prepared to deploy elsewhere around the globe in support of national objectives.

Soon after First Company arrived in Vietnam, Marine Corps officials recognized that there was more war to be fought than there were Marines to fight it. The Corps, along with the other services, began an expansion that was unparalleled in times of undeclared war. One of the "add-on" units formed to reinforce the Corps was the Third Force Recon Company, which was organized on 4 October 1965. To assist in its organization and training, the Third Company was co-located with the Second Company at Camp Lejeune.[2]

Maj Gary Wilder was assigned as commander of the Third Company with Capt William C. Floyd, executive officer; WO Don Cameron, supply officer; 1stLt Raymond Martin, communications officer; and 1stSgt Harry Martin, first sergeant. Twelve NCOs from the Second Company were reassigned to form a nucleus of experienced leaders. While 10 of the 12 later earned commissions as officers, only five survived the war.

To fill the ranks of the Third Company, a Corps-wide request was made for volunteers. Despite the rigors of reconnaissance and the promise that the unit would soon deploy to Vietnam, Marines reported to the company from around the world. A majority, including all the platoon leaders—Lieutenants Ken Jordan, Jeff Ketterson, George Stern, Dick Barba, Douglas O'Donnell, and Al Ward—came from Lejeune's 2nd Marine Division. The company ranks were also filled by several former Force Recon Marines who returned to active duty from civilian life specifically to join the company.

Priority was given to the Third Company for procurement of both equipment and personnel. Initial plans were for all supplies to be force-fed through the regular system. Wilder and Cameron soon saw that this procedure was a lengthy, inefficient process and requested permission to requisition equipment on their own authority. Their request was approved with one million dollars budgeted to outfit the company. Three months later, after 1,400 priority requisitions and the expenditure of $850,000, the Third Force Recon Company had all its authorized equipment.

Volunteers continued to join the company from other troop units, while quotas were also authorized for procuring additional Marines as they graduated from basic and airborne training. From each jump school class of 30–35 men, the Third Company was allowed to select 8–10 who were the most highly qualified and motivated. Floyd remembers, "I think that collection of Marines was probably the finest organization ever put together. Many of them are today commissioned officers in the Marine Corps and others who later got out are successful in business."[3]

While the assembly of men and equipment was going well, the Third Company was faced with one major problem—time. From past experience, the company officers and NCOs were aware that it took from a year and a half to two years to properly train a Force Recon unit. They had been given less than six months, with a target date of April 1966 for entry into Vietnam.

Two factors enabled the recon men to compress the training schedule to meet the timetable—the company knew where they were going and what type of missions would be expected of them on arrival. Unlike the peacetime Force Recon units, which had to prepare for a myriad of missions and deployments anywhere around the globe, the Third Company could eliminate any training that was not related to preparation for Vietnam.

From October to January, individual training and skill schools, such as airborne, demolitions, and scuba, were stressed. By mid-January 1966 the company strength was at 85 percent, and it deployed for seven weeks' training in the Caribbean. Working around the clock, with no liberty granted, the company concentrated on scouting, patrolling, and teamwork. The training exercise concluded with the entire company attending the Jungle Warfare School in Panama. Lieutenant Martin, the communications officer, was honor graduate, with other members of the company breaking every individual and unit record the course had to offer.[4]

By the end of March the Third Company was back at Lejeune and was prepared for deployment to the war zone. Floyd recalls, "By this time, with all the training we had undergone, the company was very tight operationally, was highly motivated, and was ready to go to war."

However, as had happened the previous year with First Company, the company would not go to war en masse but had its personnel reassigned piecemeal, to the extent that the unit would lose most of its hard-earned preparedness. The primary reason for this was that senior commanders in Vietnam were still unsure how to use Force Recon assets already in-country. Rather than bring in another company, they decided to place the Third Company on hold until its proper deployment could be determined.

For several weeks the company attempted to maintain its training level and morale as the men sat waiting at Camp Lejeune. According to Floyd, "We didn't know from day to day what was going to occur. Of course, everybody had already sent their families to places all over the country where they would stay while we were overseas. It was kind of frustrating."[5]

In those days of many requirements and limited assets, it should not be surprising that demands for well-trained troops soon began to drain the Third Company of the men it had worked so hard to prepare. In early May two platoons of the Third Company were ordered to join the 26th Marine Regiment on Okinawa, where that unit was preparing to deploy to Vietnam to join the 3rd Marine Division. Selected for the mission were the 1st Platoon commanded by Lieutenant Jordan and the 5th Platoon under Lieutenant O'Donnell. Jordan, as the senior officer, was designated commander of the unit known as the Third

Force Recon Detachment. Sailing aboard the USS *Boxer* via Norfolk and the Panama Canal, the detachment arrived at Okinawa on 25 May 1966. After more training on the island, the detachment deployed to Vietnam in August with the 26th Regiment.[6]

While the loss of the 1st and 5th fragmented the Third Company, at least those platoons were able to deploy to do the job for which they had trained. The remainder of the company was not so fortunate. Immediately after the deployment of the detachment, Major Wilder received orders to report to Vietnam to assume command of the 3rd Reconnaissance Battalion. Floyd took over what remained of the Third Company only to receive a levy for eight NCOs, including two platoon sergeants, to report to Lackland Air Force Base, Texas, to form the Corps' first two Scout Dog Platoons. Dogs and men were destined for Vietnam as soon as training was completed, but the loss of the most qualified sergeants was a high price for the Third Company to pay.

A few days later another requirement called for one officer and six NCOs to report immediately to Da Nang and join SOG's Naval Advisory Detachment. Lt Richard Barba was selected to lead the group.

The loss of critical personnel tore apart in weeks what had taken months to build. In a month's time the Third Force Recon Company deteriorated from a highly trained unit ready for war to one that had to report itself "not operationally ready."[7] Individual shortages in the company headquarters included the executive officer, first sergeant, operations chief, radio repair chief, five radio operators, and five parachute riggers. The 2nd and 6th Platoons were at zero strength, the 1st and 5th were deployed, the 4th lacked a commander, platoon sergeant, equipment NCO, two team leaders, one assistant team leader, and one scout. Only the 3rd Platoon, which Floyd had zealously protected, was still fully manned and operational.[8]

Neither Floyd nor anyone else in the unit had any idea what would happen next. As no leaves had been allowed since the company's formation the preceding October, Floyd decided to schedule time off for the remaining recon men. No sooner had the leave policy been initiated than a message from Fleet Marine Force, Pacific (FMFPac), was received stating that the III Marine Amphibious Force (III MAF) in Vietnam requested the immediate deployment of the Third Company to the war zone.[9] The III MAF had finally determined that additional Force Recon assets were needed and assumed that the Third Company was standing by at Lejeune. What they did not know was that during their period of indecision, Marine Corps Headquarters had not been able to justify tying up valuable resources and had siphoned off personnel to other priorities.

Floyd had no choice but to inform FMFPac, and remind Headquarters, Marine Corps, of the company's nonoperational status. The response, on 2 August, was for the Third Company—or what was left of it—to report to Camp Pendleton, prepare to receive replacements, resume training, and make ready to report to Vietnam by 15 January 1967.[10] All of the company's equipment was loaded on 14 flatcars and dispatched cross-country by rail. Since the transfer interrupted the men's long-awaited leave plans, Floyd was able to arrange individual travel orders, with delays en route for visits home. Equipment and men arrived at Pendleton in mid-August.

Once more plans were changed. Since the 3rd Platoon was at full strength and combat ready, it was ordered from Pendleton to Okinawa to be attached to the 3rd Battalion, 26th Marine Regiment.[11] After a few weeks of additional training on Okinawa, the platoon sailed to the Philippines for an exercise. After landing, the platoon was informed that in two hours a C-130 transport would be available to fly it to Da Nang. Major Wilder had learned of the platoon's status and by pulling a few strings at III MAF had been able to get them immediately transferred to his command.[12]

The 3rd Platoon arrived in-country on 2 October and spent a week at the 1st Reconnaissance Battalion's indoctrination center. On 10 October the platoon was reunited with the 1st and 5th Platoons, which had arrived in-country about the same time with other elements of the 26th Marines, and all three were attached to Wilder's 3rd Reconnaissance Battalion. Wilder finally had under his leadership half of the Force Recon company he had helped organize. Although under the operational control of the battalion commander, the three platoons retained their separate identity as the Third Force Recon Detachment.

Patrols from the detachment immediately began operations in the jungle 30 kilometers west of Hue. By the end of the month they had made 21 sightings totaling 255 VC and 66 VCS. They had made two contacts, and called in 16 artillery strikes. The patrols were credited with a confirmed body count of 10 and 13 probables. One early patrol of the 1st Platoon, led by SSgt James Capers, Jr., produced most of the detachment's statistics for the month. In 93 hours of patrolling, Capers's team spotted over 200 VC or VCS during seven separate sightings.

The first month of patrolling also produced the Third Force Recon Detachment's first casualty. Lieutenant O'Donnell, commander of the 5th Platoon, was killed on 21 October when the team he was accompanying engaged eight VC minutes after insertion. HM1 Lowell E. Burwell,* the team corpsman, later received the Silver Star

---

*Burwell was respected by his fellow recon men for his leadership abilities as well as his medical knowledge. He was known as "Mr. Everything" to his teammates because of his graduation from jump, mountain, jungle, and escape and evasion schools, and his qualifications in scuba, deep-sea diving, and demolitions. The Navy corpsman accompanied 30 patrols during the platoon's first seven months in-country, 25 of which resulted in contact. Only one failed to make an enemy sighting. On the five most productive patrols, Burwell's team killed 51 enemy themselves and accounted for an additional body count of 304 through artillery and

for his actions during the skirmish, which killed five of the enemy.[13]

In November the 3rd Platoon of the Third Force Recon Detachment was OPCONed to the First Force Recon Company, which was supporting the 1st Marine Division. The 1st and 5th Platoons stayed with the 3d Recon Battalion in the 3d Marine Division area of operations at Dong Ha. During the month, the platoons made 11 sightings of 153 enemy, which resulted in two contacts and 14 artillery missions. The recon men were credited with 24 killed and 33 probables at the cost of only two Marines wounded. Similar results would be recorded for the month of December.[14]

January 1967 brought the transfer of the Third Force Recon's 3rd Platoon and the detachment's headquarters to a place whose name would join such famed Marine battlegrounds as Tripoli, Guadalcanal, and Iwo Jima. At the time, Khe Sanh was an Army Special Forces Camp with only one Marine assigned, a lieutenant colonel serving as the liaison from III MAF Headquarters. He was an extremely proficient officer, but he was transferred a few days after the Third Company's arrival to become the G-2 (intelligence officer) for the 3d Marine Division. His replacement, unfortunately, had neither an understanding of the value of intelligence nor of the proficiency of Force Reconnaissance.

Special Forces DELTA Teams had been responsible for reconnaissance around the base but were too few in number to properly cover the vast area. Intelligence reports indicated an enemy buildup in the region, and the Third Force Recon Detachment was called in to help.[15] Although the siege of Khe Sanh was a year in the future, there were more than enough NVA and VC around the base in 1967

---

air strikes. He frequently acted as assistant patrol leader, and when the patrol leader, SSgt Librado L. Flores, was ill for 10 days with malaria, Burwell acted as patrol leader on two missions.

to keep the recon Marines busy. Their only problem was in getting the Marine liaison officer to believe what they were finding.

GySgt Lawrence Keen of the 5th Platoon recalls that patrols found signs of enemy activity all around the base from the beginning of 3rd Platoon's operations. They found trails so well developed that bridges with handrails had been built across streams. Closer to the Laotian border, they found roads capable of truck traffic. Within the first week a team occupying an OP on Hill 881 spotted mortar teams, wheeled vehicles, and over 1,000 enemy soldiers. When the OP requested artillery fire on truck lights and flashlights they observed in the valley that night, the liaison colonel denied the fire support, saying that the lights were probably only a few candles being used as a ruse by the small VC force in the area to draw the Marine's fire. On another occasion, Keen observed the colonel allowing a French priest and local officials into the base's Command Operations Center, which had classified map boards and status reports posted on its walls.[16]

The danger from the density of the enemy around Khe Sanh was compounded by their ability to monitor and interrupt the Marines' radio transmissions. One patrol, operating a radio relay site on Hill 950 overlooking the Khe Sanh Airstrip, had so much difficulty with enemy interference on their military radios that they resorted to civilian walkie-talkies they had procured before leaving the States. Another team, about to be inserted by CH-46 on an LZ northwest of the base, heard a woman's voice on their radio frequency saying, "Land, Marines, it will be your last landing." The chopper turned back to abort the mission, but the liaison colonel ordered the team to land. They were met on the LZ by a withering cross fire and were lucky to lift back off with no casualties.[17]

Just why the liaison officer made such poor decisions and why he failed to accept the reports of the recon teams while maintaining that there were few enemy in the area is unknown. He must have been quite sure of himself, however, because he even failed to include the detachment's patrol reports in his monthly Command Chronologies and Daily Situation Reports.

Regardless of what the liaison officer thought, the recon teams continued to find—and be found by—enemy forces up to battalion strength. One team became so hotly engaged 15 kilometers northeast of Khe Sanh on 18 January that a 30-man SPARROW HAWK reaction force had to be airmobiled in to help the patrol break contact.

The Third Force Recon Detachment's Team 5-2 ran into even more problems a few days later 20 kilometers to the northeast. After insertion at 1145 on 26 January, the team moved less than a kilometer before finding trails which showed heavy foot and vehicle traffic within the past few days. At 1400 the team established an OP, and the next few hours passed uneventfully.

At 1745 the team observed 10 enemy carrying AK-47s approaching their position. Allowing the unsuspecting NVA to enter their kill zone, the team opened fire, killing all 10. Seconds later an estimated 35 NVA opened fire on the recon men and began maneuvering to surround them. After 20 minutes of fighting that often closed to hand-grenade range, Team 5-2 decided that it was unable to break contact and requested a reaction force to assist the withdrawal.

A SPARROW HAWK platoon from A Company, 1st Battalion, 3d Marines departed the Khe Sanh Airstrip at 1815 aboard two CH-46s escorted by two UH-1s and two H-34s. When the helicopters arrived over Team 5-2, the recon Marines advised them that the ground situation was too hot to allow a landing and that the aircraft would have to go into an alternate LZ. The pilots ignored the warning and attempted to land. Both 34s were hit by machine-gun fire, one by 17 rounds of .50 and .30 caliber; it limped back to Khe Sanh. One CH-46 was hit while still in the air; it also got back but burned upon landing at Khe Sanh.

The crew, with one aviator wounded, was able to escape. Meanwhile the other CH-46 flew through the hail of bullets to land on the LZ. As its 16-man reaction force unloaded, the aircraft was hit and destroyed. The crew was able to unload and joined the reaction force.

Even with the 16 infantry Marines and the four aviators, Team 5-2 was still far from being out of trouble; during the landing, more enemy arrived. At 1945 two more CH-46s landed at Khe Sanh from Dong Ha and picked up the remainder of the reaction force. Accompanied by illumination flare ships and fixed-wing jet aircraft, they flew back to Team 5-2's position. A battery of Army 175mm artillery joined the battle after displacing from Camp J. J. Carroll to Thon Son Lam so that they were in range of the recon team.

At about 2200 one of the CH-46s tried to land the remainder of the reaction force near Team 5-2's perimeter. It was hit by small arms fire as it approached the LZ, made a crash landing, and burned. The crew of four and the 15 infantry Marines were able to escape with only one wounded. However, because the chopper went down 200 meters from the recon team, they were unable to link up because of the heavy enemy fire. Both Marine perimeters were now under attack by an estimated company of NVA. Again fighting frequently closed to hand-grenade range before the Marines time and again were able to beat them back. The enemy stayed close to the Marines not only in an attempt to overrun them but also to avoid the air strikes and artillery that were raining down on the surrounding jungle.

Despite the heavy fog that covered the LZ by then, helicopter gunships and fixed-wing aircraft continued to drop ordnance with unerring accuracy. One CH-46, in an attempt to deliver ammunition, collided on takeoff with a Huey parked on the Khe Sanh Airstrip. Both aircraft were destroyed, but there were no casualties.

During a brief lull in the battle at 0308, an H-34 was

able to reach both Marine perimeters and deliver ammunition while extracting the most critically wounded. Marines with less than life-threatening wounds stayed behind with their buddies to continue the fight.

At daylight the NVA made another assault only to be beaten back again. Under the protection of continuous air strikes, the recon team and reaction force were finally extracted at 0937. Team 5-2 returned to Khe Sanh after more that 15 hours of continuous fighting with one dead and five wounded.[18]

During the overnight battle, the assistant division commander of the 3d Marine Division flew into Khe Sanh to coordinate the battle. General Walt, III MAF commander, arrived shortly after the extraction was completed. The generals were beginning to receive and believe the Force Recon reports of the number of enemy around the base.

Immediately upon landing, Walt began asking members of the Third Force Recon Detachments how many enemy were ''out there.'' Sgt Alastair Douglas Scott, a former British paratrooper, replied, ''At least a thousand.''

Walt then asked what should be done, and Scotty recommended that additional Marines and the Army's 1st Air Cavalry Division be brought in. The liaison colonel, standing nearby, objected by stating, ''There's really only 50 or so VC out there.'' Walt's confidence in the Force Recon Marines was shown in his response. He calmly turned to the colonel and told him to be on the next plane out of Khe Sanh. The liaison officer assumed a minor position on the 3rd Marine Division staff the next day.[19]

Shortly thereafter, additional units from the 9th Marines were transferred to Khe Sanh. A patrol of the regiment's 1st Battalion made contact on its initial mission. The battles that preceded the siege of the base had begun.

As part of the buildup at Khe Sanh, the other two platoons of the Third Force Recon Detachment arrived at the end of January. During February the detachment conducted 25 patrols of five or six men each, resulting in 17 enemy sightings and five contacts.[20]

While the Third Force Reconnaissance Detachment was patrolling the jungle around Khe Sanh, the remainder of the company was still back at Camp Pendleton. Floyd pushed hard to recruit new men and to train them for deployment. Capt Jim Williams joined the company as operations officers and developed a training syllabus which eliminated submarine training while emphasizing the Jungle Warfare School in Panama.

By April the training was completed. The company flew from El Toro, California, via Midway and Guam, to land at Da Nang on 25 April 1967. That afternoon it was picked up by C-130s and flown to Phu Bai, where it was attached to the 3rd Reconnaissance Battalion. At Phu Bai the company was joined by its three platoons already in-country and the detachment ceased to exist. It was a reunion more of formality than personality. After more than eight months in Vietnam, few of the original Third Force Recon Detachment were still with the unit. Some had been evacuated with wounds, several had won battlefield commissions and moved on to other units, while the few remaining were nearing their rotation dates. Regardless of what had occurred, spirits were high, for finally the Third Force Recon Company had made it to the war zone.[21]

The recon men of the Third Company became acquainted with the war very quickly at Phu Bai. During their second night in-country, the cantonment area where they were temporarily billeted was mortared, slightly wounding 26 Marines. Fortunately only Sgt Lawrence Keen, who received shrapnel in the shoulder, was injured seriously enough to be evacuated. Keen quickly recovered, and rejoined the company a few days later.

Following a brief operation in the Hai Lang Forest, the Third Company moved north to Dong Ha, where it assumed responsibility for the area previously assigned to C

Company of the 3rd Reconnaissance Battalion. On 14 May, the Third Company, with D Company of the 3rd Recon Battalion attached, was tasked with providing recon patrols along the DMZ and near Con Thien in support of Operation HICKORY I. Many of these patrols were accompanied by scout dogs and their handlers, with 8–12 of the teams attached to the company throughout the summer of 1967. The relationship between the dog teams and the recon men was good because many of the handlers were former recon Marines who had been siphoned off from the Third Company back at Camp Lejeune to form the original Scout Dog Platoon.[22]

While the Third Force Recon Company was preparing for deployment, another Force Recon Company—the Fifth—was formed at Camp Pendleton. Organized to provide another unit, besides the Second Company, to train and supply replacements for the two companies in Vietnam, the Fifth Company was formed on 31 January 1967 with a nucleus of four officers and nine enlisted Marines. Maj R. T. Henry was in command; Capt W. C. Shaver, exec; 2ndLt T. E. Manry, communications officer; R. D. McNamara in charge of supply.

By the following June the company strength was up to 11 officers and 130 enlisted. Most of the officers and well over half the senior NCOs were Vietnam veterans with tours in Force Recon. The leaders and trainers knew what to prepare their men for and pursued a concentrated program of instruction in map reading, patrolling, forward observer procedures, and parachuting. Amphibious operations, diving, and submarine training were included, as the Fifth Company also had to maintain readiness for possible missions other than those in Southeast Asia.

On 14 November 1967 one platoon of the Fifth Company, two officers and 13 enlisted men, was transferred to the 27th Marine Regiment. The platoon deployed with the 27th to Vietnam in February 1968 and provided the regiment reconnaissance support until its return to the States in September of the same year. When the platoon deployed, the remainder of the company was redesignated as the Fifth Force Recon Company (minus).[23]

The Fifth Company continued to supply men to the recon units deployed in Vietnam until 1969, when it became apparent that Marine involvement in the war zone was winding down. Personnel strength of the company decreased each month until 15 October 1969, when the Fifth Company was formally deactivated.

CHAPTER 11

□□□□□□□□

Work on the Task Force Level

*W*HEN the Force Recon units first arrived in Vietnam, they were employed to provide reconnaissance at the regiment level. As more Marine units, including division headquarters, came in-country, the recon men progressed to supporting the divisions. Of course, this was still one headquarters down from the Force level of III MAF (Marine Amphibious Force), where, according to doctrine, they should have been assigned. However, in the massive area for which III MAF was responsible, small-unit hit-and-run engagements dominated rather than static lines and large battles. Controlling recon assets at the level where maneuver units could immediately respond to their findings was valid at the time.

The arrival of the remainder of the Third Force Recon Company in April 1967 fairly well established the reconnaissance unit assignments. By then each Marine division had an organic reconnaissance battalion as well as a Force Recon company. For the next two years the 1st Marine Division would have its 1st Recon Battalion with the First Force Recon Company under its operational control. The 3rd Reconnaissance Battalion with the Third Force Recon

Company OPCONed to it (i.e., under its operational control) was assigned to the 3rd Marine Division.

The exception to this organization was during the periods when the Force Recon Companies were detached from their division assignments so that they could provide reconnaissance for ad hoc task forces. Task forces were specially formed units composed of two to nine infantry battalions—often a mixture of both Marine and Army organizations. Usually commanded by a brigadier general who was an assistant division commander, task forces were organized to perform specific jobs. The I Corps tactical area of operations was so large that frequently a division headquarters could neither control nor support its widely dispersed units. A task force with a provisional support unit attached could provide both and therefore increase the combat capability of friendly units in the corps zone. Another advantage of task forces was their ability to respond to specific threats or to secure critical areas or waterways. Depending on which of the Marine divisions provided the major part of the task force, either the First or Third Force Recon Company was OPCONed as its recon asset. Upon completion of the task force's specific objectives, the Force Recon company returned to division control.

Force Recon support of task forces was marked by repeated successes in finding and destroying the enemy while developing new and innovative methods of patrolling. Individual acts of heroism and overall team proficiency were routine.

Maj Edwin H. Walker IV assumed command of the First Force Recon Company on 15 December 1967. Walker, a former commander of the Second Company back at Camp Lejeune and operations officer of the 1st Recon Battalion in Vietnam, was the author of the first SOP for STINGRAY and long-range reconnaissance patrols. A meticulous, detail-oriented, energetic officer, Walker was somewhat eccentric. Upon completion of his career in the Corps, Walker became an Episcopal priest.

On 4–5 January 1968, Walker moved the First Company "bag and baggage," including the rear support elements, from Da Nang to Phu Bai, where it was assigned to Task Force X-RAY, commanded by Brig Gen W. A. Stiles, until the following September.[1] Due to Walker's long hours of work and close supervision, the company was able to quickly establish a reconnaissance operating base despite the meager resources available at Phu Bai. Patrols were committed to the jungle only five days after their arrival.

The first patrol had negative sightings, while the second had eight sightings totaling 94 NVA/VC. Team LUGUNA POINT, the third patrol, was one of bravery and death. Departing Phu Bai at 1215 on 12 January, the patrol was to conduct an area reconnaissance of the Song Ta Trach region with emphasis on monitoring enemy movement toward the district headquarters at Nam Hoa.

At 1300 the following day, the patrol observed two enemy wearing black pajamas, one carrying a rifle. The team ambushed the VC, killing one.

LUGUNA POINT was moving through the jungle at 1145 on the 14th when it came upon an NVA base camp complete with bunkers and trenches. Before the team could withdraw, it was detected and took fire from four automatic weapons at point-blank range. In the initial fight, Sgt Nicholas Hawrylak, Jr., was wounded and LCpl Charles E. Harris was killed. Amid the hail of bullets the team corpsman, HM2 John L. Jackson, fought his way to the two downed Marines and was able to drag Hawrylak back to the hasty perimeter the rest of the team had formed. Exposing himself to more incoming fire, he dressed Hawrylak's chest, arm, and leg wounds.

When the team requested a med-evac helicopter, they were informed that there would be a delay of a half hour because no corpsman was available to accompany the mission. Jackson immediately volunteered to accompany the wounded Marine aboard the helicopter, and the med-evac soon was hovering over the team. Hawrylak was placed on a seat at the end of a cable and was hoisted through the trees. After he was pulled into the chopper, the cable was dropped back to the ground to pick up Jackson. When Jackson was suspended halfway between the ground and the helicopter, the enemy renewed their attack with Jackson as a prime target. Jackson fired his pistol in return as the bird gained altitude. Once on board, he administered to his patient all the way to the hospital and into the operating room. Despite serious wounds, Hawrylak survived.

In addition to the life-saving care Jackson administered to the wounded recon man, his bravery in volunteering to ascend the cable to the helicopter also likely saved the rest of the team. If they had had to wait the extra half hour for a corpsman to accompany the med-evac, the enemy would have had time to reinforce its attack. With the extra time provided by the med-evac's earlier arrival, the team was able to recover Harris's body and withdraw.

Harris was posthumously awarded the Silver Star. Jackson received a Bronze Star, while two other team members, Cpl James B. Linn and LCpl Robert Bahr, were awarded Navy Commendation Medals.[2]

The enemy offensive during Tet of 1968 found the First Force Recon Company conducting operations on the outskirts of Hue. Patrols prior to the offensive amassed detailed information concerning trails, weather, LZs, enemy strong points, and activities. Information gathered by the recon teams revealed an increase in enemy activity. The problem was that no one who was receiving the information was doing anything about it.

GySgt Bruce D. Trevathan remembers that many NVA were observed by the recon teams but that the reports were generally disregarded.[3] One of the company's platoon leaders, 1stLt Russell L. Johnson, recalls that he frequently talked with officers from the infantry battalions assigned to Task Force X-RAY, who told him that none of the patrol's findings ever made it down to their level. According to Johnson, the failure of other units to react to the patrols' findings caused a morale problem in the company. "There'd be two or more times a month, troopers would come up and ask, 'What good are we? We're going out there and getting all this information, but we never get any read-back on it. We never get any word that an operation has been planned because of it.' The information we were providing simply wasn't getting out to the units that could use it to improve their own operations."[4]

The Tet attack on Hue might not have come as such a surprise if anyone had been paying attention to the patrol reports of the First Company. These reports, forwarded to Task Force X-RAY with copies to III MAF and MACV headquarters, were quite revealing of the enemy buildup prior to Tet. The written comments by the debriefer in Patrol Report 46-68 state,

> In view of the great number of sightings made by this OP it could be assumed that Route 647 is being used by the NVA as an infiltration route into Hue City. A number of NVA were guided by local VC [indicating they were new to the area]. On numerous occasions NVA were observed talking to the local populace and then being led away. Some NVA were spotted arriving from the north, changing into civilian clothes, and then moving south. It is recommended that a sweep-and-destroy operation be held in this vicinity and that all civilian homes be searched for caches.[5]

Oddly, the first major contact during Tet by the First Company was not via a patrol but during bridge security, an unusual mission for recon. On 5 February the First Company was directed to provide support for engineers of the 1st Marine Division, who were to repair a damaged bridge within the city of Hue. A provisional platoon under the leadership of 2ndLt Howard W. Langdon, Jr., was assigned the mission.

The platoon, along with the engineers, was transported by truck to the objective. Just short of the bridge, the convoy found the road blocked. As the recon Marines dismounted to proceed up the road, they were ambushed from the front and left flank by NVA concealed in the surrounding buildings. The NVA were firing small arms, automatic weapons, mortars, and recoilless rifles. In the initial bursts, LCpl J. E. Prideaux was killed and PFC J. A. McIntosh was mortally wounded while attempting to recover Prideaux's body. Seven other recon Marines were wounded.

Langdon ordered his men to pull back. PFC Ronald S. Miller, despite having taken a bullet in the back, managed to drag another wounded Marine more than 20 meters until they were out of the kill zone. Another casualty was rescued by LCpl Andrew Q. Ventura. After reaching a relatively safe position with his injured comrade, Ventura again exposed himself to the hostile fire to retrieve another downed recon man. On the return he received a painful wound to the ankle but was still able to drag the injured Marine to safety. Miller and Ventura later received Bronze Stars for their valor at the ambush site.[6]

The recon platoon was finally able to break contact only after air strikes using 500-pound bombs leveled the built-up area protecting the NVA. Over two city blocks were destroyed in the fight. Much of the rest of the city would also be destroyed over the next weeks before the battle for Hue concluded with the annihilation of the invaders.

Once the fight for Hue was over and the Tet Offensive turned back, the First Force Recon Company continued with Task Force X-RAY in pursuit of the retreating enemy. Typical results were those posted the following August when the recon men conducted 142 patrols that made 224 sightings of 2,072 enemy. A total of 187 artillery missions

and 45 air strikes were called for, producing 224 confirmed kills.[7]

In September 1968, Task Force X-RAY completed its
mission and was disbanded. The First Force Recon Company returned to control of the 1st Marine Division. On
the recommendation of the Task Force commander, the
company was awarded the Meritorious Unit Commendation—the equivalent of the individual award of the Legion
of Merit.

While the First Company was a part of Task Force
X-RAY during the first quarter of 1968, the Third Company
was primarily engaged in conducting STINGRAY patrols in
support of the 3rd Marine Division. On 16 April the Third
Company was detached from the division and assigned to
Task Force HOTEL[8] operating out of Khe Sanh and Dong
Ha. Within five days the company was running missions
between the base and the Laotian border on patrols known
as KEYHOLES. Rather than finding the enemy and calling
in artillery and air strikes, KEYHOLE patrols called for the
Marines to conduct "pure" reconnaissance. The four-man
teams avoided contact while keeping the enemy under surveillance and reporting his activities, lines of infiltration,
supply points, and assembly areas. For the first time since
World War II, the Force Recon Marines were operating
strictly in a reconnaissance mode.

While the men of Third Company were initially skeptical and apprehensive about the KEYHOLE missions because
of the small size of the teams and consequent decreased
firepower, they learned to appreciate the new method. It
not only gained much information, but it also saved lives.
In the first two months of KEYHOLE operations, the company did not take a single casualty. One patrol located an
arms cache just east of the Laotian border near Co Roc.
Another team spotted an NVA platoon and followed it for
two days to an assembly area, an extensive bunker net-

work, southwest of Hill 881S. After the patrol was extracted, air strikes destroyed the complex and the NVA.

Other teams discovered trails and roads leading out of Laos to Ca Lu, the Ba Long Valley, and Khe Sanh itself. One road showed signs of tracked vehicles, while another had tank tracks with discarded fuel drums alongside. Still another road was 15 feet wide with a trail paralleling it a few meters into the jungle.

The key to the successful exploitation of the recon team's findings was in the rapid reaction by the infantry battalions. MajGen Raymond Davis, commander of the 3rd Marine Division, placed great confidence in the Third Company's patrol reports and committed company- and battalion-size operations to destroy the enemy that the recon men found.

The tortuously steep, densely vegetated terrain around Khe Sanh was ideal for recon operations. Although observation was limited, the small KEYHOLE teams could easily conceal themselves in their OPs or disappear into the thick growth if spotted while moving.

Insertions and extractions were also easier to conduct with the small patrols. During support of Task Force HOTEL, the Third Company borrowed an insertion method perfected by the Army's 1st Cavalry Division. The insertion flight team was made up of three UH-1 troop carriers, known as ''slicks,'' and a pair each of Huey and Cobra gunships. The slicks flew in a column, with the recon team aboard the lead bird, while the gunships remained nearby over the horizon or at a high altitude so they could come in to assist in case the slicks received ground fire. As the slicks approached the LZ, the column descended to treetop level and the lead chopper dropped down to a few feet above the ground as the recon Marines unloaded. Meanwhile the two trail slicks flew over the lead ship. As they cleared the LZ, the chopper that had delivered the KEYHOLE patrol popped back up at the trail of the formation and all three continued on their way.

Unless the enemy had direct observation of the LZ, it had no idea that an insertion had taken place. The only problem with the process was that the exit from the chopper had to be fast and well timed. Frequently the pilots misjudged their altitude because of tall elephant grass covering the LZ, and the recon teams jumped 10 or more feet to the ground.

This insertion method combined with the team's small size and excellent camouflage procedures allowed the recon Marines to find and observe the enemy almost at will—and there were plenty of NVA around Khe Sanh to be seen. According to the briefing notes of Capt George "Digger" O'Dell, Third Company Operations Officer, as he told one team before its insertion into their recon zone, "The command post of the 304th NVA Division is one grid square to your northwest. There are three suspected antiaircraft positions in the center of your box, each with 15 men plus a security force. Enemy activity is dense to the west, north, south, and east of your box. They have mortars and will call them in on you if they spot you."[9]

According to O'Dell, each team's premission briefing was held in front of a large map board. To one side of the map was a sign reading, "Let us not look back in anger nor forward in fear, but around in awareness."

Another smaller sign at the top of the map board was a bit more expressive of the Marines' feelings about the base. It simply stated, "Khe Sanh sucks."[10]

The Third Force Recon Company continued operations around Khe Sanh into the summer of 1968. Patrols penetrated deep into enemy-held areas, often operating in the midst of NVA regiments and divisions. On 15 June a four-man team led by Sgt David E. Metz was assigned to check out suspected NVA road-building efforts along the Laotian border. Twice the insertion helicopter received ground fire within 300 meters of the planned LZ and had to turn back. On the third attempt the team was able to land, only to immediately hear approaching vehicles and movement all around the LZ.

Metz quickly determined that they had set down in the middle of the 83rd NVA Regiment. He called for an immediate extraction, but a fierce firefight broke out before the helicopter could return. Only multiple air strikes and gunship runs were able to keep the enemy from overrunning the team. In the midst of the explosions, the chopper finally arrived and was able to sweep in under fire to extract the team. After the team's debriefing of the number and location of the NVA, additional air strikes pounded the enemy's positions, producing eight or more secondary explosions as ammo and fuel supplies were hit.

The determination and bravery of the team was shown by Metz's remarks at the conclusion of the debriefing: "I will take my team back into that same area within the next two to three days to assess damage and to find out if the road is still being built."

Results of missions were not always so immediately apparent as on Metz's patrol but nonetheless saved American lives at later times. One Third Company patrol in mid-June reconned an area only 5,000 meters east of the Khe Sanh base. Although no enemy were found, the patrol did discover fresh foxholes and indications that a hilltop was being used as an NVA observation post to watch Khe Sanh and nearby LZ Hawk.

The patrol's report resulted in an increase in alertness and additional defensive positions oriented toward the hilltop. Six days later it paid off when the NVA swept down from the hill to attack LZ Hawk. Because they were prepared, the defenders were ready. No Marines casualties were taken, and 15 NVA were killed.

Responsiveness by the commander and intelligence officer of Task Force HOTEL remained immediate. When patrols were extracted, the teams were flown directly to Khe Sanh, where the intelligence officer himself often sat in on the debriefings. In coordination with the task force operations officer and with approval of its commander, infantry companies and battalions were dispatched immediately to respond to the findings. For once, the right information was getting into the right hands at the right time. As a result, much of the success of Task Force HOTEL, and perhaps even the successful defense of Khe Sanh itself, can be directly attributed to the Third Force Reconnaissance Company.

The next support mission for the Third Company was as the reconnaissance element for Task Force CLEARWATER from September to October 1968. CLEARWATER, formed on 24 February 1968, was composed of Army, Navy, and Marine personnel and commanded by Navy Capt Gerald W. Smith. Its mission was to keep the territory from the Perfume River to Hue and from the Song Cua Viet to Dong Ha open from the South China Sea. This critical logistical route carried 90 percent of the supplies to Khe Sanh via the port at Dong Ha, from where they were airlifted the last 20 miles to the embattled base.[11]

Assignment to CLEARWATER offered the recon Marines a tremendous change from the jungle operations that had typified their time with Task Force HOTEL. During CLEARWATER the Third Company operated on rivers, in the surf, and among the sand dunes bordering the South China Sea. Adjustments had to be made and innovations originated to meet the new challenges. Insertions were still made by helicopter, but boats of all types were also used. Water insertions were made by beach landing from boats or by swimming ashore. One method devised for insertion from river patrol boats had each man to step off the moving boat's fantail into the water at five-meter intervals and then swim ashore.[12]

Movement and insertions had to be conducted mostly at night because of the lack of concealment. Starlight scopes, which enabled the recon men to see in the dark, were extremely useful. When operating along the sandy beaches and in the dunes, the patrol teams traded their jungle utilities for light-colored "long john"-type uniforms to blend in with the environment. Weapons and equipment were wrapped in tan-and-white tape to add to the camouflage.[13]

Upon completion of their two months of supporting Task Force CLEARWATER, the Third Company returned to the control of the 3rd Marine Division.

While the Third Company was returning to division control, the First Force Recon Company was preparing to provide support for Task Force YANKEE. Maj Roger E. Simmons, who had assumed command of the First Company in October, received orders on 7 December directing him to move the company south of Da Nang to An Hoa, to be attached to YANKEE. Proceeding by helicopter and truck convoy, the company made its way to An Hoa under the supervision of the operations officer, 1stLt Andrew R. Finlayson, who was a veteran of a previous tour with the company. A platoon from E Company, 3rd Reconnaissance Battalion, joined the First Company at An Hoa to be attached for the duration of the mission. The platoon added one officer, 23 enlisted Marines, and two Navy corpsmen to the company's strength of nine officers, 153 enlisted Marines, and eight corpsmen.[14]

NIGHT SCHOLAR A, the First Company's first patrol in support of Task Force YANKEE, was inserted 13 December to establish a radio relay on Hill 452. It evidently was a good spot for communications, because the team discovered the NVA using the site for similar purposes. NIGHT SCHOLAR A ran the enemy off the hilltop and captured a list of NVA radio frequencies in the process.[15]

There was no shortage of enemy in the An Hoa area. During the remainder of December, the company conducted 105 patrols that made 371 sightings of 2,830 enemy. In an oral history interview at the time, PFC Jack

L. Cox was asked, "Where is the enemy in the An Hoa area?"

The recon Marine replied, "Actually, he's everywhere. Every patrol that Force Recon has run out of An Hoa has had sightings. They're around bomb craters; they're dug into tunnels and bunkers; they're in the elephant grass; they're in the jungle; they're everywhere."[16]

An Hoa was strictly NVA country. No VC were sighted. The NVA appeared to be fresh troops with new gear. During the first few weeks of First Company's patrolling, the enemy appeared to be relaxed and operating in the belief that it owned the jungle; the NVA moved at sling arms with little security posted. In the first weeks of patrolling, the recon teams found an NVA hospital and three base camps. All were destroyed by artillery and air strikes.

This "easy hunting" did not last, however. As the enemy became aware of the recon Marines' presence—usually through the death of their own soldiers—they began systematic recon screens of their own that combed the brush looking for Americans. The First Company countered this by inserting farther from their normal recon zone and quickly moving off their LZs.

Compounding the problem of the large number of aggressive NVA were the dense vegetation and rugged terrain that made movement difficult. Defoliated areas, where everything green had been killed and turned brown by Agent Orange, added to the difficulties by limiting concealment. The dry, dead foliage also made it impossible to move noiselessly.

Another negative terrain factor was the limited number of LZs large enough to allow even a single helicopter to set down. Once the NVA determined that the recon Marines were patrolling their area, they began constant observation of the few LZs. When the patrols found that an ambush waited on every LZ, they tried new methods of insertion. First they attempted to lower men through the jungle canopy on the cable and seat device called a jungle penetrator (designed to extract wounded personnel). But that procedure was too slow, and it was also dangerous. On the first try at using the penetrator on 15 December, 2nd Lt J. E. Slater lost his grip, fell, and was killed.[17]

Next they tried rappeling from hovering helicopters directly into the jungle. Although much better than the jungle penetrator, this method also had its problems; the primary one was that there was no quick way to extract the Marines if they rappeled into a group of the enemy. Another problem was that as they descended on the ropes, the down-draft from the helicopter blades often swung the Marines into trees and branches, causing lacerations and abrasions. Also, equipment, ropes, and men frequently became entangled.

After experimenting with several rappeling methods, the teams finally adopted a procedure that began with two men rappeling to the ground. Once they had checked the area to be sure it was safe for the others, they radioed the chopper and then assisted the rest in their rappels by securing the ends of the ropes.

Although rappeling was a satisfactory technique for entering their recon zones, the Marines continued to look for better methods. Finlayson learned of the Special Forces' use of flexible ladders and went to the SOG compound at Marble Mountain near Da Nang to check it out. Taking along the company parachute rigger to lend advice, the two were able to secure the needed gear. The aluminum-rung ladder came in sections four feet wide and 40 feet long, with a 5,000-pound test strength. Four of these sections were placed together to form a ladder eight feet wide and 80 feet long, which was capable of inserting or extracting a team of up to eight men in a minimum amount of time. This larger-version ladder required a CH-46, while a smaller one could be used with the UH-1 for up to six men at a time.[18]

The ladder could be rolled up and stowed on the rear ramp of the CH-46. When an opening in the canopy was spotted, the chopper would hover, the ladder be kicked out, and the Marines would descend to the ground. The same procedure was followed for an extraction except that the team climbed up the ladder only high enough for all to have room on the rungs. When each man was in position, he used a snap link to secure a rope tied around his waist (called a Swiss seat) to a rung, so that if he lost his grip, he wouldn't fall. The chopper then lifted to a higher altitude and flew to a secure fire base and gently set down. This procedure, while giving the Marines a windy, somewhat scary ride, was much safer than if the CH-46 hovered long enough for the team to ascend the entire ladder. In areas where particularly dangerous insertions were planned, the recon men reversed the procedure by hooking into the end of the ladder on the outside of the chopper before takeoff. With a gentle hover on takeoff and a careful descent, it was safe and much faster.

Members of the First Company were initially a bit skeptical of the ladder. Practice in their base camp added to their confidence, but it was not until the ladder had actually been used in combat conditions that it was totally accepted. Appropriately, the first time the ladder was used was not in a routine insertion but rather during an extraction under fire.

Although the ladder system was not officially sanctioned by the Corps at the time because it had not been operationally tested by the Marine Air Wing, Simmons did not hesitate to use the ladder when one of his teams got into trouble. On Simmons's orders, the helicopter flew to a team nearly surrounded by an NVA force. The ladder was lowered into the middle of the team's small perimeter, and they were snatched from the jungle. Except for a few scrapes and bruises, no one was hurt.

In an interview the day after the extraction, Cpl Richard E. Spangler explained,

> I was on the first team that was ever on the ladder when we tried it out back at Da Nang. I didn't like it. In the first place I didn't trust it, and in the second place I didn't like the idea of being out in the open after breaking contact with the enemy. But yesterday [during the firefight] when I saw that ladder come out, I was never so glad to see anything in my life. My personal opinion of the ladder is I'm scared of it, but as far as using it to take a team out of a combat situation, I think it's about the greatest thing that's ever happened.[19]

Ladder operations allowed the First Company to penetrate areas that were not previously possible due to remoteness and lack of LZs. The ladder also was responsible for saving the lives of the recon men. On one occasion a team under fire was extracted in a mere 20 seconds, while another team in similar circumstances made it out in less than 45 seconds.

A patrol that began on 21 January 1969 illustrated the density of the NVA in the An Hoa area and the value of the ladder. Team PADDLE BOAT, under the leadership of 2ndLt L. M. Beck, was to conduct an area reconnaissance in the vicinity of Hill 551, about 15 miles southwest of An Hoa.[20]

On the second day of the patrol, the rear security man spotted five enemy soldiers trailing the team. He opened up on the NVA, wounding one and driving the others away. As the patrol moved in to capture the wounded enemy, he killed himself with a grenade rather than be taken alive. Upon searching the body the team discovered that he was an officer and paymaster. Along with some valuable documents was the equivalent of $130 in Vietnamese piasters.

The next morning PADDLE BOAT was moving across several steep ridge lines. After crossing the first obstacle, the team took a brief break at the bottom of a gulley. As Lieutenant Beck gave the signal to move out, Corporal Spangler heard a twig snap on the high ground to his left. He looked up and saw two khaki-clad NVA carrying AK-47s headed his way. Spangler initiated the contact by firing a magazine on full automatic. Before his burst was complete at least 20 NVA began pouring AK fire into the team's position from the high ground.

In the initial firing, Beck died instantly from a round in the chest. PFC Charles T. Heinemeier began firing on automatic as he assaulted the incline in an attempt to relieve some of the pressure on his teammates. He made it about 30 meters and through several magazines before he heard Sgt Norman F. Karkos shout, "I'm hit! Give me a hand." Karkos had been attempting to carry Beck's body to safety when he was struck in the arm. Heinemeier, still shooting, pulled back to help the sergeant.

By this time Spangler had traded his M-16 for an M-79 grenade launcher and was popping out the 40mm grenades as fast as he could reload. The team radioman, PFC L. D. Rose, fighting next to Spangler, took a mortal wound to the head at about the same time the team corpsman, HM H. E. Pearce, was also fatally wounded. With half the team dead and the NVA beginning to attack down the hill, all the remaining three Marines could do was run.

At the bottom of the ridge, Karkos, despite his wounds, took charge of what remained of the team. When he realized that Rose and the radio were not with them he knew that without communications they could not call for a med-evac, reinforcements, or extraction. He turned to Spangler and Heinemeier, saying, "Somebody's got to go after the radio."

In an oral history interview, Heinemeier later recalled, "Like a dumb ass I said, 'I'll go,' and ran up the hill."

With the other Marines covering him by fire, Heinemeier made it back to the contact site. When he found the dead radio operator he lifted him up to get the radio off his back and began running, rolling back down the hill. According to Heinemeier, "From what the rest of the guys told me there were rounds hitting all around me all the time, but I was so scared I never noticed them. All I could think about was getting the radio, getting it back down the hill, and getting the hell out of there.''

When Heinemeier returned, the team continued its withdrawal down the hill and on into a valley. Heinemeier recalled, ''We wanted a SPARROW HAWK [reaction team] pretty bad. We were badly shook up about losing three of our buddies. We didn't know where the enemy was. We got into the brush as much as we could and hid, and hoped that they wouldn't follow us. From what I understand, back at the company area, everybody had their gear on, ready to come out and get us. It made us feel good that they were worried about us.''

About 30 minutes later a helicopter with an external ladder arrived. Heinemeier's troubles were not yet over. He noted, ''I'd seen people use the ladder before, but I always thought, 'That's not for me.' But I was damn glad to see it. That was one of the most exciting experiences of my life. I fastened on the ladder. There wasn't room for the other two men to get on, so I unhooked and climbed up a little further. Well, the other men got on and I hadn't snapped in yet. The bird went up and some brush hit me right in the face, and knocked me off the ladder. I fell about twenty-five feet but broke my fall by landing in a tree. The chopper hovered back down for me and I got on pretty well near the bottom and snapped in again.''[21]

When the three Marines landed back at An Hoa, Sergeant Karkos refused medical attention until he could be thoroughly debriefed. Information he and the other team members provided enabled a reaction force to go back into the contact area and recover the bodies of the dead.

Karkos and Heinemeier both were awarded the Silver Star for their actions on the hillside. Escaping death once, however, did not mean safety for the remainder of a tour. On 18 August, Heinemeier received a wound to the neck on Hill 31. Three days later he died.[22]

Patrols of the First Force Recon Company continued to find the NVA in large numbers throughout their assign-ment to Task Force YANKEE. Many teams were able to infiltrate into the very center of enemy camps, stay for days, and depart without ever being detected. Such was the case for Team RECLINE in April 1969.[23]

RECLINE was an experienced, determined team. On an earlier mission it had been shot out of an insertion LZ three times before finally making it into their recon zone on the fourth try. In mid-April the team received fire and had to turn back twice before making insertion at 1305 on the 13th on an alternate LZ. 1stLt Richard E. Miller, patrol leader of RECLINE, had been assigned by Major Simmons to capture a prisoner and bring him back to the company base. The com-pany commander hoped that interrogation of the POW would help identify the NVA unit in the area and how it could cover so well the LZs that the recon Marines were attempting to use as insertion points.

Team RECLINE found their LZ to be unoccupied, but three trails, each four to six feet wide, ran along the sur-rounding tree lines. More than a dozen freshly dug fox-holes circled the clearing. The team headed south because that direction appeared to contain the thickest vegetation. They had not gone far when the point man signaled a halt. Miller crawled forward to the point man, who said he had just seen 14 enemy dressed in khakis, wearing pith hel-mets, and carrying rifles. One of the NVA was apparently in charge of dinner because he was carrying a live pig.

Miller reported the sighting to Simmons while recom-mending that his team remain at the trail to attempt a prisoner snatch. Simmons concurred but directed the lieu-tenant to wait and watch for a day to get a better idea of the number of enemy in the area before attempting to cap-ture a POW. On completion of the radio transmission, the team pulled back from the trail into a heavy growth of jungle for its overnight perimeter.

At 0630 the next morning, Miller and LCpl Terry M.

Taylor reapplied their camouflage before crawling back to the trail. Over the next four hours the two Marines counted 158 NVA walking up and down the pathway. One group was moving a cart containing mortars and rockets. Four teams passed carrying .50-caliber machine guns.

Miller realized that with the number of enemy in the area it would be impossible to safely take a prisoner. He returned to the team's perimeter, informed Simmons of his sightings, and recommended a B-52 strike be made after the team's extraction. Simmons agreed that a POW snatch was too risky, but directed Miller to continue the planned mission: four days of observation.

Taylor and Miller returned to the trail, spotting 70 more NVA before dark. Noise from a nearby stream sounded like the enemy were bathing and relaxing. All around were sounds of digging, tree cutting, and the pounding of things being built. The two Marines returned to the perimeter for the night but no one slept. Every effort was made to remain as quiet as possible.

The next morning, day three of the mission, Miller and Taylor again positioned themselves to observe the trail. Their intention was to see if the traffic on the path was a regular occurrence or only a one-time affair. Over the next four hours the question was readily answered: 120 NVA passed by.

Each day Miller had thought about moving the team's perimeter to a different location. He decided to remain in place. They had gone three days without being detected, and there seemed to be no other place nearby that the enemy did not occupy or walk through. During the third night Miller happily made plans to move to an extraction point the next morning. A call from Simmons brought the unwelcome news that no helicopters were available and that the mission was extended by a day.

As daylight broke the horizon, it was back to the trail for Miller and Taylor. Before noon they spotted 139 enemy—some who were beginning to look familiar from the previous days. Miller assumed that the team was within a battalion or regiment base camp and that they were counting and recounting many of the same NVA as they moved from place to place within their complex.

For over three days Team RECLINE had not eaten and had slept little. At 0500 on the fifth morning a heavy rain began to fall. The downpour was enough to muffle any noise they might make, so Miller signaled his men that they could break out their chow. Miller remembers, ''We had been getting hungry and thirsty. We hadn't pulled anything out of our packs. I gave the men at ease to eat as much as they wanted while it was raining and they really got into it. I think Taylor ate five cans of C-rations. I ate two LURPs and three C-rats.''

Shortly after finishing their chow the Marines began to move to the extraction point. Miller decided that the LZ used for insertion was likely under enemy observation due to the fresh preparations they had discovered on landing. An aerial observer radioed that there were several bomb craters to the north that should work.

From Miller's observation of the trail, he had decided that the NVA rarely moved in the area before 0800, so he requested the extraction for 0600. As the team carefully crossed the trail and moved toward the bomb craters, they discovered just how precarious their position had been. According to Miller,

> This is when we got a real shock. It turned out we had picked the only wooded area on the hill. When we moved we found the rest of the area looked like Golden State Park—a tree here, a tree ten meters away, but all the underbrush, all the secondary canopy down around the ground, had been cleared away. There were sleeping hooches all over the area—little lean-tos they had built. We were right in the middle of a base area, and they were just waking up.[24]

Miller's team quietly moved on through the NVA base camp. A few minutes later they reached the bomb craters, where a helicopter dropped a ladder to them. In seconds the Marines hooked on and were lifted from the jungle, leaving the enemy unaware they had been observed. Bomb strikes and artillery soon interrupted their complacency.

CHAPTER 12

━━━━━━━━

Work on the MAF Level

*D*URING the first four years of Marine involvement in Vietnam, there was a reluctance on the part
of senior commanders to employ reconnaissance units beyond the range of friendly artillery and radio communications. Despite the record of success on the few occasions
that Force Recon patrols had been allowed to exceed these
limitations, the general policy had been to assign the Force
Recon companies at the division and task force level whose
spheres of influence did not extend beyond the range of
their organic supporting arms. In essence this meant that
the III MAF commander had no reconnaissance asset
working directly for him and his staff. All the information
received at III MAF was generated by and reported
through the force's subordinate units. While this was useful in the planning process, this arrangement did not provide overall intelligence, which was critical to planning at
the MAF level.

The reasons for these distance limitations, which virtually took the "range" out of long-range patrols, were
deeply embedded in the concept of fighting the war itself.
In a war of attrition versus a war of objectives, i.e., destroying the enemy rather than taking and occupying ter-

ritory, the best use of manpower was perceived as using men to find the enemy and then attack him with air power and artillery. For the US leadership in Vietnam, technology seemed to be the solution to the question of how to fight a difficult, complex conflict.

Inherent to this concept was that a unit, regardless of size, was virtually useless if it did not have communications to call in the vast array of supporting arms. Along with this supposition it seemed reasonable that a unit outside the range of artillery, even if it did have radio contact, could not properly use the technology available to destroy the enemy. Of course, this reliance on supporting arms and technology almost disregarded the most important asset in warfare—man himself.*

Another factor that hindered the recon Marines from being allowed to operate at the force level was that in Vietnam there was an absolute, unwritten rule that the dead and missing were to be retrieved at all costs. Although all military units throughout American history have taken pride in their ability to bury their dead, a simple fact of warfare has always been that the turmoil of the battlefield and the risks taken to achieve victory do not always allow that to be possible. In Vietnam, where the enemy did not subscribe to the rulings of the Geneva Convention in the treatment of the dead and prisoners, avoidance of adding to the rolls of the missing was a high priority.**

---

*Perhaps the ultimate example of the foolish reliance on technology was the "McNamara Line" proposed by Secretary of Defense Robert McNamara. His idea was to erect an electronic sensor barrier along the DMZ which would detect the enemy infiltrating south. Once detected, the enemy was to be destroyed by supporting arms without any US troops ever being directly exposed to the enemy. The "McNamara Line" failed for two reasons. First, there were hundreds of miles of border between South Vietnam and Laos and Cambodia where the NVA could cross at will. Secondly, and most important, the electronic sensors and other gadgetry simply did not work well, if at all.

**Nearly two decades after the end of US involvement in Vietnam, one only has to look at the efforts and anguish still expended in the attempt

It was not until LtGen Herman Nickerson, Jr., assumed command of the III MAF on 26 March 1969 that the Force Recon Marines finally were given the opportunity to operate as the long-range reconnaissance patrol asset at the force level. The decision was reached by Nickerson not only because of his willingness to accept the risks involved but also because of the realization that he needed information for planning that was beyond the capability of division assets to collect. Leaving the Force Recon companies attached to the divisions was a misuse of assets that Nickerson was not willing to continue.

One of Nickerson's first actions upon assuming command was to contact the divisions, requesting an estimate of how quickly the Force Recon companies could be prepared to begin recon missions as assigned by the III MAF. LtCol Richard D. Mickelson, commander of the 1st Reconnaissance Battalion, responded for the 1st Marine Division that the First Force Recon Company was immediately available. The First Company had recently returned to battalion control after operating independently as a part of Task Force X-RAY and then Task Force YAN-KEE.[1]

No such positive response was received from the 3rd Marine Division. Upon completion of Task Force HOTEL the Third Company had become so assimilated into the 3rd Reconnaissance Battalion that it was no longer capable of operating independently.[2] Part of the absorption of the Third Company by the battalion was a result of the battle for Khe Sanh, where over 70 percent of the battalion's B Company had been killed or wounded. The commander of the 3rd Recon Battalion had exercised his authority of command to transfer many of the top officers

to account for the 2,400-plus who are listed as missing in Southeast Asia to understand the pressure on commanders to avoid actions that might result in unaccountables for their units.

from the OPCONed Third Company to replenish B Company.

Another problem that had lowered the readiness level of the Third Company was the conflict between the company and battalion commanders. Maj James E. Anderson had assumed command on 29 November 1967 and was well regarded by the Marines of the Third Company. One trooper noted, ''Major Anderson was the best commanding officer I ever served under. He was all for the troops.''[3]

Anderson was an old hand at reconnaissance, having served with the 1st Marine Division recon unit as a private in 1949–50, as a corporal with the First Provisional Brigade in the Korean War, and as a staff sergeant with the First Amphibious Reconnaissance Company at Camp Pendleton. After earning his commission, he commanded A Company of the 2nd Reconnaissance Battalion as a captain at Camp Lejeune.

Anderson differed with the commander of the 3rd Recon Battalion over the tactical deployment of the company. Another conflict between the two that caused great consternation, and one that eventually led to Anderson's transfer out of the company, was in the disposition of captured weapons. Anderson wanted to ensure that his Marines were able to take authorized captured weapons, such as SKSs (semiautomatic rifles) and pistols, home with them at the end of their tours. When SOP was followed, turning the weapons over to the division G-2, troopers were rarely able to reclaim their trophies. Eventually Anderson became so frustrated with the system that he began ignoring the policy and storing the captured weapons in his company arms room. When this was discovered on 10 May 1968, Anderson was transferred out of command.[4]

His successor, Capt William F. Snyder, though a good officer, had no prior reconnaissance experience. Much of his time in command was spent learning the complexities of the company.

Although the Third Company would rise again to its

previous level of proficiency, it was simply not prepared to answer Nickerson's call to operate independently in early 1969. Consequently, the First Force Recon Company was selected to begin operations directly for the commanding general of the III MAF. Except for a brief time at Ba To shortly after the company's arrival in Vietnam, that was the first time that a Force Recon unit was to have the opportunity to perform at the command level for which it had been organized.

On 20 May the First Company moved back to Da Nang for a period of rehabilitation and training. Besides giving the company time to prepare for its new mission, it also allowed the III MAF staff to focus on the use and support of recon assets. After a week of receiving replacements and generally relaxing, the company embarked on a rigorous training program encompassing a review of scouting and patrolling, weapons qualification, and familiarization with insertion and extraction methods such as STABO, the ladder, and rappeling. STABO was a new procedure adopted from the Special Forces: a 120-foot nylon rope with a parachute harness attached to the end. A hovering helicopter could drop STABO rigs through the jungle canopy to a team on the ground who would don the harness and be lifted out of the jungle.

Three parachute jumps were also conducted during the training period to maintain the recon Marines' proficiency in airborne operations. The jumps were also considered a reward for past service, because the recon men considered parachuting more fun than work.

The training period for the First Company was also well spent by the III MAF staff. Although doctrine called for the Force Recon companies to work at the force level, that did not necessarily mean the III MAF Headquarters staff had any idea of how to use the asset. A reconnaissance conference was held at III MAF Headquarters on 5 May to begin "educating" the staff on the capabilities and support requirements of the company. Both Simmons of the First Company and Mickelson of the 1st Recon Battalion attended to lend their expertise and advice. At the forefront of the discussions was the guidance from Nickerson that, as the III MAF commander, he would be in charge of mission tasking for the First Company.

A second recon conference, held on 12 June, dealt more with the specifics of long-range reconnaissance operations. Items of particular interest were insertion and extraction techniques and the employment of reaction forces.

On 11 June, III MAF issued Recon Operations Order 1-69, which directed the insertion of the first recon teams in support of the amphibious force to begin on 15 June. The insertion date was delayed to 17 June when it was discovered that the order did not include plans for providing aircraft to be on standby for commitment of the reaction force if needed.

The assigned area for the reconnaissance was the southwest sector of Quang Nam Province near what was known as Base Area 112. No combat or reconnaissance operations had been targeted in the area during the preceding six months. The dense, triple-canopy jungle that covered the area was believed to contain elements of NVA transportation and rear service units as well as a major tactical headquarters. Four recon teams—HANOVER SUE, MILL-BROOK, RECLINE, and PEARL CHEST—were selected for the mission. Their general assignment was to determine the location, number, and activity of any enemy in the zone. Specific tasks assigned were to capture a POW and locate major trails and enemy antiaircraft weapons—particularly any 37mm positions.

An overflight of the objective area was made on D-2 for the patrol leaders and transport pilots. Primary and secondary LZs were selected. However, because the overflight did not descend below 1,500 feet, to avoid alerting the enemy of the impending operation, it was not determined if the LZs selected were large enough for a set-down insertion. To ensure that the teams would be able to insert regardless of the condition of the LZs, each helicopter was rigged for ladder and rappel in case set-down was impossible.

An added security measure that would remain with the recon Marines throughout their work at the force level was in the area of communications. Each team was issued a KY-38, an "accessory" to the PRC-77, which scrambled transmissions. Only a receiver that also had a KY-38 using the same keys, which changed daily, could unscramble the voice messages. Within the communication net containing the KY-38s were the recon teams, a fire support coordination center, the Force Recon company command operations center, the nearest division headquarters command operations center, and III MAF Headquarters. Several relay stations were also established at various fire support bases to relay messages from the patrols when they were beyond normal communications range. When the teams' recon zones were beyond communication range of the relay station, aircraft could also have the scramblers added to their radio systems.

On the morning of 17 June the teams prepared for insertion, with plans calling for two teams to go in just after daylight and two in the late evening. The first team to attempt to land found the LZ too small and went down a ladder. An unexpected movement of the aircraft caused one Marine to lose his grip and fall to the ground, injuring his back. Another man also fell, landing on a Marine on the ground, causing a head injury. After evacuating the two, the rest of the team continued the mission. The second morning insertion was able to set down on their LZ and began their patrol with no difficulties.

Team RECLINE, consisting of patrol leader Lieutenant Ready, five enlisted Marines, a Navy corpsman, and a Kit

Carson Scout,* moved northwest off their LZ at a slow pace after the early morning insertion. Rugged terrain, exceptional heat and humidity, and innate caution restricted the team to covering only 100 meters per hour.[5]

During the first day of patrolling, RECLINE discovered several places that the enemy had used as temporary bases that were not observable from the air. Two 50-foot-diameter areas were encountered that were camouflaged from the air by vines interwoven into the tree branches, forming a thick, netlike cover. The team was confident that they had not been detected, as they frequently paused to listen for anyone following and occasionally doubled back on their path to be sure.

On the third day of the patrol, 19 June, movement became even more difficult—about 50 meters an hour—as RECLINE moved up a hill. At 1030 four NVA wearing blue uniforms and green bush hats were spotted approaching the patrol. Their relaxed, carefree manner gave no indication that they were aware of the team's presence. Before the patrol could conceal themselves, the NVA spotted them and a firefight broke out. The recon men killed three, but more NVA began to join in. Apparently the group first sighted had been the point for a larger element.

Withdrawing to the south, RECLINE attempted to break contact, but the enemy was unwilling to give up the chase as they spread out on line, carefully searching the jungle. RECLINE was not in direct communication with the company or a relay station but was able to contact one of the other teams, which passed along their messages. Since they were out of the range of artillery, air support was requested to help break contact and cover the team's extrac-

*Kit Carson Scouts were former VC or NVA who had "rallied" to the South Vietnam government. After a period of indoctrination and training they were assigned as scouts to American units. Most Kit Carsons picked up at least a little English and doubled as passable interpreters. The scouts were not regularly assigned to the Force Recon companies but did occasionally accompany patrols.

tion. An hour after the initial contact, an aerial observer was overhead directing air strikes of 250-pound bombs and napalm on the pursuing NVA. Several strikes were called so close that the RECLINE team was peppered with shrapnel from American bombs.

Helicopter gunships joined the fight, firing white phosphorus rockets to cover the extraction. A helicopter hovered over the 120-foot canopy, dropped STABO rigs to the team, and lifted them to safety. Except for minor wounds from the bomb strikes, there were no casualties.

Team MILLBROOK, under the leadership of Sgt Theodore A. Ott, was also inserted during the late afternoon of 17 June into jungle even thicker than that which RECLINE had to contend with. Nothing was found the first day or night, but the morning of the second day yielded a well-used trail. The jungle flanking the pathway was so thick that the point man hadn't spotted it until he was only three meters away.[6]

Ott decided that the best way to determine if the NVA were still in the area was to follow the trail. The usual practice in such circumstances was to parallel the path in the bordering jungle. After some deliberation Ott came to the conclusion that the vegetation was so thick that the patrol would make too much noise if it followed the usual procedure. Although he knew it was risky, Ott directed the patrol to move down the trail. MILLBROOK had moved less than a hundred meters before four NVA walked up on the rear security man, who was forced to open fire after he was spotted. He managed to kill one and probably one more before the enemy withdrew.

Ott immediately pulled his team off the trail, setting up a 360-degree perimeter. A few minutes later another group of NVA approached, but because of the dense vegetation the Marines could not determine how many. In two brief firefights over the next ten minutes the team added three more kills to its body count. A quarter hour later the enemy probed the perimeter once again. This time one soldier ventured so close that PFC Johnnie Carter was able to shoot him in the knee and elbow and then drag him into the Marines' position. With a live prisoner the patrol's objective had been met—it was time to pull out. Ott called for extraction.

Before the choppers arrived, the Marines began to take fire from three directions. During the firefight the corpsman continued to work on keeping the prisoner alive. In one NVA rush, Ott had to stand to protect the medic, killing two but taking a bullet in his stomach. Carter turned to knock down the man who shot Ott.

Seconds later a grenade landed between the wounded patrol leader and the corpsman. Carter dove between the two, grabbed the grenade and heaved it away. A few meters from his hand it detonated, showering the team with shrapnel but producing only minor wounds rather than the death it would have delivered had Carter not reacted so quickly. Carter was not deterred by the explosion, as he hastily retrieved his M-16 and blasted still another NVA who was rushing the perimeter.

Ott continued to lead his team despite his painful wound and to direct the air strikes that were now on station. The patrol leader later noted, "My wound didn't need taking care of because my web gear was pretty much putting enough pressure on it to keep the bleeding down."[7]

About 1115 the enemy again attempted to overrun the Marines' position. Attacking from two sides through the thick brush, the enemy forced the recon team to withdraw to a better position. PFC Dennis G. Murphy remained behind to cover the movement. His extremely accurate marksmanship broke up two assaults, killing at least three before the enemy began concentrating their fire on the single Marine. Murphy returned fire until he was fatally wounded, enabling the team to move to a more protected position. The NVA tried another attack on the new perimeter a few minutes later but were again beaten back.

During a lull in the fighting, Ott crawled to Murphy and

dragged his body back to the team. By 1430 the battle had been going on intermittently for six hours. Continual fixed-wing air strikes of bombs, mini guns, and 40mm had kept a wall of steel around the Marines. Major Simmons was making every effort at Da Nang to get extraction birds to MILLBROOK. He also arranged for additional aerial observers flying OV-10s loaded with white phosphorus rockets to obscure the extraction with smoke.

The extraction team was made up of two CH-46s under the command of Maj Van S. Reed. Reed's aircraft was rigged for a ladder extraction, while his wingman's chopper was fixed for STABO. Following a run of smoke rockets mixed with mini guns and 40mm, Reed swooped down to pull the team out.

According to Reed, "As we moved down we came under heavy automatic weapons fire. We continued on down until we put the helicopter right on top of the trees. We were taking occasional hits, but it was nothing real bad. I tried to contact the team on the radio because at this time we could not find their actual position due to the dense jungle canopy. I had radio problems. I could not get the team to answer me. We hovered there about five minutes."[8]

Meanwhile, unknown to Reed, the crew in the back of the helicopter had lowered the ladder. When the pilot finally made communication with the team on the ground he was told to move northwest. As he attempted to do so his crew chief informed him that the ladder was extended and they would have to climb to pull it out of the trees before moving to the team's location. Reed raised the chopper to 100 feet, giving the NVA to his flank a better shot. Eight hits were taken in the cockpit, with an equal number striking the hydraulic system. Reed was forced to pull away and nurse the damaged aircraft back to base.

Reed's wingman, Lieutenant Beasley, now took up the effort to extract the team. Waiting only long enough for more smoke-rocket-carrying OV-10s and two Cobra gunships to roll in to assist, Beasley hovered at treetop level above MILLBROOK. Although the chopper was taking fire, the STABO rigs were dropped through the canopy. By this time Ott had collapsed from loss of blood, but his Marines snapped him into a STABO harness. The same was accomplished for the less-than-willing prisoner, and the team was lifted from the jungle.

HM3 Bricher, the team's corpsman, offered the best summary of the mission after MILLBROOK's return to its company base. The young medic stated that although it was the air cover that broke the enemy's back, the most important survival factor was that the team was able to remain composed, to keep its cool, and to hang together despite the circumstances.[9]

Although two of the first four patrols in support of the MAF were aborted early due to contact, the reconnaissance accomplished what it was tasked to do. The enemy had been found, trails discovered, and a prisoner captured. Future missions in the same area were equally successful in pinpointing an NVA base camp complete with a land-line communications network near Hill 434.

During the period 9 March to 23 November 1969, patrols from the First Force Recon Company sighted 7,747 enemy. Individual awards for valor and service included two Navy Crosses, two Legion of Merits, 11 Silver Stars, 32 Bronze Stars, 21 Navy Commendation Medals, 22 Navy Achievement Medals, and 43 Purple Hearts.

The importance of the intelligence gathered by the First Company during the eight months of patrolling is reflected in their recommendation for a Meritorious Unit Citation. According to the recommendation:

Specific missions of the company ranged from the penetration of deep and long range reconnaissance patrols into the very heart of enemy controlled territory to locate enemy troop concentrations, supplies and lines of communications, to the capture of enemy personnel. In face of numerically superior enemy forces who were employing aggressive, well trained counter-reconnaissance forces, the company repeatedly reentered enemy sanctuaries, completing assigned missions and providing information vital to the subsequent fixing, interdiction and destruction of untold numbers of enemy forces. Accomplishing a total of 191 patrols, the information gathered by patrols formed the foundation and impetus for operations and massive air/artillery strikes against enemy base camps, lines of communications and supply depots. The identity and location of the newly infiltrated 90th NVA Regiment into Quang Nam Province, the egress of the 21st and 1st NVA Regiments from Quang Nam Province and subsequent return of these units was established in large measure by information gathered by the company's patrols. Intelligence gathered from information provided by these patrols went on to precipitate highly successful forays, including Operation DURHAM PEAK, by the 1st Marine Division into the Que Son Mountains and Antenna Valley area where extremely complex enemy base camps and large quantities of supplies were uncovered and destroyed. The enemy was denied a vital stepping stone to Da Nang from the south and to An Hoa from the east and his designs for offensive operations against these areas were effectively preempted. While embarked on operations for the III Marine Amphibious Force, the Company was tasked to locate the enemy's Military Region 5 and Group 44 headquarters, their related installations and supply and communications routes in the southwestern reaches of Quang Nam Province. Patrols provided a flow of heretofore unknown and extremely valuable information from the interior of the enemy's base areas. With repeated interdiction of his newly identified installations and facilities, the enemy was effectively kept off balance and rendered unable to launch his 1969 "summer offensive" of the magnitude he had intended.[10]

While the First Company was supporting the III MAF in the summer and fall of 1969, the Third Force Recon Company was rebuilding to its former proficiency. The leader of the reconstitution of the Third Company was Maj Alex Lee, who assumed command on 1 August 1969.

Part of the reason that Lee was able to get the Third Company back to "force recon standards" was the assignment of 1stLt Clovis C. "Igor" Coffman, Jr., as the company operations officer. Coffman not only had a comprehensive background in reconnaissance but was also a personal friend of the III MAF commander, General Nickerson. Experienced officers and enlisted Marines were soon reassigned to the company. Lee and Coffman began an intense training program in which the graduation exercise was an actual patrol in the jungle. Lee stressed teamwork, cooperation, and professionalism. In the amazingly brief period of two months, Lee had the Third Company back to, or possibly above, its former skill level.

Not only was the company good, but its members were also able to exceed the usual tight brotherhood felt by recon Marines. Members of the company often referred to themselves as "the family."[11] Their motto, "Anywhere, anytime—no questions asked," referred to assistance in personal matters as well as on the battlefield. Corpsman Bruce H. Norton recalls that there was such an atmosphere of absolute trust among the recon men that locks on personal lockers in the rear were never used and valuables were left unsecured on desks and bunks. Nothing ever disappeared. A kitty of several hundred dollars was formed from which any member could draw a loan and repay at his convenience. No books were kept, and the fund was always solvent.*

---

*The "family" did not cease as Marines rotated back to the States. Its members continued to keep close contact and were often aware of pro-

From the end of August to 22 October 1969 the Third Company operated in the Ben Hai River area near the DMZ. Although still formally attached to the 3rd Recon Battalion, the company worked independently in support of the Army's 1st Brigade, 5th Infantry Division (Mechanized). Much of the recon Marines' time was spent in training P Company, 75th Infantry (Ranger) to take over recon responsibilities along the DMZ. Even while accomplishing the training mission, the Third Company managed to keep at least two eight-man patrols in the field along the DMZ.

While the two Force Recon companies were doing their best to contribute to the war efforts, other events were taking place that would influence their future operations. In May 1969, President Richard M. Nixon announced a phased withdrawal of US troops in Vietnam to turn the conflict over to South Vietnamese forces. Nickerson recognized that despite the pullout, the III MAF would maintain responsibility for the same vast tactical area of operations in I Corps for some time. To prepare for this eventuality, Nickerson directed his staff to study the options and recommend how the amphibious force could continue to perform its mission as resources were reduced.

The resulting staff study, published on 22 September 1969, noted that the tactical situation of the III MAF I Corps tactical zone, combined with the requirement to continue operations for an undetermined period during which the US forces would be progressively reduced, underscored the necessity of increased intelligence and surveillance efforts using all available means.[12] Of particular interest was the study's finding that intelligence assets in

motions and transfers before they were officially released. When the company executive officer, Capt Norman Heisler, a former first sergeant and veteran of the Korean War as well as three tours in Vietnam, was killed by a drunk driver near Quantico in 1972, virtually the entire "family" turned up for the funeral.

the region lacked coordination—some were controlled by the G-2 or G-3 of the divisions, some by the Army's tactical units or Special Forces, and still others by the MAF itself. Nothing was being done to coordinate reconnaissance efforts to prevent duplication or to eliminate "blind areas" that were not covered at all.

Much of these findings was not news to Nickerson, as he was well aware of the reconnaissance status in his area of responsibility. Earlier in September, Nickerson had sent a message to Army LtGen Melvin Zais, commander of the XXIV Corps* stating,

> As you may know, I receive a detailed briefing each morning on the deep reconnaissance activities of US forces in the ICTZ [I Corps Tactical Zone]. I have noticed recently that the number of long range reconnaissance patrols maintained in the field by the 101st Airborne Division [one of XXIV Corps' subordinate units] has been minimal. I believe that you will agree that active and extensive deep reconnaissance is a vital dimension of our effort here, especially while the prospect of a diminishing number of US troops in the ICTZ.[13]

The III MAF staff study concluded that a dynamic and integrated intelligence and surveillance capability throughout I Corps was urgently needed. Nickerson took action on 16 October by directing the establishment of a Surveillance-Reconnaissance Center (SRC) to be operational by 1 November. Its mission was "to integrate

---

*The XXIV Corps (originally called the Provisional Corps) was organized on 10 March 1968 to help counter the Tet Offensive. Its commander was an Army lieutenant general with a Marine major general as deputy. The Corps contained both Army and Marine units, and although it was subordinate to the III MAF, many Marines felt that its organization was an infringement on Marine "turf" and responsibilities in I Corps.

ground, aerial, signal, and sensor surveillance information from ICTZ assets as well as from assets being employed in adjacent areas in order to provide the most meaningful and appropriate utilization of each asset in a comprehensive and dynamic surveillance/reconnaissance effort.''[14]

Nickerson was quite satisfied with the information the First Recon Company had been providing over the past five months and had been closely monitoring the rebuilding efforts in the Third Force Recon Company. He now felt it was time to get both companies working for him at the MAF level. On his directions, the Third Company was notified to report to Phu Bai on 26 October to begin operations in support of the Amphibious Force.

Initial operations by the Third Company in support of III MAF were in the Hai Van Pass area. However, this was only an interim mission while Nickerson coordinated for the company's commitment to the target from which he most desired intelligence—the A Shau Valley. The A Shau, located 30 miles southwest of Hue, had been a hotly contested region since the beginning of the war because it offered the most direct infiltration route into Quang Nam Province from Laos. Although US units had frequently invaded the valley and controlled it for varying periods of time, the cost in resources and men had always been high. Each time the Americans had focused on other objectives, the NVA had moved back into their valley strongholds. Throughout the A Shau were extensive bunker complexes, defensive positions, road networks, and supply points.

The A Shau Valley was within the area of operations of XXIV Corps, and General Zais, as the Corps commander, had been committing K and P Companies of the 75th Infantry Rangers to the area since the preceding September. In a message to Nickerson, Zais explained the difficulties anticipated in patrolling the valley: ''Employment [of patrols] is considered hazardous because artillery support will be limited to nonexistent, communications will be difficult, and weather in the coming five months [monsoon season] will impose severe restrictions on insertion, support, and extraction of teams."[15]

Upon completion of the III MAF staff study, Nickerson offered Zais the assistance of the Third Force Recon Company in the A Shau. Zais displayed no interservice rivalry in his response: "I would be delighted to employ the Marine Force Recon Company in XXIV Corps AO. I have seen it in operation along with the recon teams of the 3rd Marine Division Recon Battalion and I know these teams to be as effective as they are gallant."[16]

Since the A Shau was located within the area of operations of the XXIV Corps' 101st Airborne Division, the "Screaming Eagles" provided most of the Third Company's air and fire support. The division's 2nd Squadron, 17th Cavalry was assigned to provide the recon men helicopter support.[17]

Patrols began on 13 December with Teams TINNY and SAVVY attempting an insertion to establish a radio relay station. As they neared their LZ, the lead UH-1 was hit by 12.7mm antiaircraft fire. It crashed and burned. The six Marines and the air crew were all wounded or injured in the crash but were safely extracted by a chase aircraft of the 17th Cavalry. Another attempt to insert a radio relay team was made without incident on 21 December.

Over the next five and a half months the Third Company patrolled the A Shau Valley, producing intelligence that directed units of the 101st Airborne and air strikes, including B-52 missions, that prevented the NVA from mounting an offensive in the province during the spring of 1970. The Third Company was so successful that the NVA ultimately resorted to forming the 11A and 11B Counterreconnaissance Companies—both of which the Third Company found, identified, and partially destroyed. The NVA counterreconnaissance companies were quite sophisticated. Their operations included wearing camouflage fatigues and face paint similar to the recon Marines, employing radio direction finders and jammers, and carrying the most modern equipment and AK-47s. On several occasions the NVA even employed trained scout dogs in their attempts to ferret out the recon patrols.[18]

Initial relations between the Marines and the "sky soldiers" of the 17th Cavalry were somewhat strained. But as they continued operations together, this changed to mutual respect and admiration. One of the major events in building a tighter relationship occurred in early 1970. A patrol led by LCpl "Grape" Vineyard was inserted to conduct a bomb-damage assessment (BDA) of an air strike on an NVA bivouac site. Vineyard's team discovered bodies and pieces of bodies of an estimated 100 enemy dead. Before the patrol had finished its grisly job, an NVA patrol struck. Over the next five hours a running battle with six significant contacts took place as the recon Marines attempted to break contact. Pilots of the 17th Cav orbiting overhead were monitoring the fight on their radios and expected the team to request an extraction. When Vineyard finally called them, he asked only for an ammo resupply so the team could continue its mission. The cavalrymen were impressed.

Not all the patrols in the A Shau were as successful for the Third Company. On 5 February 1970 a six-man patrol was caught in a cross fire from well-concealed NVA in an area of dense elephant grass. Three Marines, Cpl Allen M. Hutchinson, Cpl Adam Cantu, and LCpl Daniel Savage, were killed. Two others were wounded. The sixth Marine and team radioman, Cpl Charles T. Sexton, was also hit, but a sheathed K-bar knife on his shoulder harness stopped the bullet. Although the impact of the round broke the knife in two and knocked Sexton to the ground, he was able to take charge of the team. Directing the fire of his wounded teammates while collecting and redistributing ammo and grenades, Sexton was also able to call in supporting fire and an extraction bird. For his calm actions,

Sexton was meritoriously promoted to sergeant and recommended for the Navy Cross by General Nickerson.[19]

Two days later another Third Company team got into a similar firefight. Sgt Arthur Martinez Garcia, Jr., Cpl Ted J. Bishop, and Cpl James M. Fuhrman were killed.

Despite the stubborn enemy and the losses, the morale of the Third Company was exceedingly high during operations in the A Shau Valley. Sgt James T. Keysacker captured the spirit of the company in an oral history interview at the time. "We had an outstanding commanding officer who knew what he was doing. The troops were well disciplined. They'd give us a job and tell us it had to be done, and we tried our damnedest to do it. Our supply was outstanding, chow was great, and just as a whole, everybody was just outstanding. The men I served with—I don't think there could be any better in the world. The Third Force Reconnaissance Company is the best fighting force the Marine Corps ever had."[20]

Ultimately the Third Company would lose nine Marines in the A Shau while killing 267 NVA, by body count, with the company's own weapons. Captured documents and POW interrogation reports revealed that the company was responsible for 3,000 more enemy dead as a result of artillery and air strikes that it had directed. For the period 7 December 1969 to 16 February 1970 the Third Company was awarded the Army Valorous Unit Commendation—one of only two Marine units to be so honored during the entire war.[21]

While the Third Company was patrolling the A Shau Valley, the First Force Recon Company was assigned by the III MAF to the Thuong Duc Corridor. Beginning in December 1969, the First Company would spend nine months conducting patrols and OPs. Typical of the action they found in the corridor was the patrol of Team MISTY CLOUD from 30 March to 6 April 1970. During 168 hours in the jungle, MISTY CLOUD made 20 sightings of 145 NVA/VC.

The patrol called in 12 artillery fire missions killing 10 and causing 15 secondary explosions. Four air strikes killed at least five more enemy while causing nine additional secondary explosions.

Team MISTY CLOUD also discovered that the enemy was experiencing extreme food shortages. Several areas were found where the NVA were attempting to grow their own crops. The enemy's dependence on the gardens was explained in the patrol report noting, "The great importance [with which] the enemy regards these food plots was demonstrated by the fact that when the cultivated plots caught fire due to a fire mission the enemy could be observed in the open fields trying to stop the fires while the fire missions/air strikes were in progress."[22]

During the same patrol, the recon Marines experienced extensive jamming and interference on their radios. This included the repeating of the patrol's call sign in English, various transmissions by males and females in Vietnamese, and long periods of music. Other patrols in the corridor had similar communications difficulties and learned to use code words to switch to alternate frequencies to ensure that messages got through.

Patrols in the corridor were not always so one sided. Team ABE LINCOLN was into its second day of patrolling on 19 March 1970 after several contacts with individuals or small groups of NVA. Early morning observation of a bamboo bridge across the Song Con River yielded no results, so the team continued its reconnaissance. Moving through heavy brush, the team received small-arms fire at 1040, killing the patrol leader, SSgt D. E. Ayers. The team was extracted under fire when it could not evade the enemy. Ayers' body, however, was never recovered despite later searches. The sergeant is still listed on the rolls of the MIA.[23]

In addition to their patrols, the teams of the First Company frequently manned OPs that provided an overview of the Thuong Duc River Valley. Most of these posts were occupied for only short periods. One OP, located on top of Hill 487, however, was manned for weeks at a time. The rugged mountain was covered in boulders 10–20 feet in diameter and was so steep that teams had to be inserted by ladder or by rappeling in. Although the regular use of the same OP site obviously compromised its position to the NVA, it was felt that the natural topography of the hill would prevent enemy attack.

That assumption was correct—except on one occasion. On 11 June 1970 an NVA company supported by heavy machine guns managed to scale the rocky slope in an attempt to overrun the hilltop OP. Team SANDHURST, under the leadership of Sgt James R. Chistopher, held its positions until completely surrounded. Before the NVA could make their final rush, the team was extracted by a helicopter using the SPIE* (pronounced "spy") system before sustaining any friendly casualties.[24]

One of the last missions run by the First Company in the Thuong Duc Corridor began on 31 July. Team HANS-WORTH,[25] a platoon-size patrol, was to establish a radio relay site just off its insertion LZ. For two days and nights the team spotted nothing as it routinely relayed radio messages to and from units deeper in the jungle. Several times the Marines heard movement around their perimeter but could not determine if the disturbance was caused by men or animals because of the thick vegetation.

At 0120 on the morning of 4 August, the perimeter was hit by grenades, satchel charges, and rocket-propelled grenades (RPGs) followed by automatic weapons and small-arms fire. One of the RPGs scored a direct hit on LCpl William C. Clark, killing him instantly. Another RPG seriously wounded the platoon commander, who went into

---

*The SPIE (Special Patrol Insert/Extract) system was similar to the STABO rigs. It was a 60-foot extraction line to which multiple D-rings were affixed. Using a parachute harness or a Swiss seat, the recon men could connect themselves to the D-rings with a snap link. An entire team could be snatched from the jungle in seconds.

shock and was unable to lead the platoon. Cpl James C. Holzmann, assisted by Cpl Michael L. Loren, took charge of HANSWORTH, dashing from position to position as they directed the team's counterfire and redistributed ammunition and hand grenades. The main attack of the NVA centered on the defensive position occupied by LCpl M. A. Hobbs, who beat back repeated enemy charges.

Throughout the remainder of the night the battle raged. An hour before dawn a flare ship and gunships arrived to join in the fight. At dawn, a reaction force was airlifted in to assist, causing the NVA to leave the jungle littered with bodies and drag marks where they had carried off their dead. A pool of blood only five feet in front of Hobbs's position marked how close the NVA had come to the Marines' perimeter.

CHAPTER 13

■□■□■□■□

To Expect the Unexpected: Missions, Information, Bravery, and Dangers Other Than the Enemy

PATROL reports of the Force Recon Companies reflect an almost routineness in missions assigned, information gathered, and valor exhibited. However, incidents that were unusual, nearly unbelievable, and at times outrageous did occur. The recon Marines quickly learned that in patrolling, like the Vietnam war itself, nothing was fixed or unchanging.

In addition to the usual operations of area and route reconnaissance, maintaining OPs, destroying targets of opportunity with supporting artillery and air power, and conducting bomb damage assessments, several out-of-the-ordinary missions were at times assigned and executed. These included scuba, pathfinder, demolitions, and "special" operations.

Although generally not engaged in operations along major waterways, some teams did use scuba to investigate bridge pilings, to clear rivers of obstacles and explosives, to search underwater caves and caches sites, and to implant sensors in waterways used by the enemy. In October 1967 a scuba team was formed in the First Company in response to the destruction of over 15 bridges in a six-month period along the supply routes from Da Nang to the fringes of I Corps. The team's mission was to inspect bridge pilings for charges placed by NVA frogman sappers, to defuse those that they found, and to assess damage of successful enemy sabotage.

They were also tasked with devising methods of preventing underwater attacks on the bridges. The most common techniques were the periodic dropping of concussion hand grenades into the water and having marksmen snipe at anything floating down the waterway. One method devised by First Company scuba-team member SSgt Thomas J. Vallario employed a thin copper wire placed a foot below the water's surface connected by alligator clips to an indicator light in a bridge bunker. The clips could be adjusted for two to 35 pounds of pressure. Separation by an underwater swimmer activated the indicator light.

The scuba team occasionally had to retrieve bodies from rivers and search underwater caves and cache sites. Scuba operations in the murky inland waterways required the use of only the best-trained and coolest recon Marines. In an interview at the time, Vallario explained, ''the visibility is approximately five inches, if it's that good, and it's normal reaction for a person to stay away from dark places. If a man goes down there and he's not sure of himself, he panics. He might come up into a sharp branch. Once in a while you find punji stakes in the water about two or three feet long. Another hazard is getting tangled up in vines. If you don't know what to do, and panic, you'd better hang it up. The more you twist, the more you'll get tangled.''[1]

Because of the Force Recon Marines' training in explosives, they were occasionally asked to perform demolition missions. In December 1966 a recon team was dispatched to blow up a three-strand steel cable bridge on an NVA high-speed trail out of Laos into I Corps. On other patrols the teams worked with engineers to clear hilltops for permanent OPs or to make or enlarge LZs. Demolitions were also carried on many patrols, regardless of mission, for use in destroying captured enemy weapons and equipment that could not be extracted.

Although official pathfinder functions were eliminated from Force Recon responsibilities before their arrival in Vietnam, the companies still were called upon a few times to perform the function. On 18 July 1967, Team DOGMA was inserted into a Happy Valley LZ to see if the area was secure and then to guide in the 1st Battalion, 7th Marines. DOGMA, composed of patrol leader 2ndLt Thomas W. Williamson, 11 enlisted Marines, and a corpsman, detected a VC force lying in wait around the LZ. The team's direction of gunships on the enemy before the infantry Marines' landing saved helicopters as well as men.[2] A similar operation was conducted two years later, in July 1969, by the 5th Platoon of the First Company in support of the 1st ARVN Ranger Group near Fire Base Ryder.[3]

Because the enemy in I Corps used land-line wire communications between major bases, the recon Marines were dispatched at times to tap into these systems. Equipped with Surveillance Device 4-114A, the patrols tapped into the lines, recorded the conversations, and delivered the tapes to intelligence channels for translation.[4]

Various sensor devices were given to the recon teams on special missions to place along trails, in assembly areas, and in temporarily abandoned bunker complexes.[5] These sensors, monitored from receiving stations at fire bases or from aircraft, could detect movement or any disturbance on the ground. Some of the devices contained audio sensors so sensitive that they could monitor the enemy's conversations. Although the sensors seldom lived up to the expectations of the technocrats in Da Nang and Saigon, they did prove useful on occasion—particularly in the stay-behind mode, after the Marines moved on, to determine if the enemy reoccupied the region.

Another technique that the recon Marines experimented with was borrowed from the DELTA teams of the Special Forces. Roadrunner missions involved dressing and arm-ing a Kit Carson Scout to look like an NVA soldier and letting him "run the trails." A recon team shadowed the Roadrunner from the nearby jungle. When the Kit Carson encountered a group of NVA or VC, he gave a cover story of being a courier new to the area and attempted to learn about enemy activity there. If the enemy seemed important enough or had enough information, on a signal from the Roadrunner the recon team attacked or took a POW.[6]

Force Recon teams were always alert for the opportunity to take a live prisoner, because much could be learned during interrogation. However, the capture of an enemy soldier was difficult for two reasons. First, the recon teams were quite vulnerable themselves because of their small numbers and their deployment far from other friendly units. Second, the NVA and VC were near fanatical in their resistance to capture and often chose to die fighting rather than become a prisoner.

Although the capture of a POW was a secondary mission of practically every patrol, it was somewhat unusual for a team to be primarily assigned the taking of a prisoner. Most of the POWs brought in by the recon men were a byproduct of successful ambushes, where a wounded enemy was quickly grabbed from the kill zone and extracted along with the patrol. When a specific prisoner snatch was assigned, a great deal of planning and preparation went into its execution.

One such POW operation began with the return of a recon patrol of the First Company under the leadership of Lt William J. Peters in July 1969. Peters reported to Company Commander Maj Roger Simmons that the team's recon zone contained a heavily used trail frequented by small groups of NVA. Simmons approved the plan to reenter the area and to attempt a POW capture using Peters' team reinforced by a team led by Lt Charles L. Lowder.[7]

The two lieutenants spent the next day brainstorming the operation, conducting a map reconnaissance, comparing data on the terrain in the zone, and preparing their plan. Early the next day they briefed their combined team, which was labeled HEAD COLD. The following day was occupied with detailed rehearsals and inspections. Particular attention was given to practicing the system of dot and dash codes transmitted by keying their radio handsets that would be used for communications between the security and snatch elements. Different codes were devised so that information on the number of enemy sighted and their direction of movement could be communicated silently. Binding and gagging were also practiced so the prisoner could be secured and silenced after capture.

Team HEAD COLD was inserted on 9 August 1969. By the following morning it had reached the trail identified by Peters on the previous patrol. A four-man element was left in place on the trail. Security teams, each composed of two men, moved up and down the trail and positioned themselves to provide early warning. Peters, Lowder, and two other Marines set up a few feet from the trail between the security elements to make the snatch.

A half hour after all elements were in position, one of the security teams reported in code that six NVA were approaching. When the enemy reached the snatch team, Peters jumped onto the trail in front of them as Lowder did the same to their rear. Both lieutenants yelled in Vietnamese for the group to surrender. The startled NVA, making no effort to give up, began shooting and running in all directions. Peters recalls, "in the initial firefight, Lieutenant Lowder killed two of them, I killed one. Another NVA that had run down the trail was turned back by our security, and I chased him and tackled him. This all happened rapidly. There were still rounds going off. I wrestled the NVA to the ground and in the ensuing fight was kicked in the face and various places, but I finally overpowered him and subdued him to some extent."

The team corpsman came to Peters's assistance, but the NVA remained uncooperative. He continued to struggle as he scratched and kicked in his attempt to escape. Before they finally got the enemy soldier secured, he managed almost to bite off the corpsman's thumb.

Soon after the prisoner was finally bound and gagged, the team began hearing movement coming down the trail. One of the security elements popped its Claymores on the lead elements of the NVA reaction force and joined the rest of the team on the preplanned withdrawal route. Covered by fixed-wing air strikes, the team managed to outdistance its pursuers despite the added weight of the prisoner, whom they alternated carrying over their shoulders. At 1150 they were extracted by STABO, and then delivered their prisoner to interrogators at An Hoa.

Perhaps the most unusual mission ever assigned to the recon Marines was one that also dealt with prisoners— Americans rather than the enemy.[8] In late 1966, an NVA defector reported that he had been a guard at a POW camp in the Nam Dong area that contained four Americans, two Australians, and 24 ARVNs. This information was passed through the MACV Joint Personnel Rescue Center to the CIA station in Hue and the III MAF headquarters.

The mission to check out the rallier's story was given to the 3rd Recon Battalion and its attached Third Force Recon Company. Volunteers were solicited to make up a seven-man team that would be led by Capt Ken D. Jordan and Lt James Capers. Also accompanying the operation, code named DOUBLETALK, were the NVA rallier as a guide, an interpreter, and a corpsman.

After several delays due to weather and the Christmas truce, DOUBLETALK was inserted on 14 January 1967. An elaborate support system of radio relays, air cover, and a reaction force were standing by. Moving slowly, and frequently having to hide from numerous NVA patrols, the team reached the POW camp the next day. There were no signs of any prisoners. Apparently the entire camp had been moved several weeks previously—likely at the time the enemy realized that one of their guards had gone over to the other side.

While the recon men were taking pictures of the abandoned camp to turn over to intelligence channels, several enemy approached, only to be shot down by the team security element. DOUBLETALK withdrew and was extracted with no friendly casualties.

Despite the occasional assignment of these rather exotic missions and the impressive body count routinely achieved by the Force Recon Marines, their primary accomplishment was in the information they gathered for intelligence analysis in the planning for larger operations. Maj Bryon A. Norberg, head of the Ground Recon Sub Unit of the III MAF G-2 Collection Section, best summarized the accomplishments of the Force Recon companies by stating,

From where I sit, I can only say that their contribution in terms of intelligence information collected, intelligence information which can be acted upon, has been vital to the performance of our overall mission here in I Corps. The reconnaissance elements which we have had out in the field have been in a position to continually monitor the activities of the NVA and the VC. They have been capable of reporting to us the movements that were being made by enemy units. These reports have often times made the difference between having a thorough and precise understanding of what the NVA intention in any area might or might not be.[9]

Force Recon patrols throughout the war regularly went into the jungle, found the enemy, observed his movements, determined his intentions, evaluated his morale, and reported this information. Usually the recon teams were able to accomplish those tasks without the enemy's being aware that the Marines had invaded its territory and, in essence, that Force Recon was "out-guerrilla-ing the guerrillas." While the patrol reports of the Force Recon companies are marked by repetitious observations of the enemy, the recon men were well aware that each patrol offered the opportunity for the unusual as well as the routine.

One unexpected patrol finding was the occasional observation of abnormally large enemy groups. A four- or six-man patrol, lying concealed in the jungle, felt it was routine to spot groups of 10 to 20 enemy walking only a few meters from its position. Yet even when the numbers jumped to the hundreds, often taking hours to pass, the coolness of the Force Recon Marines, the ability simply to count, wait, and report, was routine.

One team from the Third Company counted over 200 NVA on 26 December 1966 while in support of Operation SIERRA. On the same operation, a patrol from the First Company spotted 230. The following January, near Chu Lai, a team of the 2nd Platoon of the First Company made 13 sightings of 674 NVA/VC in a period of 48 hours. In the same area another patrol spotted 194 while still another team counted 145.[10]

Observations of large enemy elements continued throughout the war. In June 1969, Team HANOVER SUE made three sightings totaling 420 NVA/VC in a single day. Two months later a patrol spotted 364 enemy equipped with Soviet-made flame throwers, mortar tubes, and crates of ammunition. Between 5 and 10 September 1967, Team SWIFT SCOUT observed 928 enemy.[11]

Numbers alone were not the only significant findings. Lying in wait on ambush or moving on patrol, the recon Marines never knew what unexpected spotting they might make. Several patrols near the Laotian border, including Team LUNCH MEAT on 4 September 1969, spotted Caucasians with the NVA. Although each sighting was made when the enemy were too numerous for the Marines to attempt a kill or a capture, it was assumed that the Caucasians were advisors or observers from communist bloc countries. Chinese advisors, identified by their uniforms, were also spotted, but once again the large security forces accompanying them prevented the recon men from bringing in a body as proof.

By going into the "backyard" of the enemy, the Force Recon Marines periodically discovered elaborate base camps and bunker complexes. A patrol of the First Company in January 1967 found a complex complete with a training site containing classrooms, blackboards, and a library.[13] One First Company patrol on 5 July 1969 was surprised to come upon in the jungle two 20-foot-long clotheslines complete with drying laundry.[14]

On 2 January 1970, 1st Lt John J. Holly, First Company patrol leader of a six-man team operating in the Hai Van Pass area, discovered two recently used base camps containing equipment and documents of intelligence value. Upon moving into a third camp a few hours later, Holly's point man surprised an NVA monitoring a radio in a hut. After a brief firefight, the team seized the radio and frequency codes from the dead operator.[15]

In the search of the remainder of the base camp, Holly's team found a hospital, secret documents on troop locations, an ammunition dump, and a clothing supply hut. Knowing the enemy would soon return, Holly selected the most vital material to take along, destroyed the rest, and requested an emergency ladder extraction. As the team move to a suitable location for the extraction, the returning enemy attempted to surround the small patrol. Using the terrain for the maximum protection, Holly deployed his Marines in a defensive perimeter. Upon arrival of the extraction birds, the NVA directed heavy fire at both the team and the helicopters. Disregarding his own safety, Holly repeatedly exposed himself as he directed the hovering helicopter into the best position to ensure that the team as well as the captured documents and equipment were extracted.

Occasionally the patrol teams found the unexpected and were able to have an immediate impact in protecting American lives and property. On 18 May 1967, a Third

Company patrol under the leadership of Lt S. K. Harnett was occupying an OP northeast of Dong Ha Mountain when they spotted an NVA unit beginning to launch 120mm rockets toward Cam Lo and the Rock Pile. Artillery requested by the recon Marines destroyed the launchers, their crews, and additional rockets not yet fired. A few minutes later another rocket launcher position was spotted that was also destroyed by an artillery barrage.[16]

Another team from the Third Company averted an attack on Con Thien by being in the right place at the right time. Moving toward an OP about three kilometers from the fire base near the DMZ, the team spotted 15 NVA advancing on Con Thien. Remaining hidden in the jungle, the patrol spotted groups of 5–20 additional NVA heading in the same direction until at least a reinforced company had passed their position. Over the next three and a half hours the recon Marines directed artillery, air strikes, and gunships on the assembling NVA that ultimately numbered over a battalion in strength. Finally, compromised by the growing number of enemy, the team called for extraction after having two men wounded—but not before adjusting a final air strike that destroyed three mortar positions. Captured documents and prisoner interrogations later revealed that the enemy was planning a coordinated attack on Con Thien before the recon Marines depleted their numbers and sent the survivors running back across the DMZ.[17]

Some of the findings by the recon Marines were even more unpredictable than the "usual" unexpected observations. In January 1969, Team CANDY TUFT of the Third Company discovered a valley stream three feet wide and a foot deep that was not depicted on their maps. Closer inspection revealed that the stream was actually a handdug canal that was being used as a water-covered trail. Recon teams kept the "stream" under observation over the next few weeks.[18] In early February, Team DRIVING

FORCE caught 200 NVA heavily laden with weapons and ammunition moving down the water-covered pathway. An artillery fire mission of 150 high-explosive rounds shreaded the ranks of the enemy while causing six secondary blasts.[19]

The First Company found a similar enemy effort at deception near the Laotian border. A wide trail easily observable from the air was the frequent target of aerial photography missions. Despite the fact that there was seldom any enemy spotted on the trail from the air, a recon team was inserted to check it out. What they discovered were two parallel paths hidden under the jungle canopy just off the main trail. While the pathway observable from the air was seldom used, the recon Marines found the hidden paths to be quite active.

While the patrol easily understood the purpose of one trail as a ruse with the other for actual use, the presence of the third path close to the one within the jungle at first confused them. The trails were too close together to have been made by either vehicles or carts. Several hours of watching the hidden jungle paths provided the answer. An enemy soldier soon appeared, walking on one trail while guiding his heavily laden bicycle on the other.[20]

More enemy trickery was discovered by the Third Company in the A Shau Valley. Aerial photography and observers saw nothing on a main road except several destroyed trucks lying on their sides or in a ditch. On the ground, the recon Marines found an entirely different situation as they observed the road from a hilltop OP. Just after nightfall the NVA came out of the jungle, turned the trucks back upright, and took off to run supplies from Laos to their valley cache site. At dawn the trucks returned, the NVA off-loaded, tipped the trucks back over, removed a tire or two for verisimilitude, and melted back into the jungle to await nightfall and another supply run.

When the patrol returned and made its report, the photo interpreters refused to believe the account by the Marines.

The team returned to the A Shau with 35mm cameras, took pictures of the NVA trucks in action, and delivered the evidence to the photo unit. Some of the interpreters were still unconvinced. Wayne Morris, a lieutenant in the company at the time, recalls that many people did not believe the Marines' story of the trucks and that this caused bitterness among the recon men. According to Morris, "If you saw a Third Force man and wanted to get him angry, all you had to say was, 'There are no trucks in the A Shau Valley'—and then duck!"[21]

One observation that was as unexpected as any other, and likely more so, was the rare patrol that produced no sighting of the enemy at all. Of course, the lack of enemy activity in a particular area was important intelligence information in itself. Inserting a few recon teams into a region to see if the enemy was occupying it was a much better use of manpower then committing an infantry battalion or regiment for the same purpose.

A good example of this economy of force that the Force Recon companies provided occurred during a patrol by Team CAPE HORN of the First Company on 29 January 1970. The team's mission was a reconnaissance of Route 614, which was thought to be the main NVA supply route from Laos into Quang Nam Province. Traffic was suspected to be so heavy that the route had been labeled the "Yellow Brick Road." Air strikes and artillery were periodically directed along the track.

In less than four hours of patrolling after insertion, CAPE HORN found Route 614 to be no longer in use by the NVA. Landslides covered the road in places, and erosion had cut it in others. No effort had been made to fill in or bypass bomb craters. Vegetation was reclaiming the roadway, and there were no tracks of vehicles or even bicycles present. Except for signs of light foot traffic, all of which were at least two weeks old, there was no evidence of the enemy.

Subsequent patrols along the Laotian border during the following weeks revealed that Route 610 had become the new NVA main supply route. Artillery and air strikes that had been doing nothing but blowing holes in the ground along Route 614 were redirected to real targets on Route 610.[22]

Although individual acts of valor were the "unexpected that was expected," to the point that they were almost routine, bravery was not a subject of great concern or discussion among the recon Marines. Bravery was a difficult phenomenon for the recon men to distinguish, for reconnaissance patrolling was valor in itself. "Courageous" is only one adjective that can be given to men who willingly went far from other friendly units, deep into enemy territory, in small, lightly armed groups. Bravery was a characteristic exhibited by every recon Marine in volunteering to join the unit to begin with.

Most American servicemen in Vietnam responded to the question of how long they had been in-country by giving the number of days since their arrival—or more commonly, the number of days until their departure. The response of the recon Marines was never given in days but rather in the number of patrols in which they had participated.

In studying the hundreds of citations for Navy Crosses, Silver Stars, and other valor awards earned by the Force Recon Marines, a single commonality is reflected in each. When extraordinary heroism was required to accomplish a mission or to ensure the safety of the rest of the team, each recon Marine exhibited valor with no thought of glory but rather the overall welfare of the team.

For the Force Recon Marines, the risks taken and the courage required were rewards in themselves. "For those who fight for it, life has a flavor the protected never know" is a quote often associated with the war. There are numerous claims to its origin, the most common one being "seen on a bunker during the siege of Khe Sanh." In fact, the quote was penned by an anonymous member of the

Third Force Recon Company on the back of C-ration carton. It was nailed on one of the company's bunkers at Khe Sanh.

Other slogans and mottoes that appeared on Force Recon walls or were quoted by the recon Marines at one time or another during the war also reflect their attitude: "You never live until you've almost died"; "Only the good die young—and we are"; "Where the Divisions go, we've been"; "Search, discover, destroy"; "We may be few but we've done it many"; and "The eyes and ears of the Corps."[23]

In addition to the NVA and VC, many more dangers in the jungle confronted the recon Marines. Disease, infection, accidents, weather, and the terrain presented threats to health and life. Although a certain number of nonbattle casualties are inevitable anytime a military force is placed in a war zone, some injuries and deaths were more unexpected than others.*

Team ROCK MAT from the First Company experienced perhaps the most unusual, frightening patrol that resulted in a nonhostile death. The company intelligence debriefer noted in his report that although many teams returned after having encountered great dangers, the men of ROCK MAT were more rattled than any previous patrol that he had debriefed.[24]

The team departed the company base on the morning of 7 May 1970 for a helicopter insertion in the mountainous region near Bach Ma, about 16 miles south of Phu Loc. Nightfall found the team atop a densely vegetated razorback ridge at the 3,116-foot level. Slopes of the ridge were extremely steep, peaking to the top, which was only six meters wide. Because of the narrowness of the ridge line, the patrol set up on line for their nighttime position rather

---

*Of the over 58,000 Americans who died in Southeast Asia, more than 10,000 perished from nonhostile causes. Deaths by accidents or disease accounted for over 1,600 of the Marines' loss of nearly 14,000 during the war.

than form a perimeter. The patrol leader, Sgt R.C. Phleger, took a position at the extreme end of the line.

At 2000 the team heard movement in the surrounding brush followed by two screams from Phleger. After more sounds of a violent struggle descending down the slope, the jungle again grew silent. The assistant patrol leader, Cpl Jerry T. Smith, swiftly took charge of the team and led a search of the immediate area. In the moonless dark they could find nothing, and they spent the remainder of the night restlessly awaiting the sunrise.

At dawn the team discovered a bloody trail along with paw prints and claw marks of a big cat. Following the trail, the Marines came across the patrol leader's rifle, gas mask, and other gear. A bit farther on they found Phleger's body. Later, while evacuating the remains, the team heard a loud growl and saw fleeting glimpses of a 400–600-pound tiger. The team shot at the cat but did not bring it down.

After extraction of ROCK MAT, other teams from the Third Company were inserted into the same area to find and kill the tiger. A few days later they were successful. The dead tiger was lifted out of the jungle and returned to the company base camp.

Another report of a tiger stalking a recon team was made on 1 May 1969. A patrol of the Third Company found tiger tracks throughout its recon zone and on two occasions heard the animal within 10 meters of its positions. On one approach the team used CS gas to scare away the cat.[25]

Although the Marines and the other armed services stressed safety in training and in combat, an environment of lethal weapons, explosives, and high-performance vehicles and aircraft sets the scene for accidents. Regardless of the amount of coordination and attention to detail, it was impossible to totally prevent injuries and deaths that were not a direct result of hostile action.

The largest single loss of life of Force Recon Marines happened not in battle but in a helicopter accident. On 11 June 1967 a seven-man team from the Third Company was en route to an insertion near the DMZ when their CH-46 exploded in midair from unknown causes and crashed into the jungle. The recon Marines and four crew members all perished.[26]

Helicopters could also be dangerous for other reasons. On 18 August 1969, PFC F. McLaughlin of the First Company's Team MINK COAT was struck in the head by the rotor of a CH-46 that landed on an incline during an extraction near Hill 953. McLaughlin died a few hours later in the Navy Hospital at Da Nang.[27]

Friendly air and artillery was "friendly" only if it landed in the correct locations. Cpl P.J. Murphy of the First Company was killed on 15 May 1968 by an off-target artillery round that landed in the patrol's night position.[28] A team of the 6th Platoon, Third Company avoided destruction by a B-52 strike which dropped its bombs in the wrong location on 21 August 1967 only because a chance encounter with an NVA force had caused them to move an hour earlier.[29]

Some of the accidents suffered by the recon Marines were their own fault. On 16 January 1969, a nervous new member of Team FOREFATHER mistook a fellow recon Marine—returning to the perimeter after emplacing Claymore mines—for the enemy. Fortunately, the resulting gunshot wound was not serious.

Weather and terrain were often as dangerous as the war itself. Team BAGSHAW of the First Company was occupying an OP on Hill 452 during a thunderstorm on 11 July 1967. At 1815 a bolt of lightning struck the patrol's perimeter, detonating 10 Claymore mines and at least that number of frag grenades and causing an explosion so great that one Marine was blown out of the perimeter and off a nearby cliff. Two Marines, LCpl L.T. Stowe and LCpl

A. Allen, were killed, and six other recon men were wounded.[30]

A lesson on the dangers of lightning had been learned the hard way by the recon Marines. On future operations, explosives were segregated from the team during thunderstorms. However, this procedure did not always guarantee safety. When caught in a lightning storm on 25 June 1970, Team MOVEABLE, from the 5th Platoon of the First Force Recon Company, stashed all its ordnance. Although there were no explosions, a lightning bolt struck the middle of the team's position, knocking several Marines unconscious and stunning the rest for several minutes. Sgt David J. Wickander was instantly killed.[31]

Perhaps the most consistent enemy the recon men faced in Vietnam was not the NVA or VC but the terrain of the country itself. Teams often found the jungle so thick or the mountains so steep that their movements were restricted to no more than 100 meters an hour. One patrol near Da Nang in December 1966 was accompanied by a scout dog team. Shortly after insertion the patrol leader was forced to call for an extraction for the dog and his handler because, "The terrain is too thick and movement too difficult for the dog." After the dog's extraction the team continued its mission.[32]

At times the jungle offered more than just discomfort and hardship. Team MOTOR of the First Company encountered several groups of NVA while on patrol in a mountainous region 30 miles west of Da Nang. Each time it was able to break contact with the enemy and continue the mission. Accompanying the patrol was the senior NCO of the company, GySgt Vincent R. Thornburg. Although Thornburg's duties were at the company base, he periodically went along on patrols to better understand what his men were up against. On 3 February 1970, Team MOTOR engaged another NVA force and again broke contact. During its hasty withdrawal, an embankment gave way, plunging Thornburg down a 150-foot cliff. Thornburg was conscious for 45 minutes before he died of his injuries. Although he was in extreme pain, he suffered quietly so as not to give away the team's location to the pursuing NVA.[33]

CHAPTER 14

▪▫▪▫▪▫▪▫

Notable Patrols—
Extraordinary Men

*F*OR the Force Recon Marines the definition of a good patrol was quite simple—it was one that the team returned from with no casualties. If the team managed to gather some useful information or achieve a body count—which they usually did—it was an even better patrol. In contrast, any patrol that resulted in a friendly loss of life or wounded Marines went on the negative side of the patrol's account ledger.

Although the vast majority of the Force Recon patrols were in the good or the better category, some of the most notable operations are those that were marked by close combat, extraordinary bravery, and nearly unbelievable survival despite odds overwhelmingly in favor of the enemy. While every patrol conducted by the recon Marines deserves to have its story told, there is neither space nor in some cases ample records to adequately relate all their accomplishments. The following examples are but a representation of the dedication, daring, and deeds of the recon men.

Of all the patrols accomplished by the Force Recon Marines, only one resulted in the awarding of the Medal of

Honor to a team member. The same patrol also marked the largest number of recon Marines killed or wounded by combat action on a single operation.[1]

Team BOX SCORE of the Third Force Recon Company reached its assigned recon zone six miles northwest of Dong Ha on 15 February 1968 by walking from the nearest fire base. Composed of eight men including patrol leader 2ndLt Terrence C. Graves, six enlisted Marines, and a corpsman, BOX SCORE had a rather typical mission—to determine enemy activity, engaging what enemy they found with supporting fires, locating LZs and trails, and attempting to capture a prisoner.

By the afternoon of the 16th, the team had reached an area overlooking a small stream pocked with bomb craters. Hearing voices in the thick brush across the waterway, the team crossed the stream to set up an ambush in a bomb crater alongside a trail. Within minutes seven NVA walked down the pathway. When the enemy was within five meters of the ambush, the recon men opened up, killing all seven. In the brief firefight, the NVA were barely able to return fire; however, two of the rounds they managed to get off struck Cpl Danny M. Slocum, tearing away shin and muscle from his thigh but not producing life-threatening wounds.

While the team medic, HM3 Stephen R. Thompson, was treating Slocum, Graves hastily searched the bodies and found a diary along with other documents. The patrol leader then called for med-evac for the wounded Marine and began moving the team to a better point to bring in the helicopter. Box SCORE made it only a few meters before the team was raked by automatic weapons fire from two different directions. Graves organized the team into a hasty perimeter as the Marines returned fire. Several of the NVA machine guns were knocked out by accurate M-79 grenade launcher fire by Cpl Robert B. Thomson, though Thomson had been unable to spot the exact position of the automatic weapons until PFC Michael P. Nation exposed himself to mark their positions with tracer rounds for Thomson to zero in on.

The silencing of the enemy machine guns brought only a brief lull to the fighting. Every minute, more NVA joined the battle, until at least two companies were ringing the eight-man patrol. Despite the number of NVA, Graves had to move his team to a better position from which to fight and hopefully be extracted. As the lieutenant directed in air strikes and gunships to cover their movement, the team began inching its way to the top of a small knoll. At one point a CH-46 attempted to land near the team but took several hits and had to lift off.

As the CH-46 flew out of range, the NVA again concentrated their firepower on the recon team. Graves took a bullet in the thigh, but an inspection by Doc Thompson revealed that the bone was not broken. After a quick bandaging, Graves was back on the radio coordinating the supporting fires. No sooner had the corpsman finished with the lieutenant than Corporal Thomson yelled that he too had been hit. A bullet had penetrated the Marine's left side and shattered the pelvic bone before lodging in the abdominal cavity. Doc Thompson recalls, ''He said, 'I'm blacking out, Doc, I'm blacking out.' Then he passed out on me, and I think at that moment he died. I started closed-chest cardiac massage and mouth-to-mouth resuscitation. While I was doing this, Lopez [PFC A. S.] yelled, 'Doc, Emrick's [LCpl Steven E.] hit, I think he's dying.' I looked over and said, 'Nation [who had been cross-trained by Thompson in medical procedures], just do what you can.' ''

Nation alternated between treating Emrick and doing his best to fight off the NVA. According to Nation, ''Emrick kept saying, 'Get the radio off.' That was what he was talking about; he wasn't worried about himself. Lopez finally got it off by snapping off the bottom of the pack. Then Emrick said, 'Oh my God,' and that's the last thing

he said. I started to give him mouth-to-mouth. Lopez said
he could still feel a pulse.''

There was no letup in the NVA fire despite the repeated
runs by fixed-wing aircraft and helicopter gunships. Graves
continued to fight as he directed the team to make another
attempt to move to higher ground. With Doc Thompson
and PFC James E. Honeycutt dragging Thomson and with
Nation and Lopez carrying Emrick, Graves and Slocum
provided covering fire despite their wounds. A few minutes later BOX SCORE reached the low grassy ridge that was
large enough for a set-down extraction. Although the patrol was then in a good position for extraction, the ridge
they occupied was paralleled by two higher hills—both
occupied by the NVA—only 100 meters away.

The fight by the eight Marines against several hundred
NVA had been going on for over an hour and a half. Another CH-46 made an attempt to reach the team but took
heavy fire and had to regain altitude. Capt David Underwood, orbiting the fight at 1,000 feet in his H-34, radioed
that he was coming in to make the extraction. Flying behind a Huey gunship for covering fire, Underwood came
in at treetop level through a guantlet of small-arms and
machine-gun fire, touching down only a few meters from
the team. Intense fire immediately centered on the H-34,
shattering the side windows and some of the pilot's instrument panel gauges. More rounds were slamming into the
fuselage and fuel pods. Although practically every warning light was lit up on the still operational parts of the
instrument panel, Underwood stayed at the controls, waiting for the recon team to climb aboard.

Dragging, pulling, and crawling through the elephant
grass, the Marines loaded the aircraft as Graves continued
to return the NVA fire. Three long minutes passed as the
recon men ensured that their wounded buddies were pulled
onto the aircraft that was now profusely leaking fuel and
was in danger of exploding. Nation later stated, ''I guess
Lieutenant Graves saw how bad the plane was hit and re-

alized if the chopper didn't leave then it wouldn't be leaving at all, because I saw him waving at the pilot and yelling 'get' or 'get out.' He did this realizing that he might get hit again and his chances of getting back were pretty slim, but he wanted to make sure that the rest of us made it back. What Lieutenant Graves did is the bravest thing I've ever seen.''

As Underwood began to lift the crippled chopper, the NVA ran out of their protected positions for better shots. One burst strafed the bird, a bullet hitting Lopez in the thigh and glancing off the bone and into the Marine's stomach. As the helicopter gained a few feet of altitude, Slocum and Honeycutt realized that Graves was being left behind. With no words exchanged between the two, both Marines jumped from the helicopter to help their lieutenant. With the loss of weight of the two men, Underwood was able to gain altitude quickly and nurse the bird to the nearest medical facility. More than 20 bullet holes were later counted in the aircraft.

Meanwhile, Underwood's wingman, Capt Carl Bergman, was attempting to pick up the remaining recon men. Three passes through the NVA fire failed to find the Marines, but on the fourth try Bergman spotted the trio and set his H-34 down near them. The chopper immediately came under intense automatic weapons fire from NVA so close that initially Bergman could not distinguish between the sounds of the outgoing from his door gunners and the incoming from the enemy. A shout from the cargo compartment revealed that the crew chief had been wounded and that the fuel cells were hit and leaking. Bergman was forced to lift off before the remaining members of box score were able to fight their way to the helicopter.

Graves, Slocum, and Honeycutt continued to return fire as they made still another attempt to move to a more advantageous position. The NVA dropped two mortar rounds near the trio but did no damage. Suddenly a UH-1 pilot spotted an opening and swooped in almost on top of the

Marines. The Huey hovered just off the ground as the recon men threw their gear aboard and pulled themselves into the aircraft. Cross fire from the NVA zeroed in on the chopper as it attempted to lift off. Graves was hit again, as was the copilot, who slumped over the controls. The Huey nosed over and crashed on its side into the jungle.

Slocum found himself on top of "a heap of bodies." As he crawled out of the helicopter, 15–20 NVA were sweeping toward him on line. The enemy spotted the Marine and opened fire as he turned and ran toward a nearby stream. Hitting the streambed at a dead run, Slocum was able to elude his pursuers.

By then, darkness was closing in on the battle area. A reaction force consisting of a platoon of B Company, 1st Battalion, 4th Marines air-landed near the crashed Huey to rescue any survivors. Before they reached the downed aircraft, they too became engaged with the NVA from three directions and suffered one killed and four wounded. Unable to proceed, the platoon formed a defensive perimeter.

Slocum heard the firefight from his hiding place near the stream but decided to remain in place. He later recalled matter-of-factly, "I didn't want to go back over there. There was a firefight going on and I didn't want to get shot anymore."

At daylight the next morning, the remainder of B Company was lifted in and finally reached the crashed chopper to report that Graves and Honeycutt were dead and Slocum missing.

The missing Marine's problems were not yet over. In his attempt to link up with B Company, the infantry Marines mistook him for an NVA and called in artillery on him. Slocum states, "It didn't bother me; I got down in a hole."

When the infantrymen started toward Slocum's hole, not wanting to take any more chances, he headed in the opposite direction. Finally a chopper spotted him and coordinated his joining up with B Company. Slocum was evacuated to the Naval Hospital in Cam Ranh Bay where after two and a half months he recovered from his wounds and eventually rejoined the Third Company. Thomson, Lopez, and Emrick were not so fortunate. All three died of their wounds either aboard Underwood's helicopter or within hours after reaching the evacuation hospital.

Slocum, Doc Thompson, and Bergman later received the Silver Star. Thomson's Silver Star and Honeycutt's Navy Cross were both awarded posthumously. Underwood also had earned a Navy Cross. On 2 December 1969, in the office of the Vice-President of the United States, Spiro Agnew presented the Medal of Honor posthumously to the family of Lieutenant Graves.

While some recon teams such as BOX SCORE gained notoriety for a single patrol, others earned their reputation for sustained successful operations. Such was the story of Team KILLER KANE of the First Force Recon Company in 1967.

During the first few months of 1967, KILLER KANE conducted routine patrols in the Hiep Dup Valley area, producing valuable intelligence information. The team, under the leadership of 1stLt Andrew R. Finlayson, gained a reputation for good judgment and caution. On 25 March an incident occurred to Team COUNTERSIGN, also of the First Company, that would have a great effect on future operations by KILLER KANE.

COUNTERSIGN had been inserted on the 24th and had seen little of the enemy the first day. On the second day of the mission, the team detonated a booby-trapped mine that killed the patrol leader, Capt Eric Barnes, and the assistant patrol leader, Sgt Godfred Blankenship. The team's third in command, Corporal Watson, took charge and continued the mission with the four replacement recon Marines that arrived on the helicopter that evacuated the bodies.[2]

Finlayson later reflected on the impact of the booby-trap

incident and how it changed his focus from reconnaissance to combat patrolling. "Eric was a gifted officer who was literally loved by his men and had the utmost respect. He had just come back from R&R in Hawaii when he was killed. The patrol was to have been his last one, since it was the policy of the unit not to allow captains to be patrol leaders [Barnes had recently been promoted]. His death resulted in my changing the tactics employed by my platoon from then on. I was so incensed by Eric's death that I planned a revenge mission. Corporal Watson [was] an Irish citizen and veteran of eight years' service with the British Royal Marines [before joining the USMC], including combat in Kenya, and I planned our conspiracy carefully."[3]

Finlayson requested permission to operate in the same general area where Barnes and Blankenship had been killed and to take half of the dead captain's team to act as guides. KILLER KANE was assigned a recon box three kilometers square south of Barnes's zone, but Finlayson had no plans to stay in the assigned area. During the insertion he convinced the pilots to land his team north of the intended LZ so that they were very near the trail leading from Antenna Valley to the Hiep Dup Valley, where the two Marines were killed.

KILLER KANE moved quickly to the trail and, after a brief recon to check security, set up an ambush. Finlayson recalls, "I had told Corporal Watson that we weren't interested in prisoners, but just in avenging Eric. It didn't take long." Revenge, however, did not include noncombatants. Several groups of unarmed civilians were permitted to pass unmolested by the hidden Marines. Finally two VC armed with rifles approached and Watson initiated the ambush, killing both. Since no large enemy elements were thought to be in the area, the patrol cleared the trail of the bodies and reassumed its ambush position. Four hours later two more enemy were killed. One of the VC carried an officer's pistol and a dispatch case containing numerous names of undercover agents in Antenna Valley. Finlayson wanted to remain in the ambush, but two engagements from the same position was risky enough. The team and the valuable documents were extracted.

Upon return to the company base camp, Finlayson remembers, "We celebrated with beer on the back porch of our hootch at Camp Reasoner and sang Irish drinking songs with Corporal Watson. Thus began the nine-month saga of KILLER KANE, the team that initiated contact with the enemy at every opportunity. During this time, KILLER KANE participated in 34 long-range reconnaissance patrols, with 181 confirmed kills by artillery and air strikes, 254 probable kills by arty and air, and 42 confirmed kills by small arms, and *nine* POWs."[4]

KILLER KANE led all Force Recon teams in body count for well over a year. When *Newsweek* magazine came looking for a story on the recon Marines, it was Finlayson they sought to interview.[5]

Typical of the use of their own firepower as well as artillery and air to kill the enemy was a patrol that KILLER KANE began on 15 May 1967. Operating from an OP on Hill 203, overlooking the Hiep Dup Trail, the team spotted seven enemy on the path. Using small arms and M-79 grenades, they killed one by body count and got another four probables. A short time later, KILLER KANE spotted approximately 100 VC carrying packs and rifles and approaching from the same direction. Finlayson called in 80 rounds of eight-inch artillery, killing 16 more. An aerial observer, following the lieutenant's directions, was able to spot the fleeing enemy and direct air strikes of napalm and rockets, killing at least 15 more. KILLER KANE was extracted the next morning, having accounted for over 30 dead without ever having a shot fired at them in return.[6]

Not all missions were quite as easy for KILLER KANE. On 3 July 1967 the team took fire as it attempted to insert into its primary LZ. The insertion was aborted and the pilots moved to the secondary LZ, where it also received fire. When the pilots queried Finlayson if they should return to base, he told the aviators to locate another LZ.[7]

KILLER KANE was finally able to insert in a small clearing atop Hill 582. Although it received a few rounds going in, no casualties were sustained. Finlayson immediately moved the team off the LZ and into the thickest vegetation he could find. Setting up in a perimeter, the recon Marines spent the night with no one removing his pack or web gear in case the team had to move out quickly if detected.

The next morning the patrol found trails, huts, and cultivated garden plots throughout its zone. On one trail, complete with steps cut into embankments and logs with handrails crossing streams, KILLER KANE spotted three VC. The point man fired, killing at least one, as the patrol pulled back, popping CS gas to cover its withdrawal.

In the early afternoon, the team set up a perimeter in thick elephant grass to take a break. Ten minutes later something moving through the grass caused the team to freeze in place. A single VC parted the vegetation to find his face inches from the barrel of a Marine's rifle. At point-blank range the VC was knocked backward "like a rope had been tied around his waist and yanked back."

Finlayson concluded that a large enemy force was in the area, so he moved the team back near the insertion LZ in case it had to make a hasty extraction. That night the Marines heard voices, drums, and signal shots, but the enemy was unable to find the patrol's hidden position. By the next morning the Marines decided that the enemy had likely given up its search and moved to another area. They knew they were wrong in their assumption when they heard a canteen strike against metal outside their perimeter and then the sounds of men moving through the brush. The team stayed quiet, allowing the VC to get to within a few feet of its position before opening up. In the first 20 seconds, five enemy were killed. After a 15-minute firefight, which often closed to hand-grenade range, the VC pulled back. KILLER KANE, with two Marines wounded by grenade fragments, moved to the LZ and was extracted.

Other patrols by KILLER KANE produced valuable intelligence information as well as consistently high body counts. On 21 July 1967, the team was inserted into Happy Valley to conduct screening operations for advancing infantry forces of the 7th Marines in support of Operation PECOS.[8]

On the second morning of the patrol, KILLER KANE was moving east when the point man heard voices and halted the team. According to Finlayson,

"At first I thought these voices were so loud that they couldn't be VC; they must be Marines operating in the area, because they obviously felt very secure. However, after checking my map I decided no friendly units were in this area. We moved up very carefully, very slowly, until we came upon four VC sitting around a fire. We heard other voices indicating there were more, but we had no idea how many there were at this time. I called up my machine gunner, who came forward and set up with the point and backup man and myself. The four of us opened fire about simultaneously. After about ten minutes of intensive fire—we had complete fire superiority, the enemy only returned two bursts of automatic weapons fire during the entire exchange—we slacked up a bit, threw hand grenades and gas grenades down into the ravine below. Five men, myself included, moved down into the ravine in order to assess what damage we had done."

A search of the contact area revealed two bodies along with discarded weapons and equipment that seemed to lie everywhere. Finlayson continues, "The recovery of the equipment and weapons was facilitated by the hasty departure of the VC. Evidently, they had no stomach for fighting, and they retreated hastily back up the stream that ran through this ravine to the north. After we had recovered all the gear and had gotten to the top of the ridge line again and set up a defense, we began to take stock of what we had captured. Some of the captured equipment consisted of two Chinese light machine guns, one AK-47 assault rifle, and two anti-tank rocket launchers. We also had 16 packs, 850 pounds of rice, 15 pounds of medical equipment and several cooking utensils, knives, web gear, gas masks, 140 uniforms, 15 sweatshirts, and various other items."[9]

More important than the weapons and equipment were the 40 pounds of documents captured. The documents, including codes, unit designations, diaries, and serialized equipment lists, revealed that KILLER KANE had hit an element of the 402nd Sapper Battalion. That was the first time any recon unit had encountered the VC unit. Once everything was extracted, the team continued its mission. It was later determined that the contact had produced the largest haul of equipment, weapons, and intelligence of any recon patrol to that point of the war.

The rare days that the members of KILLER KANE were at the company base rather than in the jungle, they were often spotlighted to brief visiting dignitaries and high-ranking officers on their patrol successes. Throughout Finlayson's leadership, it led all III MAF reconnaissance teams in body count. The end of the team finally came not due to any action on the part of the enemy but due to the normal rotation back to the States as its members completed their tours. When Finlayson departed Vietnam, he was awarded the Bronze Star. His citation stated in part, "With a daring and a flair normally reserved for fictional accounts, Lieutenant Finlayson accumulated a year-long remarkable record. Behind the radio call sign KILLER KANE, his thoroughly professional patrol time after time closed with the enemy and achieved outstanding results."

* * *

Some force Recon teams were best known for an individual within their ranks. A good example of such a recon Marine was SSgt Roy A. Fryman. While most of the Force Recon Marines in Vietnam were in their teens or early twenties—especially in the latter years of the war—Fryman was an "old hand" who had initially joined the First Company in 1959.

When Fryman—a graduate of scuba, airborne, mountain, ski, amphibious reconnaissance, and escape and evasion schools—reached Vietnam, he was not assigned to a recon unit. After five months he secured a reassignment to the First Company in early 1968, soon proving that he was where he belonged. He earned the Navy Cross, the Silver Star, two Bronze Stars, and three Purple Hearts during his time with the company. His dedication was so strong that when his rotation date arrived, Fryman was in the jungle on patrol and was extracted only one day before the departure of his "freedom bird."[10]

Fellow recon Marine GySgt Bruce D. Trevathan recalls that Fryman was a man without fear, who often proclaimed he thought it was good when the enemy fired at him because he then knew exactly where they were.[11]

Much of the personal bravery exhibited by Fryman was accomplished in taking care of his fellow recon men on Team SENATOR. On 26 February 1968, while moving along a hillside, SENATOR received fire from two directions. Fryman placed his assistant patrol leader in charge of moving the team, including two wounded Marines, to a nearby LZ for extraction while he stayed behind to cover the withdrawal. Exposing himself to fire, Fryman engaged the enemy with his M-16 while he also adjusted artillery onto the VC's positions. At the last minute, Fryman broke contact and dashed to the LZ just in time to be extracted with the rest of the team.

During a patrol the following month, SENATOR had two minor engagements on 28–29 March. Several days passed with no action until 3 April, when the team, from an OP, spotted several VC walking down a trail. A few moments later, six more came into view followed by a column of 223 VC/NVA carrying AK-47s, machine guns, crew-served weapons, and mortars. Fryman called in an artillery mission that made direct hits on the enemy formation. At one point, Fryman crawled to within 50 meters of the impacting artillery rounds to ensure his adjustments continued to destroy the enemy.

While SENATOR was moving to an extraction LZ, Fryman spotted a dazed VC. A foot race developed, with Fryman winning as he captured the enemy soldier along with his weapon. When the team neared the LZ, a gunship pilot reported spotting another VC hiding nearby. Fryman shortly added another prisoner to the team's accomplishments.

Later that month, on 29 April, Fryman was leading his team on patrol through the southeastern portion of the Phu Loc Valley when he discovered a well-used trail and heard voices. He quickly deployed his men and, as two NVA appeared on the trail, personally initiated the ambush, killing one with his M-16. During the brief firefight, an enemy grenade landed by Fryman and three other Marines. The patrol leader picked up the grenade and threw it back toward the trail, killing the second NVA. Although Fryman suffered a concussion from the explosion, he refused medical aid and moved forward to search the dead enemy. After recovering weapons, equipment, and documents, he concealed the bodies in the jungle along the side of the trail.

Anticipating that other NVA would come to investigate the firing, Fryman established another ambush 100 meters south. Twenty minutes later three NVA were sighted coming down the pathway. Again triggering the ambush, Fryman killed one and wounded another. Exposing himself on the trail, Fryman dragged the wounded enemy into the bush to be treated by the team's corpsman, HM2 Michael W. Robertson. As the team moved to the nearest LZ, team radioman Cpl Thomas J. Schaub called for a med-evac to retrieve the wounded NVA.

While waiting for the evacuation helicopter, Fryman deployed three-man security teams to the north and south. Minutes later he heard fire from the southern team. Disregarding his own safety and quickly moving to join them, Fryman jumped into the fight, taking on three NVA with an automatic 18-round burst from his M-16 and following that up with a CS grenade. He then boldly grabbed another wounded prisoner and dragged him back toward the team's perimeter.

Before the med-evac arrived, more NVA began to close around the Marines' position, and a gunship pilot radioed to Fryman that the enemy was attempting to surround the team. Fryman realized that they couldn't wait for the helicopter and began moving the team cross-country. Despite several running gun battles, the team was able to elude the enemy and reach another LZ where it and its prisoners, captured equipment, and documents were extracted. Team SENATOR had managed not to sustain a single casualty.*

As a platoon leader, 1stLt Wayne E. Rollings accompanied or led many patrols during his tour with the First Force Recon Company in 1969. Recon Marines of that period remember that any patrol that Rollings was on was a notable one—some more so than others.

On 26 March 1969, Rollings led a 10-man team, REPORT CARD, on a mission into the Duc Duc District. When the team spotted a well-used trail, it set up only meters off the pathway with the intention of capturing a prisoner. During the first half hour of observations, 31 NVA passed by. The number of enemy in the area caused Rollings to give up his plan to take a POW. He decided instead to ambush an officer or NCO to gather documents. NVA Number 32 walking down the trail seemed to meet the requirement. He was wearing a new uniform, sported a pith helmet, and carried an AK-47.

---

*For his actions on the patrol, Fryman was awarded the Navy Cross and was meritoriously promoted to Gunnery Sergeant. Fryman returned to Vietnam for a second tour in 1969 and was killed as the result of hostile action in the Que Son Valley on 23 August.

With a single rifle burst, the NVA was killed, but his body yielded nothing of any intelligence value. Hiding the body, REPORT CARD waited for more NVA to enter their kill zone. Minutes later two more appeared, only to meet the same fate as Number 32. While the Marines were searching the bodies, more and more NVA began coming out of the jungle, forcing the Marines to withdraw. Soon 80–100 enemy were giving chase. Rollings placed the team in a defensive position where the men could meet each enemy probe with M-79 fire and hand grenades. The team did not use small arms unless an enemy was in plain sight. Over the next three hours, Team REPORT CARD, with the assistance of air strikes, beat back each enemy attack. Finally, after 10 more NVA were killed, the enemy withdrew, leaving no Marine casualties.

After the team's extraction, Rollings said, ''I learned that with a small unit, if you can keep good 360-degree security, you can hold off a very large force that outnumbers you considerably, and suffer few or no casualties.''[12]

Back in the same general area on 11 April 1969, Rollings was leading Team LUNCH MEAT.[13] Shortly after nightfall, the patrol spotted as many as 35 flashlights in the valley below its hillside position. Apparently the enemy had found the team's trail and was out to find the Marines. Rollings allowed the enemy to get within 100 meters before bringing in volley after volley of 155mm artillery. Throughout the remainder of the night, the NVA, estimated to number at least 75, attempted to overrun the Marines' perimeter. Each time artillery, gunships, and the firepower of the recon men drove them back.

At daybreak the NVA pulled back long enough for LUNCH MEAT to begin moving to an extraction point. Enemy patrols were soon in pursuit, and a running firefight took place over the next two and a half hours before the team was extracted. At one point an NVA force caught up with the recon team, and Rollings went to the center of the action to engage the enemy and cover the team's withdrawal.

Rollings's audacity was repeated on future operations. On 9 September, he led Team GRIM REAPER into an area so saturated with enemy that in one hour they counted 364 NVA.[14] Members of the team were able to penetrate one enemy complex so quietly that one of their findings was a man and woman having intercourse in a bunker. The recon Marines left the couple undisturbed—at least for the moment. As soon as Rollings was convinced that he knew the exact extent of the enemy's fortifications, the team withdrew and called in air strikes to destroy the complex.

On 18 September, Rollings was again leading GRIM REAPER on a recon mission 30 miles southwest of Da Nang.[15] In a small clearing that the team could not avoid due to the terrain, the team point man spotted an NVA ambush. After only one round was expended, the Marine's rifle malfunctioned. Rollings ran forward to take up an exposed position between the point man and the NVA. Although the enemy small-arms fire tore into his clothing, pierced the crown of his bush hat, and ripped the gas mask off his web belt, he stood his ground firmly while firing at the NVA. When fragments of an enemy grenade struck him in the face and legs, he continued to stand resolute as he answered the NVA's fire, killing seven and routing the others.*

Another example of a patrol deemed notable because of the dedication and bravery of its leader was Team TEA

---

*By the completion of his tour, Rollings had earned a Navy Cross, a Bronze Star, and other decorations. He remained in the Corps after the war, continuing to meet any and all challenges—particularly those of a physical nature. On 1 April 1975, while assigned to the United Nations Tiberias Control Center in Israel, Rollings set the record for nonstop, continuous motion, hands-behind-the-head, straight-legged, elbow-touching-opposite-knee sit-ups. In a period of 15 hours and 32 minutes the former recon Marine managed to perform 35,000 sit-ups.

TIME of the First Company. On 23 April 1969, under the leadership of Sgt Joseph R. Crockett, TEA TIME was inserted south of Lang Son Kol to conduct a reconnaissance.[16] On the third morning of the patrol, LCpl M.G. Ellis, PFC C. T. Heinemeier, and PFC D. J. Oliver moved from the team's hillside OP down to a stream to fill canteens. While the Marines were at the water, they saw a lone NVA downstream carrying 100 pounds of rice. Although the recon men attempted to remain concealed, the enemy soldier spotted them. A four-round burst from an M-16 killed him but attracted 30–40 of his comrades, who pursued the three Marines as they scrambled back up the hill.

No sooner had the water party rejoined the team than three NVA approached the perimeter. They were killed before they could return fire. More NVA followed, but Crockett kept them at bay over the next hour as air strikes dropped bombs and napalm. The patrol leader requested an immediate extraction but was informed that all air assets were being diverted to another team that had taken casualties.

When TEA TIME lost its air support, Crockett switched to artillery to keep the NVA from overrunning his position. But the artillery was not enough, and the NVA, reinforced by several heavy machine gun teams, renewed its attack. Initial bursts of the machine guns' cross fire from the northwest and southwest killed PFC Oliver and wounded five others so severely that they were unable to continue the fight. Once the enemy realized that only two Marines were still returning their fire, they mounted another assault. Crockett grabbed an M-79 and, with a wounded Marine handing him rounds, began to shred the enemy formation. His first round killed one NVA with a direct hit and wounded four others. When Crockett ran out of M-79 ammo, he ran from wounded Marine to wounded Marine, gathering hand grenades and heaving them toward the NVA, single-handedly breaking up the attack.

The dazed NVA withdrew to a safer distance but continued to fire sporadically on the patrol. TEA TIME's troubles were not nearly over, however. Flames that had been started by a napalm run slowly crept up the hill, and the enemy seemed to help it in hopes they could burn the Marines out of their positions. Crockett later reported, "The fire would almost die and then there'd be a large hiss and explosion, like someone pouring gas on a fire. They slowly just brought the fire up the hill right into my position."

Crockett exposed himself to the enemy fire in an attempt to extinguish the advancing flames with his fatigue jacket. Finally, realizing that he couldn't stop the burning vegetation, Crockett began carrying the wounded Marines to safer locations. Again and again the flames approached the wounded, but the patrol leader repeatedly moved his men to safety—all the while attending to their wounds, returning NVA fire, and coordinating the team's extraction on the radio.

When the evacuation helicopters and a reaction force arrived overhead, Crockett tied a brightly colored air panel to his body and moved to an exposed clearing to mark TEA TIME's position. The first helicopter to attempt a landing took .50-caliber machine gun fire, wounding the pilot in the leg. Gunships finally silenced the enemy so that the choppers could land. Crockett refused to be evacuated with the rest of the team and volunteered to stay behind with the reaction force to search for enemy dead and wounded.

Crockett was later awarded the Navy Cross for his actions on the fire-swept hillside. More meaningful to the sergeant, however, was the simple statement by PFC J.B. Denton in his award recommendation for his team leader. Denton wrote, "He saved my life."

CHAPTER 15

The Final Days—And Beyond

V_{IETNAM} was a unique war in American history. No clearly articulated national objective was ever established, nor was a strategy devised for achieving this undefined task. Furthermore, it was a conflict where US servicemen were committed without the involvement of the Congress. As the war dragged on, even the support of the American people was lost.

The job of the Marine Corps and the men of Force Recon was not to question the validity of the war or of the way it was fought. Following lawful orders and upholding the fighting traditions of the Corps were the objectives of the Marines in Vietnam—and their success in these tasks cannot be questioned. While victory was denied the Marines and other armed services in Southeast Asia, feats of valor, hardship, and dedication were added to their proud histories.

The conclusion of Force Reconnaissance efforts in support of the Vietnam War came from neither victory nor defeat. The end was influenced by factors from both within and without the Marine Corps. Outside the war zone was a war-weary nation that no longer supported US involvement in Vietnam. President Richard M. Nixon was elected in 1968 on the platform of "peace with honor" and the promise of withdrawing American troops from the war zone. By May 1969 his negotiations with the North Vietnamese, influenced by an increase in the bombing of the North, enabled the President to announce the first pullouts of American units. Timetables were soon revealed that left commanders in Vietnam faced with the task of quickly reducing the troop strength of over a half million men.

Actions within the III MAF also influenced the eventual stand-down of the Force Recon companies. By the end of November 1969, the 3rd Marine Division was withdrawn from the war zone to Okinawa. By 9 March 1969 the Army's XXIV Corps commanded more units than the III MAF and became the senior headquarters over the remaining Marines.

More important to the decline of the Force Recon companies was the departure of Gen Herman Nickerson and the assumption of command of the III MAF by Lt. Gen Keith B. McCutcheon. Nickerson had been recon's biggest supporter and had been instrumental in the Force Recon companies' working at the III MAF level. Although there is no direct confirmation in official or unofficial documentation, the feeling among the recon men was that McCutcheon was "antirecon" and did not like the idea of an "elite within an elite." Still others felt that Lieutenant General Zais, who was still in command of the XXIV Corps, did not share Nickerson's appreciation for the Force Recon companies and pushed for their demise after the departure of the III MAF commander.[1]

Whatever the politics back home or the personalities of the commanders in I Corps, the Third Force Reconnaissance Company was stood down with virtually no notice and even less fanfare on 10 March 1969. The Third Company recon men were extracted from their recon zones in the A Shau Valley to Phu Bai, where there was time only for one brief party before they were reassigned. A dozen of the recon men were transferred to the First Company, while half that many were reassigned to Hoi An to train members of the 2nd Republic of Korea Marines in reconnaissance techniques. The remainder of the Third Company was spread out among the remaining infantry regiments in the III MAF.

From 10 March to 10 July 1970, the Third Company was "carried at zero strength," meaning that while the unit remained officially active, no one was assigned to it. On 10 July, 1stLt T. S. Hodge and SSgt Frank Schemmel were assigned to the company to supervise the closing out of the unit's records and accounts. Their initial place of duty was aboard the USS *Vancouver*, which sailed from Vietnam for San Diego on the same day the two Marines were assigned to the company. Arriving in California on 1 August, Hodge and Schemmel moved to Los Flores at Camp Pendleton to complete the closeout of the company. On 27 August 1970, in accordance with provisions of the 5th MEB's Operation Order 2-70, the Third Force Reconnaissance Company was deactivated.[2]

Although the phased pullout of US troops from Vietnam and the departure of General Nickerson also affected the First Force Recon Company, its slowdown was more gradual than the "sudden death" of the Third Company. The First Company continued operations in the Thuong Duc Corridor for six months after the stand-down of the Third Company. However, each month found the company strength declining, from a high in March of 15 officers and 177 enlisted Marines to 10 officers and 74 enlisted men by 1 August.[3] The number of patrols and the resulting enemy sightings and contacts during the period decreased proportionately.

The remaining members of the First Company were extracted from the Thuong Duc Corridor on 10 August 1970 to assume a stand-down status at Da Nang. Unlike the Third Company, the First Company was not scheduled for deactivation, but was to be reassigned to Camp Pendleton and remain on the active rolls. During out-processing, the company strength was further reduced by the transfer of the newest arrivals to other units in-country. By the time the company was prepared for embarkation, only four officers, three staff NCOs, and 25 enlisted Marines remained to carry the unit's colors back to the States.[4]

On 24 August the First Company, under command of Capt Norman D. Centers, was OPCONed to the 5th MEB and immediately boarded the USS *St. Louis*. Sailing via Okinawa, the First Company arrived in Long Beach on 11 September and moved to Los Flores at Camp Pendleton.[5] Like most returning Vietnam veterans, the First Company received no welcome-home parade or ceremony of any kind.

During the first six months after the return of the First Company, the unit strength was never more than 35. With the winding down of US efforts in Vietnam, the overall strength of the services was reduced, as were budget allocations for training and refitting. On 14 April 1971, the First Company moved to the Del Mar area of Camp Pendleton, where on 10 May, Capt Danny L. Cook assumed command. Cook, a former enlisted parachute rigger in the company, began seeking volunteers and focusing the unit on training requirements despite the austerity of the times.[6]

Although the company was never to have more than one-half of its authorized personnel assigned, a rigorous training program including parachuting, rappeling, recon techniques, scuba, and amphibious skills was undertaken. Physical conditioning was emphasized, and the company trained for the "next war" using pre-Vietnam doctrine and manuals rather than rehashing the last one. By the summer of 1971 the company was able to embark on operational team training. Joint field exercises with the Army's Special Forces followed, which concluded with Operation CABLE RUN III in Arizona's Tonto National Forest on 1–20 February 1972.[7]

In May 1972, the 3rd Marine Division, then stationed on

Okinawa, requested that a Force Recon Platoon be attached to its Reconnaissance Battalion. Because of the limited manning of the First Company, the transfer was merely a paper transaction. With the authorization for the unit, the 3rd Marine Division formed the platoon with volunteers from its own 3rd Reconnaissance Battalion. The Sixth Platoon, First Force Recon Company, was formally activated at Onna Point, Okinawa, on 1 July 1972.[8] It was attached to the 3rd Recon Battalion, which was commanded by a former member of the Second Force Recon Company, Maj George Douse.

The years following the Vietnam War were difficult times for all the services. Money was tight, authorizations for personnel were down, the popularity of the military with the public was at an all-time low, and the "all volunteer" system which replaced the draft offered unique problems all its own.

Despite their accomplishments in Vietnam, many in the Marine Corps command structure felt that the Force Recon companies should be reduced along with the rest of the Corps. Some of the nonsupporters of Force Recon were considered to be "honest brokers" whose concerns for cutbacks were in the best interests of the Corps as a whole. Others were more directly "antirecon" and still held to the long-term belief that there was no room for an elite within an elite. As for the Force Recon men of the time, most recall that no former company members or supporters were in decision-making positions at Marine headquarters. With no one to represent their cause, the men knew that their future was questionable.

One of the major monetary problems in retaining the First Force Recon Company was the expense of reequipping and modernizing the unit for possible future battlefields. The post-Vietnam development of simple, shoulder-fired, heat-seeking, antiaircraft missiles signaled the end of the unrestricted use of helicopters. New techniques and equipment, including free-fall parachutes, adaptable aircraft, and recovery devices such as the Fulton Sky Hook, would have to be modernized and purchased. Other gear developed since the war, such as the Emerson closed-circuit scuba system, which eliminated the problem of bubbles rising to the surface, needed to be secured.

As for the requirement to reduce the total number of Marines on active duty, even the supporters of Force Recon admitted that the reconnaissance companies were vulnerable to the cutback. Some suggested a compromise: combine Force Recon with the division recon battalions rather than lose the long-range recon capability altogether.

Personnel reductions and austere budgets were not the only pressures to reduce the Force Recon Companies. Some of the critics of Force Recon revived the prewar idea that the information provided by long-range reconnaissance could be provided by other components, such as the CIA. Still others were enamored with the growing array of electronic sensors, the emergence of satellite surveillance, and the various new airborne detecting and observation devices. Although that school of thought had proven inaccurate in Vietnam and other wars, some felt there no longer needed to be a "man on the ground" to gather intelligence.

Another factor that influenced the antirecon factions was the post-Vietnam reorganization of the services that took away much of the Marine Corps' strategic planning responsibilities. The Marine Amphibious Forces were no longer responsible for preparing plans, but rather were charged with executing plans produced and coordinated by the Joint Chiefs of Staff level of the National Military Command Center.

While most of the focus of Force Recon reductions centered on the First Company, the Second Company was also considered for deactivation on occasion. Fortunately for the Second Company, not deploying to Vietnam had allowed it to maintain fairly stable in personnel and in updating equipment. Their stability was also assisted by the post-Vietnam concentration on rebuilding forces focused on Europe to counter the Warsaw Pact threat. Since the Second Company was on the East Coast and was dedicated to supporting actions in the Atlantic, it received priority in training, personnel, and other resources.

Whatever the official reasons—and none were given at the time or since—the First Force Recon Company was alerted on 15 July 1974 for deactivation, to occur prior to 1 October of the same year.[9] Simultaneously, the Sixth Platoon attached to the 3rd Marine Division on Okinawa was to be stood down. The formal message announcing the demise of the company was not news to its members. A few days before, MajGen Kenneth Houghton, the commander of the 1st Marine Division, had returned to Camp Pendleton from a general officers' conference in Washington, D.C., and informed the company of the impending announcement. It was ironic that Houghton was the bearer of the news; as a captain, the general had led the reconnaissance unit in Korea that was the predecessor of the First Company.

On 13 September the First Company made its final parachute jump on Camp Pendleton's Tower Drop Zone from a CH-53. Upon completion of the airborne exercise, the recon men returned to their company area and began turning in gear and equipment. Many of the Marines were transferred to other units during the next few days. Classified records of the company were burned, while unclassified files, including many detailing service in Vietnam and the support records for valor awards, were unceremoniously thrown in the trash.*

The First Company's final ceremony was held on the morning of 26 September in front of the troop billets. Although the unit colors were paraded, they were not of-

*LtCdr Ray Stubbe, stationed at Camp Pendleton at the time, reverently retrieved the discarded records. Many of those files from the trash are the basis for this narrative.

ficially cased, since that regretful chore was not to take place officially until the last day of the month. The ceremony was a simple one. No bands played and no reporters covered the event. A few former members of the company—those stationed at Pendleton or retired in the local area—quietly observed the end of First Force.

An anonymous message scrawled on the blackboard of the company briefing room perhaps best portrayed the feelings of the recon Marines: "The finest are always the FIRST to go. Long live Force!"

Monday, 30 September 1974, was a typical misty, foggy Del Mar day. In the late afternoon the four remaining Marines assigned to the First Company assembled in front of the orderly room. The company commander, Maj Gene D. Hendrickson, assisted by his first sergeant and observed by the other two recon men, cased the colors of the First Force Reconnaissance Company. An era marked by dedication, bravery, tenacity, and sacrifice had come to an inauspicious conclusion.

To one side of the area where the colors were cased was a trash bin. On top was a discarded sign that had once hung on the wall of the company's operation section. After the colors were cased, one of the Marines walked to the refuse heap, retrieved the sign, dusted it off, and carried it away. Even in the late evening light, the faded letters could be made out: "If everyone could be Force Recon, it wouldn't be Force Recon."[10]

AFTERWORD

THE traditions, expertise, and "can do" attitude of the Force Recon Marines were continued for the next decade and a half by the Second Company. Memories of the First Company lived on only in the hearts of its former members and in the minds of young officers who had witnessed the accomplishments of the company in Vietnam.

As time passed and the junior officers were promoted to the Corps' senior leadership positions, many encouraged the reactivation of the First Company. Adding another Force Recon company to the Corps was also encouraged by the US overall reemphasis on special operations, warfare in the Mideast, and the increase in hostilities in Central America. In early 1987, Headquarters, Marine Corps directed the reactivation of the First Company. On 27 May, the colors of the First Force Reconnaissance Company were unfurled by the new company commander, Maj Gordon Nash. Bands played, generals spoke, and reporters wrote and took pictures. Standing proudly to one side were veterans of the company from Vietnam and times prior to the war.

APPENDIX A

○○○○○○○○○

Force Reconnaissance Company Table of Organization to Number M-4623—19 April 1967

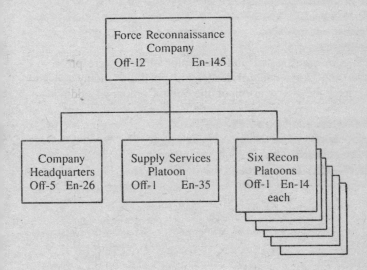

Notes:
1. The Company Headquarters consists of a Headquarters Section, an Operations Section, and a Communications Section.
2. The Supply and Services Platoon consists of a Platoon Headquarters, a Supply Section, a Mess Section, a Parachute Maintenance and Re-

pair Section, a Medical Section, a Motor Transport Section, and an Amphibious Equipment Maintenance Section.
3. The Six Reconnaissance Platoons each consist of a Platoon Head-quarters and three four-man recon teams.

APPENDIX B
■□■□■□■□■□

Commanding Officers, First Force Reconnaissance Company

Amphibious Reconnaissance Company, Corps Troops, Amphibious Corps, Pacific Fleet
     Capt James J. Jones   07 Jan 43–25 Aug 43

Amphibious Reconnaissance Company, V Amphibious Corps
     Capt James J. Jones   25 Aug 43–14 Apr 44

Amphibious Reconnaissance Battalion, V Amphibious Corps
     Maj James J. Jones   14 Apr 44–26 Aug 44

Amphibious Reconnaissance Battalion, Fleet Marine Force, Pacific
     Maj James J. Jones   26 Aug 44–24 Sep 45

Amphibious Reconnaissance Company (Pacific Coast)

Capt Robert W. Taylor	11 Jan 54–30 Mar 54
Capt Theodore R. Wall	31 Mar 54–06 Apr 54
Capt Howard G. Holt	07 Apr 54–24 Apr 54
Maj Robert E. McClean	25 Apr 54–16 Sep 54
Maj Philip E. Booth	17 Sep 54–31 Jan 55
Capt John L. Eareckson	01 Feb 55–06 Mar 55
Capt Fred L. Parks	07 Mar 55–30 May 55
Capt Joseph A. Goss	31 May 55–17 Jul 55
1stLt Evan L. Parker, Jr.	18 Jul 55–27 Jul 55
Maj Eugenous M. Hovatter	28 Jul 55–03 Jun 56
Capt Evan L. Parker, Jr.	04 Jun 56–10 Sep 56
Capt Michael M. Spark	11 Sep 56–18 Jun 57

First Force Reconnaissance Company

Maj Bruce F. Meyers	19 Jun 57–15 Jan 59
Capt Herman J. Redfield III	16 Jan 59–22 Jun 59
Maj John D. Counselman	23 Jan 59–24 Jun 60
Maj Robert G. Hunt, Jr.	25 Jun 60–10 Apr 61
Maj James S. McAlister	11 Apr 61–03 Oct 62
Maj Tom Gibson	04 Oct 62–31 Aug 63
Capt Patrick J. Ryan	01 Sep 63–11 Sep 63
Maj Robert R. Dickey III	12 Sep 63–11 Dec 64
Maj Herman A. McDonald, Jr.	12 Dec 64–08 Jul 65
Maj Malcolm C. Gaffen	09 Jul 65–27 Dec 65
Capt William C. Shaver	23 Dec 65–14 Mar 66
Maj Dwain A. Colby	15 Mar 66–04 Sep 66
Maj Bill B. Lowery	05 Sep 66–08 Apr 67
Maj Michael D. Cerreta, Jr.	09 Apr 67–16 May 67
Capt Albert K. Dixon II	17 May 67–19 Sep 67
Capt Daniel J. Keating	20 Sep 67–14 Dec 67
Maj Edwin H. Walker	15 Dec 67–01 May 68
Maj James V. Sullivan	02 May 68–02 Oct 68
Capt W. M. Lingenfelter	03 Oct 68–05 Oct 68
Maj Roger E. Simmons	06 Oct 68–03 Oct 69
Maj William H. Bond, Jr.	04 Oct 69–04 Jun 70
Maj Dale D. Dorman	05 Oct 70–04 Aug 70
Capt Norman B. Centers	05 Aug 70–10 Sep 70
1stLt John J. Holly	11 Sep 70–02 Nov 70
1stLt John G. Baker	03 Nov 70–09 May 71
Capt Danny L. Cook	10 May 71–13 Oct 72
Capt Phillip E. Prince	14 Oct 72–05 Jul 73
Maj Gene D. Hendrickson	06 Jul 73–30 Sep 74 (deactivated)
Maj Gordon Nash	27 May 87– (reactivated)

APPENDIX C
■□■□■□■□

Commanding Officers, Second Force Reconnaissance Company

Maj J. Z. Taylor	Jun 58–Jun 59
Maj P. X. Kelley	Jun 59–Aug 60
Maj D. M. Twomey	Aug 60–Jun 62
Maj J. E. Conroy	Jun 62–Jan 64
Maj J. H. Carothers, Jr.	Jan 64–Jul 65
Maj W. H. Rice	Jul 65–Aug 65
Maj D. J. Norris	Aug 66–Jul 67
Maj J. J. Clancy	Jul 67–Apr 68
Maj W. R. Wildprett	Apr 68–Jul 70
Maj R. C. Prewitt	Jul 70–Nov 70
Maj B. A. Green	Nov 70–Jul 71
Capt A. G. Little	Jul 71–Nov 71
Maj R. J. Reynolds, Jr.	Nov 71–Aug 72
Capt W. Harley	Aug 72–Sep 72
Maj K. R. Wakefield	Jul 73–Jul 73
Maj T. C. Taylor	Jul 73–Jul 75
Capt F. S. Blair	Jul 73–Jun 76
Maj J. Caper, Jr.	Jun 76–Jun 78
Maj W. E. Rollings	Jun 78–Jan 80
Capt R. E. Nelson	Jan 80–Feb 81
Maj J. W. Smyth	Feb 81–Jul 82
Capt A. D. Walker	Jul 82–Aug 82
Maj K. A. Conry	Aug 82–Nov 84
Maj J. R. Crockett	Nov 84–Nov 86
Maj W. A. Woods	Nov 86–

APPENDIX D

━━━━━━━

Commanding Officers, Third Force Reconnaissance Company

Maj Gary Wilder	04 Oct 65–06 Jun 66
Maj W. C. Floyd	06 Jun 66–28 Nov 67
Maj J. E. Anderson	29 Nov 67–10 May 68
Capt W. F. Snyder	10 May 68–01 Dec 68
1stLt R. M. Harden	01 Dec 68–15 Jan 69
Maj R. W. Holm	15 Jan 69–13 May 69
Maj O. R. Kartchner	14 May 69–31 Jul 69
Maj Alex Lee	01 Aug 69–10 Mar 70
(Cadried at zero strength)	10 Mar 70–10 Jul 70
1stLt T. S. Hodge	10 Jul 70–27 Aug 70
	(deactivated)

APPENDIX E

━━━━━━━━

Officer in Charge, Third Force Reconnaissance Detachment

Capt Kenneth D. Jordan	26 Apr 66–26 Mar 67
Capt W. D. Mooney	27 Mar 67–26 Apr 67

APPENDIX F

Commanding Officers, Fifth Force Reconnaissance Company

Maj Richard T. Henry	31 Jan 67–03 Jan 68
Maj J. D. Clews	04 Jan 67–21 Mar 69
Maj W. C. Shaver	22 Mar 69–15 Oct 69
	(deactivated)

APPENDIX G

Honor Roll, Vietnam First Force Reconnaissance Company

Cpl L. H. Merrell	23 Apr 65	Faxon, TN
LCpl R. P. Sisson	16 Dec 65	Hulberton, NY
LCpl W. R. Moore	16 Dec 65	Richmond, CA
Cpl R. S. Joy	16 Dec 65	Abernathy, TX
LCpl J. P. Dowling	29 Jan 66	Madison, WI
SSgt K. R. Hall	24 Apr 66	Keene, NH
LCpl V. J. Ford	29 Apr 66	Upper Darby, PA
HM2 L. W. Carper	17 May 66	Winchester, VA
Cpl J. W. Schuster	02 Jun 66	Altonna, PA
Capt E. M. Barnes	25 Mar 67	Windsor, CT
Sgt G. Blankenship	26 Mar 67	Vicey, VA
2ndLt W. E. Martin	03 Jun 67	Prescott, AZ

LCpl R. A. Williams	07 Jun 67	Greenville, SC
LCpl L. T. Stowe	11 Jul 67	North Edwards, CA
LCpl A. Allen	11 Jul 67	Philadelphia, PA
LCpl R. D. Whelchel	07 Sep 67	Liberal, KS
LCpl W. A. Gilmore	07 Sep 67	Alexandria, LA
LCpl T. F. De Gray	17 Oct 67	Milwaukee, WI
Sgt A. T. Jensen	17 Oct 67	Hales Corners, WI
Sgt J. E. Huff	27 Oct 67	Huntsville, AL
LCpl C. E. Harris	14 Jan 68	Norfolk, VA
PFC J. A. McIntosh	05 Feb 68	East Boston, MA
LCpl J. E. Prideaux	05 Feb 68	Brighton, CO
Cpl P. J. Murphy	15 May 68	Levittown, NY
Cpl J. W. Lyons	05 Jun 68	Phoenix, AZ
Sgt R. G. Dorsett	29 Jun 68	Superior, AZ
Sgt C. L. Walton	07 Nov 68	San Jose, CA
PFC J. W. Sincere	22 Nov 68	East Hartford, CT
2ndLt J. E. Slater	15 Dec 68	Marshalltown, IA
2ndLt L. M. Beck	23 Jan 69	Paoli, OK
PFC L. D. Rose	23 Jan 69	Herlong, CA
HN H. E. Pearce	23 Jan 69	Stanhope, NJ
PFC D. J. Oliver	23 Apr 69	Manassas, GA
PFC F. McLaughlin	18 Aug 69	Chatham, VA
LCpl C. T. Heinemeier	21 Aug 69	Bunker Hill, IL
GySgt V. R. Thornburg	03 Feb 70	Los Angeles, CA
Sgt R. C. Phleger	07 May 70	London, OH
Sgt D. J. Wickander	20 Jun 70	Caldwell, OH
LCpl W. M. Clark	04 Aug 70	Runnells, IA

(Note: There is evidence in the records of the company that one other Marine died on 28 December 66, two others on 29 December 66, and one more on 17 May 1966. However, a detailed search of the files, and interviews with the former recon men, have failed to reveal the accuracy of the reports or the men's names.)

Missing in Action

1stLt J. T. Egan	21 Jan 66	Mountainside, NJ
LCpl E. R. Grissett	22 Jan 66	San Juan, TX
HM2 M. L. Laporte	05 Sep 67	Los Angeles, CA
SSgt D. E. Ayers	19 Mar 70	Alderwood Manor, WA

The lack of an "Honor Roll" for the Third Company is not an oversight. It is an impossibility. As the above note indicates, the authors cannot be sure of the complete accuracy of the First Company list. No data, including after-action reports, is complete enough to come up with a list for Third Company—despite the authors' desire and efforts to do so.

APPENDIX H
○○○○○○○○○

Honors, First Force Reconnaissance Company

Presidential Unit Citation with One Bronze Star
    As part of the 3rd Marine Division   08 May 65–15 Sep 67
    As part of the 1st Marine Division   16 Sept 67–09 Jan 68
                    and
                    08 Sep 68–31 Oct 68

Navy Unit Citation with Two Bronze Stars
    As part of 3rd Recon Battalion   31 Oct 65–07 Dec 65
                    and
                    27 Dec 65–15 Mar 66
    As part of Task Force YANKEE   27 Dec 68–18 Mar 69
    As part of 1st Recon Battalion   01 Jan 70–01 Mar 70
    (Sub Unit #1, First Force Recon Co.)   01 Jan 70–31 Dec 70

Meritorious Unit Commendation with One Bronze Star
                    10 Jan 68–07 Sept 68
                    02 Mar 70–10 Aug 70

National Defense Service Streamer with One Bronze Star

Vietnam Defense Service Streamer with Two Silver and Three Bronze Stars
    Vietnam Defense Campaign   24 Oct 65–24 Dec 65
    Vietnamese Counteroffensive   25 Dec 65–30 Jun 66
    Campaign
    Vietnamese Counteroffensive Phase II   01 Jul 66–31 May 67
    Vietnamese Counteroffensive Phase III   01 Jun 67–29 Jan 68
    Tet Counteroffensive   30 Jan 68–01 Apr 68
    Vietnamese Counteroffensive Phase IV   02 Apr 68–30 Jun 68
    Vietnamese Counteroffensive Phase V   01 Jul 68–01 Nov 68

Vietnamese Counteroffensive Phase VI	02 Nov 68–22 Feb 69
Tet '69 Counteroffensive	23 Feb 69–08 Jun 69
Vietnam Summer–Fall 1969	09 Jun 69–31 Oct 69
Vietnam Winter–Spring	01 Nov 69–30 Apr 70
Sanctuary Counteroffensive	01 May 70–30 Jun 70
Vietnam Counteroffensive Phase VII	01 Jul 70–24 Aug 70

APPENDIX I
========

Honors, Second Force Reconnaissance Company

National Defense Service Streamer with One Bronze Star

APPENDIX J
========

Honors, Third Force Reconnaissance Company

Presidential Unit Citation	
As part of the 3rd Marine Division	25 Apr 67–15 Sep 67
Navy Unit Commendation	
As part of the 3rd Recon Battalion	16 Sep 67–31 Jul 68
Meritorious Unit Commendation	
As part of the 3rd Recon Battalion	01 Aug 68–30 Sep 68
Valorous Unit Commendation (Army)	07 Dec 69–16 Feb 70
Vietnam Cross of Gallantry with Palm	25 Apr 67–20 Sep 69
National Defense Service Streamer	

Vietnam Service Streamer with One Silver Star
and Four Bronze Stars

Vietnam Counteroffensive Phase II	01 Jul 66–31 May 67
Vietnam Counteroffensive Phase III	01 Jun 67–29 Jan 68
Tet Counteroffensive	30 Jan 68–01 Apr 68
Vietnam Counteroffensive Phase IV	02 Apr 68–30 Jun 68
Vietnam Counteroffensive Phase V	01 Jul 68–01 Nov 68
Vietnam Counteroffensive Phase VI	02 Nov 68–22 Feb 69
Tet '69 Counteroffensive	23 Feb 69–08 Jun 69
Vietnam Summer–Fall 1969	09 Jun 69–31 Oct 69
Vietnam Winter–Spring	01 Nov 69–30 Apr 70

Republic of Vietnam Meritorious Unit Citation (Civil Actions Medal,
First Class, Color with Palm)

APPENDIX K
●●●●●●●●

Honors, Fifth Force Reconnaissance Company

National Defense Service Streamer

SOURCE NOTES
╳╳╳╳╳╳╳╳╳╳╳

(Sources annotated "HMD" are on file at the History and Museums Division, Headquarters, US Marine Corps, Building 58, Navy Yard, Washington, D.C. Copies of interviews conducted and documents listed as "in the personal papers of" have also been forwarded to the History and Museums Division.)

CHAPTER 1: An Elite within an Elite

1. Russ Martin, *Happy Hunting Ground*, New York: Atheneum, 1968, pp. 197–218.
2. Data from personal papers of Maj James Steele, 15 October 1974, and telephone interview of Steele on 20 February 1988.
3. Lesson Plan, 1962, in personal papers of LtCol Patrick Ryan.
4. LtGen Raymond G. Davis, "Military Operations in Counterinsurgency," Presentation for CIRADS-4, Fort Bliss, Texas, 15–17 September 1970.
5. Maj Bryon A. Norberg, Oral History Collection No. 4383, HMD.
6. Letter of Col William Weise, 11 April 1975, and telephone interview of BrigGen Weise, 20 February 1988.

CHAPTER 2: The Early Days—Beginnings Through World War II

1. Capt Harry Allanson Ellsworth, *One Hundred Eighty Landings of United States Marine Corps, 1800–1934*, Washington, D.C.: HQMC, 1974, pp. 72–74, 114, 151–52.

2. Maj Dion Williams, *Naval Reconnaissance: Instructions for the Reconnaissance of Bays, Harbors, and Adjacent Country*, Washington, D.C.: GPO, 1906.

3. Maj Dion Williams, *Naval Reconnaissance: Instructions for the Reconnaissance of Bays, Harbors, and Adjacent Country*, 2nd ed., Washington, D.C.: GPO, 1917.

4. For materials on Ellis vide: Maj Earl Ellis, *Advanced Base Defense During the Present War*, Ellis file, HMD. Maj Earl Ellis, "Bush Brigades," Marine Corps *Gazette*, March 1921, pp. 1–15. Maj E. H. Ellis, *Advanced Base Operations in Micronesia*, HMD, Archives 9558. Maj Frank O. Hough, "Personalities—Men Who Differed," Marine Corps *Gazette*, November 1950. Lynn Montross, "The Mystery of Pete Ellis," Marine Corps *Gazette*, July 1954. LtCol P. N. Pierce, "The Unsolved Mystery of Pete Ellis," Marine Corps *Gazette*, February 1962, pp. 34–40. Mark Sufrin, "The Story of Earl Ellis," *Mankind* Magazine, April 1970, pp. 70–76. W. L. White, "The Disappearance of Earl Ellis," *Reader's Digest*, September 1960. John L. Zimmerman, "The Marines' First Spy," *Saturday Evening Post*, 23 November 1946. LtCol John J. Reber, "Pete Ellis: Amphibious Warfare Prophet," U.S. Naval Institute *Proceedings*, November 1977, pp. 53–64.

5. Division of Fleet Training, Office of Naval Operations, U.S. Navy, *Landing Operations Doctrine*, 1938, F.T.P. 167, Washington, D.C., 1938.

6. Letter from RAdm A. W. Johnson, Commander Attack Force, to Commander, Reconnaissance Group, 28 February 1938. Subject: Reconnaissance to be conducted on Puerto Rico, HMD.

7. Letter from 2ndLt Kenneth D. Bailey, Co. F, 5th Marines, to CG, 1st Marine Brigade, FMF, 5 March 1938. Subject: Puerto Rican Reconnaissance, HMD.

8. MajGen W. P. Upshur, "Brief Outline of the Problems, Forces Used and Initial Dispositions, Fleet Landing Exercise No. 6," HMD.

9. BrigGen H. M. Smith, ''Summary of the Problem,'' appended to the Upshur report, HMD.

10. 1stLt Leo B. Shinn, ''Amphibious Reconnaissance,'' Marine Corps *Gazette*, April 1945, p. 50.

11. Biography microfiche file, James L. Jones, HMD.

12. CG, Amphibious Corps, Pacific Fleet, Corps Intelligence Order Number 4-42, *Reconnaissance Patrols Landing on Hostile Shores*, 29 October 1942, HMD.

13. Table of Organization D-817, promulgated by CMC letter 2385-60, 21 December 1942, HMD.

14. Orders, Rear Echelon, 5th Amphibious Corps, Camp Elliott, California. Subject: Orders to permanent duty beyond the seas, 10 September 1943, in personal papers of James L. Jones.

15. For materials on Apamama vide: CNO, USN, *Dictionary of American Naval Fighting Ships*, vol. 5, Washington, D.C.: GPO, 1970, p. 28. Capt James R. Stockman, *The Battle for Tarawa*, 1947, p. 63, HMD. CO, Recon Co., VAC, *Action Report, Galvanic*, HMD. VAdm George C. Dyer, *The Amphibians Came to Conquer: The Story of Admiral Richmond Kelly Turner*, Washington, D.C.: GPO, 1971, p. 633. Holland M. Smith and Percy Finch, *Coral and Brass*, New York: Charles Scribner's Sons, 1949. Theodore Roscoe, *United States Submarine Operations in World War II*, Annapolis, MD: U.S. Naval Institute, 1949. Sgt Frank X. Tolbert, ''Apamama, a Model Operation in Miniature,'' *Leatherneck*, February 1945. Samuel Eliot Morison, *Aleutians, Gilberts, and Marshalls, June 1942–April 1944—History of United States Naval Operations in World War II*, vol. 7, Boston: Little, Brown, 1962. Robert Leckie, *Strong Men Armed*, New York: Ballantine, 1962. Russ Martin, *Line of Departure: Tarawa*, Garden City, NY: Doubleday, 1975. Interview of James L. Jones, 8 June 1975.

16. For materials on Majuro vide: CO Amphibious Recon Co., *War Diary, Operations of Reconnaissance Company on Sundance Atoll*, 16 March 1944, HMD. Dyer, op. cit. Cdr Francis Fane, *The Naked Warriors*, New York: Appleton-Century-Crofts, 1956. Sgt Francis X. Tolbert, ''The 'Recon Boys' at Majuro,'' *Leatherneck*, June 1945, p. 15. Interview of Jones, op. cit.

17. For materials on Eniwetok vide: *War Diaries, Sundance*, op. cit. Dyer, op. cit. CO, Amphibious Reconnaissance Com-

pany, *Action Report Downside Operation, Reconnaissance Company, V Amphibious Corps*, 18 March 1944, HMD.

18. HQ., VAC, Corps GO No. 30-44. Subject: Commendation, Amphibious Reconnaissance Company, for Action in the Central Pacific, 19 March 1944, in personal papers of James L. Jones.

19. Marine Corps dispatch 102102, 11 April 1944, HMD.

20. Readiness Report, Amphibious Reconnaissance Battalion, Fifth Amphibious Corps, 30 June 1944, HMD.

21. For materials on Tinian vide: Dyer, op. cit. Smith, op. cit. Fane, op. cit. Jeter A. Isley and Philip A. Crowl, *The United States Marines and Amphibious War*, Princeton, NJ: Princeton University Press, 1951. Maj Carl W. Hoffman, *The Seizure of Tinian*, Washington, D.C.: HQMC, 1951. Fletcher Pratt, *The Marines' War*, New York: William Sloane Associates, 1948.

22. Commendation from MajGen A. D. Bruce, 77th Infantry Division, to CG FMFPAC, 21 April 1945, with Endorsement 330.13, 21 April 1945, in personal papers of James L. Jones.

23. Commendation, HQ, Tenth Army, signed by Gen Joseph W. Stilwell, to: FMF Force Reconnaissance Battalion, in personal papers of James L. Jones.

24. Cdr E. A. Felt, "Coast Watching in World War II," US Naval Institute *Proceedings*, September 1961, pp. 72-79.

25. 1stLt R. B. Firm, Letter to Maj Guy Richards, undated, "Reconnaissance" file, HMD.

26. Col William F. Coleman, "Amphibious Reconnaissance," Marine Corps *Gazette*, December 1945, p. 23, and Sgt Francis X. Tolbert, "Advance Man," *Leatherneck*, March 1945, pp. 3-5.

CHAPTER 3: The Challenges of Peace and the Rebirth of Force

1. *USMC, Report, Organization of the Fleet Marine Force War and Peace*, Quantico, VA, 1 December 1948, HMD.

2. Navy Historical Division, CNO, USN, *Dictionary of American Fighting Ships*, vol. 5, Washington, D.C.: GPO, 1970, p. 261.

3. For materials on D Company, 5th Marine Regiment development of amphibious reconnaissance vide: MSgt Steven Marcus, "Submarine Safari," *Leatherneck*, October 1954,

pp. 16–21. Frederick Simplich, "Here Come the Marines," *National Geographic Magazine*, November 1950, pp. 653–54. Camp Pendleton *Scout*, 2 December 1949, pp. 1 and 8. Interview of MajGen Kenneth Houghton, San Diego, California, 18 November 1975. Interview of SgtMaj Neal D. King, Washington, D.C., 19 May 1975. Interview of LtCol Ernest DeFazio, Oceanside, California, 12 September 1974.

4. For materials on USMC reconnaissance in Korea vide: Lynn Montross and Capt Nicholas A. Canzona, *The Inchon-Seoul Operation—U.S. Marine Operations in Korea, 1950–1953*, vol. 2, Washington, D.C.: HQMC, 1955, pp. 190–94. Capt Walter Karig, Cdr Malcolm Cagle, and LtCdr Frank A. Manson, *Battle Report, The War in Korea*, New York: Rinehard and Co., 1952, p. 286. CO, USS *Perch*, Letter to CNO. Subject: Report of First War Patrol, 6 October 1950, HMD. Interview of MajGen Kenneth Houghton, op. cit.

5. Peter Kalischer, "The Marine's Remarkable Foreign Legion," *Colliers*, 25 October 1952, pp. 96–101.

6. Interview of Brig Gen Regan Fuller, Camp Pendleton, California, 29 September 1975.

7. Interview of LtCol Ernest L. DeFazio, op. cit.

8. Col Robert E. Cushman, Jr., "Amphibious Warfare Tomorrow," Marine Corps *Gazette*, April 1955, p. 32.

9. Lynn Montross, *Cavalry of the Sky: The Story of U.S. Marine Combat Helicopters*, New York: Harper & Brothers, 1954, pp. 168–70.

10. For materials on MCTU #1 vide: MCTU #1 files, HMD. TSgt Robert A. Suhosky, "Test Unit One," *Leatherneck*, July 1956, p. 59. Raymond V. B. Blackman, ed., *Jane's Fighting Ships, 1959–60*, New York: McGraw-Hill, 1959, p. 371. Camp Pendleton *Scout*, 16 February 1956, p. 1, and November 1956, p. 5. Interview of Col Bruce F. Meyers by telephone, 21 April 1975. Interview of Joseph Z. Taylor, U.S. State Department, Washington, D.C., 22 May 1975.

11. CO, MCTU #1, letter, 12 May 1955, HMD.

12. CO, MCTU #1, letter, 3 October 1955, HMD.

13. CO, MCTU #1, letter, 13 February 1956, HMD.

14. For materials on Donald E. Koelper vide: Washington, D.C., *Evening Star*, 19 February 1964. Maj H. D. Brad-

shaw, *United States Marine Corps Operations in the Republic of Vietnam*, manuscript, HMD. Capt Robert H. Whitlow, *The Advisory and Combat Assistance Era, 1954–1964—U.S. Marines in Vietnam*, Washington, D.C.: HQMC, 1977, p. 138.

15. MCTU #1 files, HMD, and taped comments of Col Bruce F. Meyers, Seattle, Washington, 25 July 1977.

16. Camp Pendleton *Scout*, 24 January 1957, p. 1. Interview of SgtMaj Neal D. King, op. cit. Interview of Joseph Z. Taylor, op. cit.

17. CO, MCTU #1, letter, 19 February 1957, HMD.

18. Taped comments of Col Bruce F. Meyers, op. cit.

19. Interview of SgtMaj Neal D. King, op. cit.

20. For materials on formation of First Force Reconnaissance Company vide: Maj Bruce F. Meyers, "Force Recon," Marine Corps *Gazette*, May 1961, pp. 48–53. MSgt Robert E. Johnson, "Triple Threat," *Leatherneck*, March 1959, p. 16. BrigGen H. Nickerson, "Force Recon—By Land, Sea, and Air," Marine Corps *Gazette*, February 1959, pp. 44–48. Camp Pendleton *Scout*, 6 February 1958, p. 6.

21. For materials on Marine skydiving vide: TSgt Allen G. Mainard, "Sky Diver," *Leatherneck*, May 1957, pp. 80–95. "Sky Diver," Marine Corps *Gazette*, January 1957, pp. 40–41. CO, MCTU #1, letter, 7 May 1957, HMD. CMC, letter, 25 October 1957, HMD. Interview of Joseph Z. Taylor, op. cit.

22. For materials on Fulton Sky Hook vide: Interview of BrigGen P. X. Kelley, Camp Pendleton, California, 6 November 1975. Interview of SgtMaj Dionicio Garcia, Camp Pendleton, California, 1 October 1974. Quantico *Sentry*, 26 June 1964, pp. 5 and 8. Camp Lejeune *Globe*, 9 September 1965, p. 13. CO, First Force Recon Company, letter, 11 June 1962, HMD.

23. Interview of Maj James McAlister, Oceanside, California, 21 November 1974.

24. CO, First Force Recon Company, report to CG, 1st Marine Division. Subject: FMF Organization Test Program, 10 February 1961, HMD.

25. Interview of Maj James E. Reilly, Camp Pendleton, California, 11 October 1974. Interview of James Steele, El Toro, California, 15 October 1975. Interview of SgtMaj Neal D. King, op. cit.

26. Camp Pendleton *Scout*, 22 September 1961, p. 3.
27. Camp Pendleton *Scout*, 3 March 1961, p. 1. Interview of LtCol Patrick G. Collins, Oceanside, California, 16 June 1975.
28. For materials on Donald N. Hamblen vide: Camp Pendleton *Scout*, 13 September 1963, p. 1. "Toughest Marine," *Look*, 5 May 1964, p. 36. Al Stump, "He Parachutes with One Leg," *Saga*, January 1964, pp. 12–16, 79–81. Mark Sufrin, "The One-Legged Marine Who Wouldn't Give Up," *Male*, January 1964, pp. 35, 50, 54, 56. *Newsweek*, 23 September 1963, p. 36. *Congressional Record, 1963*, p. A5921. *New York Times*, 12 September 1963, p. 16L. San Diego *Union*, 12 September 1963, p. 1. SSgt Donald Hamblen, "I Lost a Leg, But I'm Still a Marine Jumper," *Family Weekly*, 23 February 1964, pp. 14–15. CNO, letter to SSgt Donald Hamblen, 13 September 1963, in personal papers of Hamblen. Interview of 1stSgt Donald Hamblen, Oceanside, California, 25 October 1974.

CHAPTER 4: Vietnam—The Curtain Rises

1. CMC, letter to CG, FMFLant and CG, FMFPac, 10 May 1960, HMD.
2. MCLFDC, letter to CG, FMFlant and CG FMFPac, 16 September 1960, HMD.
3. CO, First Force Recon Company, report to CG, 1st Marine Division, Subject: FMF Organization Test Program, 10 February 1961, HMD.
4. Interview of Col John D. Counselman, Fallbrook, California, 19 April 1975. CG, FMFPac, *Quarterly Combat Readiness Report of Ground Units, 1 February 1961*, HMD.
5. Cdr, 7th Fleet, LOI, Operation TULUNGUN, 13 December 1961, HMD.
6. Ibid.
7. Interview of Maj James McAlister, Oceanside, California, 21 November 1974.
8. Letter from Capt Patrick Ryan to FMFPac, in personal papers of LtCol Patrick Ryan.
9. Interview of Maj David Whittingham, Santa Ana, California, 21 October 1974.
10. Officer in Charge, Detachment, First Force Recon Company, letter to CO, First Force Recon Company, 25 October 1963, copy in personal papers of Maj L. V. Bearce.

11. Coordinator, MarCorLandForDevActs, Marine Corps
    School, Quantico, VA, letter. Subject: Table of Organiza-
    tion, Force Recon Company, 25 October 1963, HMD and
    GySgt Mel Jones, "Recon All the Way," *Leatherneck*, Oc-
    tober 1963, pp. 19–25, 82–83.

12. US House Committee on Armed Services, *United States–
    Vietnam Relations, 1945–1967*, prepared by the Depart-
    ment of Defense, Washington D.C.: GPO, 1971 (com-
    monly known as the "Pentagon Papers.")

13. Interview of Maj L. V. Bearce, Camp Pendleton, Califor-
    nia, 16 October 1974.

14. Interview of MSgt James B. Schmidt, Camp Pendleton,
    California, 12 April 1976, and debriefing reports, Team
    CANCER, in personal papers of Maj L. V. Bearce.

15. Interview of Maj L. V. Bearce, Camp Pendleton, Califor-
    nia, 2 December 1974.

CHAPTER 5: Force Recon Arrives

1. Maj Michael R. Lamb, "Chronology of Significant Activities—Sub Unit #1, November 1963 to November 1964,"
   HMD.

2. Interview of Maj David Whittingham, Santa Ana, California, 21 October 1974, and Capt David Whittingham, Oral
   History Collection No. 81, HMD.

3. Ibid. and Letter from Capt Whittingham to Mrs. Merrell,
   30 April 1965, in personal papers of Maj Whittingham.

4. Capt Patrick G. Collins, Oral History Collection No. 42,
   HMD.

5. CG, 3rd Marine Division, letter, 25 November 1964, HMD
   and FMFPac, 1st Endorsement, 11 January 1965, HMD.

6. LtCol Roy Van Cleve, Oral History Collection No. 144,
   HMD.

7. Interview of LtCol Patrick G. Collins, Oceanside, California, 16 June 1975.

8. Ibid.

9. Interview of Maj David Whittingham, Santa Ana, California, 24 December 1974.

10. Whittingham, Tape 81, op. cit.

CHAPTER 6: First Force Finds Frustration

1. Interview of 1stSgt C. O. Fowler, Camp Pendleton, California, 2 December 1974.

2. Interview of GySgt Clarence Johnson, Camp Pendleton, California, 1 October 1974.

3. First Force Recon Company, Command Chronology, September, October, and November 1965, HMD.

4. GySgt Gus A. Koch, Oral History Collection No. 643, HMD.

5. Cpl George P. Solovskoy, Oral History Collection No. 416, HMD.

6. Interview of MSgt James B. Schmidt, Camp Pendleton, California, 12 April 1976.

7. Solovskoy, Tape 416, op. cit.

8. FMFPac, Report of CincPacFlt Amphibious Conference, 12 March 1966, HMD.

9. First Force Recon Company, Command Chronology, December 1965, HMD, and Jack Shulimson, *U.S. Marine Operations in the Republic of Vietnam, July–December, 1965*, manuscript, 1971, HMD.

10. Interview of SgtMaj Maurice Jacques, Camp Pendleton, California, 19 August 1975.

11. For materials on patrol at Ba To vide: Ibid. First Force Recon Company, Command Chronology, Operations Order and After Action Report 1-65, HMD. Interview of Sgt David Foster, Camp Pendleton, California, 14 and 19 November 1974. Interview of Capt Johannes Haferkamp, Oceanside, California, 1 March 1975. Interview of Fowler, op. cit. *Newsweek*, 10 January 1966, p. 24. Message, III MAF to COMUS MACV, 020314 Jan66, HMD.

12. First Force Recon Company, Command Chronology, December 1965, HMD. Interview of Capt John Freitas, Oceanside, California, 16 March 1975.

13. Solovskoy, Tape 416, op. cit.

14. Interview of LtCol Patrick G. Collins, Oceanside, California, 16 June 1975.

15. Interview of Maj L. V. Bearce, Camp Pendleton, California, 16 October 1974.

16. Cpl R. E. Belinski, Oral History Collection No. 2715, HMD.

17. HM3 Harvey E. Messier, Oral History Collection No. 2970, HMD.

18. 2ndLt Joseph K. Taussig, Oral History Collection No. 1508, HMD.

19. Koch, Tape 643, op. cit.

20. Sgt Joseph R. Crockett, Oral History Collection No. 4074, HMD.

21. Cpl John T. Morrissey, Oral History Collection No. 1712, HMD.

22. Solovskoy, Tape 416, op. cit.

23. Koch, Tape 643, op. cit., and Sgt Richard A. Van Deusen, Oral History Collection No. 44, HMD.

24. Koch, Tape 643, op. cit.

25. Maj Robert Rogers, *Journals of Major Robert Rogers*, reprint ed., introduction by Howard H. Peckham, New York: Corinth Books, 1961, p. 46.

26. Company Officer's School, Basic School, Marine Barracks, Quantico, VA, *Scouting and Patrolling, 1923–1924*, p. 20.

27. First Force Recon Company, Command Chronology, 20 January–28 February 1966, HMD, and Solovskoy, Tape 416, op. cit.

28. 1stSgt Clovis C. Coffman, Oral History Collection No. 4097, HMD and Maj D. A. Colby, "Four Rules for Recon," Marine Corps *Gazette*, December 1966, pp. 48–49.

29. Coffman, Tape 621, op. cit.

30. Koch, Tape 643, op. cit.

31. Letter of Maj George W. T. O'Dell, 4 May 1977.

32. Ibid.

33. 1stLt Russell L. Johnson, Oral History Collection No. 4425, HMD.

CHAPTER 7: Anatomy of a Patrol

1. For material on patrol procedures vide: 1stLt Andrew R. Finlayson, Oral History Collection Nos. 1243 and 1877, HMD. Sgt Theodore A. Ott, Oral History Collection No. 4383, HMD. 1stLt Richard E. Miller, Oral History Collection No. 4074, HMD. Letter of Maj George W. T. O'Dell, 4 May 1977. Maj George W. T. O'Dell, "Lessons Learned in Vietnam," Marine Corps *Gazette*, April 1973, p. 50. 1st Recon Battalion, Operations Order and Patrol Report 547-67, HMD. First Force Recon Company, Patrol Report 143-69, HMD.

2. First Force Recon Company, After Action Report, Operation PRAIRIE, HMD and First Force Recon Company, Operation Order and Patrol Report Nos. 289-67, 337-67, and 352-67, HMD.

CHAPTER 8: 1966 to Stingray

1. First Force Recon Company, Command Chronology, 20 January–28 February 1966, Encl. 12, After Action Report, DOUBLE EAGLE, HMD.

2. Capt J. L. Compton, Oral History Collection No. 339, HMD.

3. First Force Recon Company, Command Chronology, Patrol Report, 21–22 January 1966, HMD.

4. First Force Recon Company, Command Chronology, 20 January–28 February 1966, Encl. 22, After Action Report, DOUBLE EAGLE II, HMD.

5. Interview of Capt James Haferkamp, Oceanside, California, 1 March 1975, and First Force Recon Company, Command Chronology, April 1966, HMD.

6. First Force Recon Company, Command Chronology, May 1966, HMD.

7. First Force Recon Company, Command Chronology, June 1966, HMD, and interview of WO2 James Doner, Camp Pendleton, California, 17 December 1974.

8. GySgt Billy M. Donaldson, Oral History Collection No. 1281, HMD.

9. Maj D. A. Colby and Maj B. N. Bittner, "Recon's Artillery," Marine Corps *Gazette*, January 1967, pp. 49–51, and Maj D. A. Colby, "Four Rules for Recon," Marine Corps *Gazette*, December 1966, pp. 48–49.

10. First Force Recon Company, Operations Order and Patrol Report 45-66, HMD.

11. First Force Recon Company, Command Chronology, August 1966, HMD.

12. Ibid.

13. First Force Recon Company, Operations Order and Patrol Report 70-66, HMD, and Maj Duane Colby, Oral History Collection No. 307, HMD.

14. Interview of Haferkamp, op. cit.

15. Committee on Veteran's Affairs, U.S. Senate, 93rd Congress, 1st Session, Committee Print No. 15, *Medal of Honor Recipients*, 1893–1973, Washington, D.C.: GPO, 22 October 1973, pp. 879–80.

16. Interview of Haferkamp, op. cit.

17. First Force Recon Company, After Action Report, Operation PRAIRIE, HMD.

18. FMFM 2-2, *Amphibious Reconnaissance*, 12 December 1963, Para. 203c(1).

19. Maj L. V. Bearce, "Mission of Force Reconnaissance Company," Individual Research Project, Quantico, VA, April 1970, HMD.

20. Capt Francis J. West, Jr., "Stingray '70," U.S. Naval Institute *Proceedings*, November 1969, pp. 26–37.

21. HQMC, G-3, Point Papers, WestPac, 16 August 1966, p. 2, HMD.

22. HQMC, G-3, Point Papers, WestPac, 19 December 1966, p. 1, HMD.

23. HQMC, G-3, Point Papers, WestPac, 3 January 1968, pp. 1–2, HMD.

24. West, "Stingray," op. cit., p. 29.

25. Sgt Gary L. Arnold, Oral History Collection No. 701, HMD.

26. Sgt D. W. Carson, Cpl Daniel Costa, and LCpl Nicholas F. Novatney, Oral History Collection No. 1053, HMD.

27. 1stLt Robert F. Drake, Oral History Collection No. 1334–35, HMD.

CHAPTER 9: The Only Three Combat Jumps in Marine Corps History

1. Capt David Whittingham, Oral History Collection No. 81, HMD.

2. Capt Jerome T. Paull, Oral History Collection No. 222, HMD.

3. 1st Recon Battalion, After Action Report, Operation KANSAS, 28 June 1966, HMD.

4. Paull, Tape No. 222, op. cit.

5. GySgt Maurice J. Jacques and Sgt Johannes Haferkamp, Oral History Collection No. 307, HMD, and interview of Capt Johannes Haferkamp, Oceanside, California, 1 March 1975.

6. 1st Marine Division, Message, 170340Z June 66, HMD.

7. Interview of Haferkamp, op. cit.

8. Capt Francis J. West, Jr., *Small Unit Action in Vietnam, Summer 1966*, New York: Arno Press, 1981, pp. 15–39.

9. For materials on combat jump by Team CLUB CAR vide: 1st Recon Battalion, Operations Order and Patrol Report 494-67, HMD. 1st Recon Battalion, Company Bulletin 1500. Subject: Parachute Operations Schedule 5-67, 2 August

1967, HMD. GySgt Walter M. Webb et al., Oral History Collection No. 1598, HMD. Interview of Capt Lawrence Livingston, Camp Pendleton, California, 15 December 1974. Interview of GySgt Bruce D. Trevathan, Camp Pendleton, California, 18 November 1974.

10. Interview of Trevathan, op. cit.
11. First Force Recon Company, Operations Plan and Patrol Report 334-69, HMD, and 1stLt Wayne E. Rollings, Oral History Collection No. 4688, HMD.

CHAPTER 10: Third Force Recon Company
Goes to War

1. Interview of GySgt Lawrence Bell, NAB Coronado, California, 4 November 1974, and interview of Cpt Lawrence Livingston, Camp Pendleton, California, 15 December 1974.
2. Taped interview of LtCol William C. Floyd, Okinawa, 18 September 1975.
3. Ibid.
4. Ibid.
5. Ibid.
6. III MAF incoming SPECAT Exclusive message file, January–June 1966, HMD, and FMFPac, Command Chronologies, January–June 1966, HMD.
7. FMFPac, Situation Report #422, 26 May 1966, HMD.
8. Floyd tape, op. cit.
9. III MAF misc. message file, January–December 1966, HMD.
10. CMC, message, 121135Z August 66, HMD.
11. CG, FMFPac, message, 160003Z August 66, HMD.
12. Interview of GySgt Lawrence Keen, NAB Coronado, California, 4 December 1975.
13. 3rd Recon Battalion, Command Chronology, October 1966, Operations Order and Patrol Reports 77-66 and 80-66, HMD.
14. First Force Recon Company, Command Chronology, November–December 1966, HMD.
15. Interview of Keen, op. cit.
16. Ibid.
17. Ibid.
18. 3rd Recon Battalion, Command Chronology, January 1967,

HMD, and III MAF, message to CMC, 281342Z January 67, HMD.

19. Interview of Keen, op. cit.
20. 3rd Recon Battalion, Command Chronology, February 1967, HMD.
21. Floyd tape, op. cit.
22. Ibid.
23. Fifth Force Recon Company, Command Chronology, complete file, HMD.

CHAPTER 11: Work on the Task Force Level

1. Interview of GySgt Bruce D. Trevathan, Camp Pendleton, California, 18 November 1974.
2. First Force Recon Company, Command Chronology, January 1968, HMD.
3. Interview of Trevathan, op. cit.
4. 1stLt Russell L. Johnson, Oral History Collection No. 4425, HMD.
5. First Force Recon Company, Operations Order and Patrol Report 46-68, HMD.
6. Interview of Trevathan, op. cit.
7. First Force Recon Company, Command Chronology, August 1968, HMD.
8. For materials on Task Force HOTEL vide: 3rd Recon Battalion, Command Chronology, April 1968, HMD. Sgt David E. Mertz et al., Oral History Collection No. 2918, HMD. Cpl David A. Miller et al., Oral History Collection No. 3256, HMD.
9. From the personal papers of LtCol George O'Dell.
10. Personal observations of Ray Stubbe.
11. Cdr S. A. Swarztrauber, "River Patrol Relearned," U.S. Naval Institute *Proceedings*, May 1970, pp. 129–32.
12. 1stLt P. F. Kelly, Oral History Collection No. 3155, HMD.
13. Interview of Lt John R. Vandrasek, Jr., Camp Pendleton, California, 29 November, 1974.
14. First Force Recon Company, Command Chronology, December 1968, HMD.
15. First Force Recon Company, Operations Order and Patrol Report 1-68, HMD.
16. PFC Jack L. Cox et al., Oral History Collection No. 3846, HMD.

17. First Force Recon Company, Operations Order and Patrol Report 2-68, HMD.
18. Letter of Maj A. R. Finlayson, 5 May 1977.
19. Cpl Richard W. Spangler et al., Oral History Collection No. 3846, HMD.
20. First Force Recon Company, Operations Order and Patrol Report 27-68, HMD, and Spangler Tape No. 3846, op. cit.
21. Ibid.
22. Interview of GySgt Robert Boland, San Diego, California, 18 March 1975.
23. First Force Recon Company, Operations Order and Patrol Reports 120-69 and 143-69, HMD, and 1stLt Richard E. Miller, Oral History Collection No. 4074, HMD.
24. Ibid.

CHAPTER 12: Work on the MAF Level

1. LtCol Richard D. Michelson, Oral History Collection No. 4383, HMD, and interview of Col Richard D. Michelson, MCRD, San Diego, California, 18 November 1975.
2. Letter of Maj James Anderson, 9 August 1977.
3. Sgt Kenneth Lee Smith, Oral History Collection No. 4387, HMD.
4. Anderson letter, op. cit.
5. First Force Recon Company, Operations Order and Patrol Report 215-69, HMD.
6. First Force Recon Company, Operations Order and Patrol Report 217-69, HMD, and Sgt Theodore A. Ott et al., Oral History Collection No. 4383, HMD.
7. Ibid.
8. Maj Van S. Reed et al., Oral History Collection No. 4383, HMD.
9. HM3 Bricher et al., Oral History Collection No. 4383, HMD.
10. First Force Recon Company, letter. Subject: Meritorious Unit Commendation Recommendation, 10 March 1970, HMD.
11. Interview of 2ndLt Bruce H. Norton, Camp Pendleton, California, 11 and 13 August 1975.
12. III MAF, letter, Subject: Deep Surveillance and Reconnaissance Study, 22 September 1969, HMD.
13. III MAF, message, 030929Z September 69, HMD.
14. FMFPac, message, 081841Z December 69, HMD.

15. CG, XXIV Corps, message, 210431Z September 69, HMD.
16. CG, XXIV Corps, message, 010145Z October 69, HMD.
17. Third Force Recon Company, Command Chronology, December 1969, HMD.
18. Interview of LtCol Alex Lee, Camp Pendleton, California, 19 August 1975.
19. Third Force Recon Company, letter. Subject: Letter of Continuity, 20 March 1970, HMD.
20. Sgt James T. Keysacker, Oral History Collection No. 4921, HMD.
21. U.S. Army, General Order No. 2, Hq., Department of the Army, 17 January 1973.
22. First Force Recon Company, Operations Order and Patrol Report 24-70, HMD.
23. First Force Recon Company, Command Chronology, March 1970, HMD.
24. First Force Recon Company, Operations Order and Patrol Report 49-70, HMD.
25. First Force Recon Company, Operations Order and Patrol Report 96-70, HMD, and interview of GySgt Robert Boland, San Diego, California, 18 March 1975.

CHAPTER 13: To Expect the Unexpected:
Missions, Information, Bravery, and Dangers Other Than the Enemy

1. SSgt Thomas J. Vallario, Oral History Collection No. 879, HMD, and First Force Recon Company, Operations Order and Patrol Report 37-69, HMD.
2. 2ndLt Thomas W. Williamson et al., Oral History Collection No. 1444 and 1445, HMD.
3. First Force Recon Company, Command Chronology, July 1969, HMD.
4. For materials on wiretapping vide: Sgt John McDonough and Cpl Theodore A. Ott, Oral History Collection No. 3846, HMD. Sgt Ronald W. Peters and Cpl Ronald L. Williamson, Oral History Collection No. 4015, HMD. First Force Recon Company, Operations and Patrol Reports 261-69 and 275-69, HMD.
5. 3rd Recon Battalion, Command Chronology, August 1969, HMD.
6. Interview of GySgt Robert Boland, San Diego, California, 18 March 1975.

7. Lt Charles L. Lowder and Lt William J. Peters, Oral History Collection No. 4505, HMD.

8. 3rd Recon Battalion, Command Chronology, January 1967, HMD and LtCol Gary Wilder and Capt Kenneth D. Jordan, Oral History Collection No. 399, HMD.

9. Maj Byron A. Norberg, Oral History Collection No. 4383, HMD.

10. 1st Recon Battalion, Command Chronology, December 1966 and January 1967, HMD.

11. First Force Recon Company, Operations Order and Patrol Reports 221-69, 250-69, and 270-69, HMD.

12. First Force Recon Company, Operations Order and Patrol Report 265-69, HMD.

13. 1st Recon Battalion, Command Chronology, January 1967, HMD.

14. First Force Recon Company, Operations Order and Patrol Report 223-69, HMD.

15. First Force Recon Company, Command Chronology, January 1970, HMD.

16. 3rd Recon Battalion, Command Chronology, May 1967, HMD.

17. Cpl Ernest L. Wilkinson, Oral History Collection No. 3156, HMD.

18. 3rd Recon Battalion, Command Chronology, January 1969, HMD.

19. 3rd Recon Battalion, Command Chronology, February 1969, HMD.

20. Interview of Boland, op. cit.

21. Interview of Capt Wayne Morris, Camp Pendleton, California, 2 September 1975.

22. First Force Recon Company, Operations Order and Patrol Report 8-70, HMD.

23. From the diary of LtCdr Ray Stubbe, Khe Sanh, January 1967 to February 1968.

24. First Force Recon Company, Operations Order and Patrol Report 50-70, HMD.

25. 3rd Recon Battalion, Command Chronology, May 1969, HMD.

26. 3rd Recon Battalion, Command Chronology, June 1967, HMD.

27. First Force Recon Company, Operations Order and Patrol Report 253-69, HMD.

28. First Force Recon Company, Operations Order and Patrol Report 193-68, HMD.

29. 3rd Recon Battalion, Command Chronology, August 1967, HMD.

30. First Force Recon Company, Operations Order and Patrol Report 346-67, HMD.

31. First Force Recon Company, Operations Order and Patrol Report 68-70, HMD.

32. 1st Recon Battalion, Command Chronology, December 1966, HMD.

33. CG, III MAF, message, 210024Z February 70.

CHAPTER 14: Notable Patrols—Extraordinary Men

1. For material on Medal of Honor Patrol vide: 3rd Recon Battalion, Command Chronology, February 1968, HMD. Capt George O'Dell et al., Oral History Collection No. 3761, HMD. Taped interview of Cpl Danny Slocum, Capt David Underwood, et al., in personal papers of Maj George O'Dell. Medal of Honor File, 2ndLt Terrence C. Graves, HMD.

2. 1st Recon Battalion, Command Chronology, March 1967, HMD.

3. Letter of Maj A. R. Finlayson, 5 May 1977.

4. Ibid.

5. *Newsweek*, 21 August 1967, pp. 40–41.

6. 1st Recon Battalion, Command Chronology, May 1967, HMD, and 1stLt Andrew R. Finlayson, Oral History Collection No. 827, HMD.

7. 1st Recon Battalion, Operations Order and Patrol Report 352-67, HMD and 1stLt Andrew R. Finlayson, Oral History Collection No. 1243, HMD.

8. 1st Recon Battalion, Operations Order and Patrol Report 390-67, HMD.

9. 1stLt Andrew R. Finlayson, Oral History Collection No. 1467, HMD.

10. Vietnam Citations, Reel 53 and 55, HMD.

11. First Force Recon Company, Operations Order and Patrol Report 62-68, HMD, and interview of GySgt Bruce D. Trevathan, Camp Pendleton, California, 19 November 1974.

12. First Force Recon Company, Operations Order and Patrol Report 106-69, HMD, and Lt Wayne E. Rollings et al., Oral History Collection No. 4074, HMD.

13. First Force Recon Company, Operations Order and Patrol Report 142-69, HMD.

14. First Force Recon Company, Operations Order and Patrol Report 287-69, HMD.

15. First Force Recon Company, Operations Order and Patrol Report 275-69, HMD.

16. First Force Recon Company, Operations Order and Patrol Report 158-69, HMD, and Sgt Joseph R. Crockett et al., Oral History Collection No. 4074, HMD.

CHAPTER 15: The Final Days—and Beyond

1. Telephone interview of Capt Clovis Coffmann, Jr., 22 August 1975.

2. Interview of SSgt Frank Schemmel, Camp Pendleton, California, 20 August 1975, and Third Force Recon Company, Command Chronology, 10 July to 27 August 1970, HMD.

3. First Force Recon Company, Command Chronology, August 1970, HMD.

4. Ibid.

5. Ibid. and III MAF, message, 270058Z August 70, HMD.

6. Camp Pendleton *Scout*, 11 June 1971, p. 3, and 2 July 1971, pp. 6–7.

7. First Force Recon Company, Command Chronology, 1971–73, HMD.

8. FMFPAC, message, 120529Z May 72, HMD.

9. CMC, message, 151921Z July 74, HMD, and 1st Marine Division Letter of Instruction 602-74, HMD.

10. Personal observations of LtCdr Ray Stubbe.

BIBLIOGRAPHY

Books

Appleman, Roy E., James M. Burns, Russell A. Gugeler, and John Stevens. *Okinawa: The Last Battle*. Washington D.C.: Government Printing Office, 1948.

Asprey, Robert B. *War in the Shadows: The Guerrilla in History*. Garden City, N.Y.: Doubleday, 1975.

Baclagon, Col Uldaricos. *Lessons from the Huk Campaign in the Philippines*. Manila: M. Colcol, 1956.

Bartley, LtCol Whitman S. *Iwo Jima: Amphibious Epic*. Washington D.C.: HQMC, 1954.

Beaumont, Roger A. *Military Elites: Special Fighting Units in the Modern World*. Indianapolis: Bobbs-Merrill, 1974.

Blackman, Raymond V. B., ed. *Jane's Fighting Ships, 1959–60*. New York: McGraw-Hill, 1959.

Boggs, Charles W., Jr. *Marine Aviation in the Philippines*. Washington D.C.: Government Printing Office, 1951.

Bond, LtCol P. S., Maj E. B. Garey, Maj O. O. Ellis, Capt T. L. McMurray, and 1stLt E. H. Crouch. *Scouting, Patrolling and Musketry: A Complete Course of Practical Training for Small Infantry Units*. Baltimore: New Military Press, 1932.

Callwell, Col C. E. *Small Wars, Their Principles and Practice*. London: His Majesty's Stationery Office, 1906.

Colby, C. B. *Frogman: Training, Equipment and Operation of Our Navy's Undersea Fighters*. New York: Coward-McCann, 1954.

Corson, William R. *The Betrayal*. New York: W. W. Norton, 1968.

Crowl, Philip A., and Edmund B. Love. *Seizure of the Gilberts and Marshalls*. Washington, D.C.: Government Printing Office, 1955.

Elliot-Bateman, Michael, ed. *The Fourth Dimension of Warfare*. New York: Praeger, 1970.

Ellsworth, Capt Harry Allanson. *One Hundred and Eighty Landings of United States Marines, 1800–1934*. Washington, D.C.: HQMC, 1974.

Fane, Cdr Francis D. *The Naked Warriors*. New York: Appleton-Century-Crofts, 1956.

Feldt, Cdr Eric A. *The Coast Watchers*. New York: Oxford University Press, 1946.

Field, James A. *History of United States Naval Operations, Korea*. Washington, D.C.: Government Printing Office, 1962.

Foster, Maj Willard O. *Modern Reconnaissance*. Harrisburg, PA: Military Service Publishing Co., 1944.

Frank, Benis M., and Henry I. Shaw, Jr. *History of U.S. Marine Corps Operations in World War II*. Washington, D.C.: HQMC, 1968.

Geer, Andrew. *The New Breed: The Story of the U.S. Marines in Korea*. New York: Harper & Brothers, 1952.

Gleason, James, and Tom Waldron. *Midget Submarine*. New York: Ballantine, 1975.

Halsey, FAdm William F., and LtCdr Julian Bryan, II. *Admiral Halsey's Story*. New York: Whittlesey House, 1947.

Heinl, LtCol Robert D., and LtCol John A. Crown. *The Marshalls: Increasing the Tempo*. Washington, D.C.: HQMC, 1954.

———. *Soldiers of the Sea: The United States Marine Corps, 1775–1962*. Annapolis, MD: US Naval Institute, 1962.

Hoffman, Maj Carl W. *The Seizure of Tinian*. Washington, D.C.: HQMC, 1951.

Hough, Frank O. *The Island War*. Philadelphia: J. B. Lippincott, 1947.

Hough, LtCol Frank O., and Maj John A. Crown. *The Campaign on New Britain*. Washington, D.C.: HQMC, 1952.

Isley, Jeter A., and Philip A. Crowl. *The U.S. Marines and Amphibious War*. Princeton, NJ: Princeton University Press, 1951.

Johnstone, Maj John H. *Marine Corps Historical References Series, No. 32, United States Marine Corps Parachute Units*. Washington, D.C.: HQMC, 1962.

Karig, Capt Walter, Cdr Malcolm Cagle, and LtCdr Frank A.

Manson. *Battle Report: The War in Korea*. New York: Rinehart, 1952.

Kelly, Col Francis J. *Vietnam Studies: U.S. Army Special Forces, 1961–1971*. Washington, D.C.: Department of the Army, 1973.

Lanning, Michael Lee. *Inside the LRRPS: Rangers in Vietnam*. New York: Ivy Books, 1988.

Leckie, Robert. *Strong Men Armed*. New York: Ballantine, 1962.

McChristian, MajGen Joseph A. *Vietnam Battle Studies: The Role of Military Intelligence, 1965–1967*. Washington, D.C.: Department of the Army, 1974.

McMillan, George. *The Old Breed: A History of the First Marine Division in World War II*. Washington, D.C.: Infantry Journal Press, 1949.

Metcalf, Clyde H. *A History of the United States Marine Corps*. New York: G. P. Putnam's Sons, 1939.

Meid, LtCol Pat, and Maj James M. Yingling. *U.S. Marine Operations in Korea, 1950–1953*. Washington, D.C.: HQMC, 1972.

Miller, Col Ellis B. *The Marine Corps in Support of the Fleet*. Quantico, VA: Marine Corps Schools, 1933.

Montross, Lynn. *Cavalry of the Sky: The Story of U.S. Marine Combat Helicopters*. New York: Harper & Brothers, 1954.

Moskin, J. Robert. *The U.S. Marine Corps Story*. New York: McGraw-Hill, 1987.

Nichols, Charles S., Jr., and Henry I. Shaw, Jr. *Okinawa: Victory in the Pacific*. Washington, D.C.: Government Printing Office, 1955.

Pearson, LtGen Willard. *Vietnam Studies: The War in the Northern Provinces 1966–1968*. Washington, D.C.: Department of the Army, 1975.

Pratt, Fletcher. *The Marine's War*. New York: William Sloane Associates, 1948.

Rogers, Maj Robert. *Journals of Major Robert Rogers*. New York: Corinth Books, 1961.

Roscoe, Theodore. *United States Submarine Operations in World War II*. Annapolis, MD: U.S. Naval Institute, 1949.

Russ, Martin. *Happy Hunting Ground: An Ex-Marine's Odyssey in Vietnam*. New York: Antheneum, 1968.

———. *Line of Departure: Tarawa*. Garden City, NY: Doubleday, 1975.

Smith, LtGen Holland M., and Percy Finch. *Coral and Brass*. New York: Charles Scribner's Sons, 1949.

Stanton, Shelby L. *Vietnam Order of Battle*. New York: Galahad Books, 1986.

Stockman, Capt James R. *The Battle for Tarawa*. Washington, D.C.: HQMC, 1947.

Updegraph, Charles L. *Marine Corps Historical Reference Pamphlet, U.S. Marine Corps Special Units of World War II*. Washington, D.C.: HQMC, 1972.

Vagts, Dr. Alfred. *Landing Operations, Strategy, Psychology, Tactics, Politics, from Antiquity to 1945*. Harrisburg, PA: Military Service Publishing Co., 1946.

Walt, Gen Lewis W. *Strange War, Strange Strategy*. New York: Funk & Wagnalls, 1970.

West, Capt Francis J. *Small Unit Action in Vietnam: Summer, 1966*. Washington, D.C.: HQMC, 1967.

Williams, Maj Dion. *Naval Reconnaissance: Instructions for the Reconnaissance of Bays, Harbors, and Adjacent Country*. Washington, D.C.: Government Printing Office, 1906.

———. *Naval Reconnaissance: Instructions for the Reconnaissance of Bays, Harbors, and Adjacent Country*. 2nd ed. Washington, D.C.: Government Printing Office, 1917.

Zimmerman, John L. *The Guadalcanal Campaign*. Washington, D.C.: Government Printing Office, 1949.

Periodicals

Anon. "Scouting and Patrolling," Marine Corps *Gazette*, 27:5 (September 1943), 30–31.

Anon. "Sky Diver," Marine Corps *Gazette*, 41:1 (January 1957), 40–41.

Anon. "Toughest Marine," *Look*, 28:9 (5 May 1964), 36.

Bearce, L. V. "Reconnaissance in FMF for the 70s," Marine Corps *Gazette*, 54:10 (October 1970), 20.

Beardsley, Sgt Frank. "Silver Lances," *Leatherneck*, 49:6 (June 1965), 26–31.

Bowen, SSgt Bob. "Lockout," *Leatherneck*, 52:9 (September 1969), 20–25.

Carpenter, Col J. B., Jr. "Division Recon Battalion: No, But. . . ." Marine Corps *Gazette*, 47:3 (March 1963), 40–42.

Colby, Maj D. A. "Four Rules for Recon," Marine Corps *Gazette*, 50:12 (December 1966), 48–49.

—— and Maj B. N. Bittner. "Recon's Artillery," Marine Corps *Gazette*, 51:1 (January, 1967), 49–51.

Coleman, Col William F. "Amphibious Reconnaissance," Marine Corps *Gazette*, 29:12 (December 1945), 22–25, and 30:1 (January 1946), 13–15.

Cushman, Col Robert E., Jr. "Amphibious Warfare Tomorrow," Marine Corps *Gazette*, 39:4 (April 1955), 32.

Darby, Cpl Reuben U. "It Happened on Patrol," *Reader's Digest*, 92:550 (February 1968), 79–82.

Davis, MajGen R. G., and Lt J. L. Jones, Jr. "Employing the Recon Patrol," Marine Corps *Gazette*, 54:5 (May 1969), 40–45.

Donlon, Cpl Tom. "Recon Team in Narrow Escape," *Sea Tiger*, 4:23 (7 June 1968), 4.

Fable, Capt Eric B. "Recon or Raider the Key," Marine Corps *Gazette*, 52:10 (October 1968), 44–46.

Feldt, Cdr Eric A. "Coastwatching in World War II," United States Naval Institute *Proceedings*, 87:9 (September 1961), 72–79.

Geer, LtCol Prentice S. "Wanted: Eyes for the Troops," Marine Corps *Gazette*, 25:1 (March 1941), 38–39.

Head, R. M. "Do Not Confirm or Deny," Marine Corps *Gazette*, 38:2 (February 1954), 48–49.

Hodierne, SP4 Bob. "When a 'Good Outfit' Gets Axed," *Stars and Stripes*, Pacific ed. (circa March 1970).

Hudson, BrigGen L. C. "Reconnaissance—Key to the Concept," Marine Corps *Gazette*, 40:8 (August 1956), 28–30.

Jones, GySgt Mel. "Recon All the Way," *Leatherneck*, 46:10 (October 1963), 82–83.

Judge, Cdr Cyril B. "Commandos and Their Methods," United States Naval Institute *Proceedings*, 70:497 (July 1944), 843–49.

Kleber, Capt Victor A., Jr. "The Eyes Have It," Marine Corps *Gazette*, 33:9 (September 1949), 16–19.

Kalischer, Peter. "The Marines' Remarkable Foreign Legion," *Colliers*, 130 (25 October 1952), 96–101.

Knowlton, S. "Case for the 2-Man Recon Teams," Marine Corps *Gazette*, 41:4 (April 1957) 54–55.

Logvinenko, LtCol A. "Hunter Squads," *Infantry Journal*, 52:1 (January 1943), 46–47.

MacMichael, Capt David C. "The Amphibious Patrol," Marine Corps *Gazette*, 41:10 (October, 1957), 60–63.

McMillan, George. "Scouting at Cape Gloucester," Marine Corps *Gazette*, 30:5 (May 1946), 24–27.

Mainard, TSgt Allen G. "Sky Diver," *Leatherneck*, 40:5 (May 1957), 108.

Marcus, MSgt Steven. "Submarine Safari," *Leatherneck*, 37:10 (October 1954), 16–21.

Martinez, Sgt Dave. "Marines, NVA Race for Top of Hill,"*Sea Tiger*, 4:22 (31 May 1968), 1.

Martin, Cpl Paul G. "We Stalk the Enemy," Marine Corps *Gazette*, 37:5 (May 1953), 28–32.

Masters, J. M. "Minimize Uncertainty: The Three Headed Spook," Marine Corps *Gazette*, 42:6 (June 1958), 20–26.

Meyers, Maj Bruce F. "Force Recon," Marine Corps *Gazette*, 45:5 (May 1961), 48–53.

Nickerson, BrigGen H. "Force Recon—by Land, Sea, and Air," Marine Corps *Gazette*, 43:2 (February 1959), 44–48.

Pettus, PSgt Francis C. "A Four Day Patrol," Marine Corps *Gazette*, 28:6 (June 1944), 26–30.

Pickett, R. "Recon for Regiments," Marine Corps *Gazette*, 45:4 (April 1961), 48–49.

Richards, Guy. "Jungle Patrolling," Marine Corps *Gazette*, 29:1 (January 1945), 68–71, and 29:2 (February 1945), 21–24.

Ryan, Maj P. J. "Defending Scuba's Value," Marine Corps *Gazette*, 50:8 (August 1966), 59–60.

Saski, Sgt Larry. "Recon Team Elusive," *Sea Tiger*, 4:6 (19 April 1968), 5.

Sexton, Maj Martin J. "Mission for Recon," Marine Corps *Gazette*, 37:10 (October 1953), 23–24.

Shoup, Capt D. M. "Scouts! Information Please," Marine Corps *Gazette*, 24:1 (March 1940), 22–23.

Shinn, 1stLt Leo B. "Amphibious Reconnaissance," Marine Corps *Gazette*, 20:4 (April 1945), 50–51.

Simplich, Frederick. "Here Come the Marines," *National Geographic Magazine*, 98:5 (November 1950), 647–72.

Smith, LtGen Holland M. "The Development of Amphibious Tactics in the U.S. Navy," Marine Corps *Gazette*, 30:6 (June 1946), 13–18, 30:9 (September 1946), 43–47, 30:10 (October 1946), 41–46.

Stump, Al. "He Parachutes with One Leg," *Saga*, 27:4 (January 1964), 12–18 and 79–81.

Sufrin, Mark. "The One Legged Marine Who Wouldn't Give up," *Male*, 14:1 (January 1964), 35, 50, 54, and 56.

——. "The Story of Earl Ellis," *Mankind*, 2:6 (April 1970), 70–76.

Suhosky, TSgt Robert A. "Test Unit One," *Leatherneck*, 39:7 (July 1956), 28–32.

Tolbert, Sgt Frank X. "Advance Man," *Leatherneck*, 2:3 (1 March 1945), 3–5.

——. "Apamama—A Model Operation in Miniature," *Leatherneck*, 28:2 (February 1945), 26–27.

——. "Deadly Teams Emerge from this Academy," *Leatherneck*, (October 1943), 17.

——. "The 'Recon Boys' at Majuro," *Leatherneck*, 2:11 (1 June 1945), 14–15.

Tompkins, Rathvon M. "To Win by Air," Marine Corps *Gazette*, 31:1 (January 1947), 8–15.

del Valle, MajGen P. "Tactical Possibilities of Airborne Attack," Marine Corps *Gazette*, 31:12 (December 1947), 22–25.

Waters, A. B. "The Price of Intelligence," Marine Corps *Gazette*, 38:7 (July 1954), 34–43.

Watson, William R. "The S-2's Crystal Ball," Marine Corps *Gazette*, 36:6 (June 1952), 34–37.

Watts, Lt James J. "The Combat Swimmer," U.S. Naval Institute *Proceedings*, 95:11 (November 1969), 26–37.

White, Capt John A. "Parachute Troops," Marine Corps *Gazette*, 24:2 (June 1940), 11–14.

Wilkinson, James B. "Recon Battalion: No, ..." Marine Corps *Gazette*, 47:2 (March 1963), 36–39.

Williams, R. C. "Amphibious Scouts and Raiders," *Military Affairs*, 13:3 (Fall 1963), 150–151.

Woessner, LtCol H. "Employment of Recon," Marine Corps *Gazette*, 43:12 (December 1959), 50–53.

Wyatt, LCpl Steve. "20 NVA Succumb to Accurate Rifle of Recon Marines," *Sea Tiger*, 3:49 (8 December 1967), 1.

Zimmerman, B. L. "Island Coastwatcher," Marine Corps *Gazette*, 30:1 (January 1946), 16–18.

Official Military Manuals and Publications

U.S. Army. FM 21-50, *Ranger Training and Ranger Operations*. January 1962.

U.S. Army. FM 21-76, *Survival, Evasion, and Escape*. March 1968.

U.S. Army. FM 57-38, *Pathfinder Operations*, with Change No. 1. July 1970.

U.S. Army. TC 1-4, *Rappelling from Helicopters*. September 1968.

U.S. Marine Corps. AM-15, *Amphibious Reconnaissance*. 1951.

U.S. Marine Corps. FMFM 2-1, *Intelligence*. 1967.

U.S. Marine Corps. FMFM 2-2, *Amphibious Reconnaissance*. 1963.

U.S. Marine Corps. FMFM 6-1, *Marine Division*. 1969.

U.S. Marine Corps. FMFM 6-2, *Marine Infantry Regiment*. 1969.

U.S. Marine Corps. FMFM 8-1, *Special Operations*. 1968.

U.S. Marine Corps. FMFM 8-2, *Counter-Insurgency Operations*. 1967.

U.S. Marine Corps. M-0078, *Motorized Reconnaissance*. 1939.

U.S. Marine Corps. MCS 3-1, *Combat Intelligence*. 1948.

U.S. Marine Corps. NAVMC-3310, *Guide for Reconnaissance of Landing Areas*. 1944.

U.S. Marine Corps. NAVMC-4101, *Amphibious Operations, Intelligence*. 1948.

U.S. Marine Corps. NAVMC-4115, *Amphibious Operations, Employment of Underwater Demolition Teams*. 1946.

U.S. Navy. NAVPERS 16120, *A Handbook of Amphibious Scout and Raider Training*. 1944.

U.S. Navy. FTP 167, *Landing Operations Doctrine*. 1938.

Official USMC Records*

Advanced Research Projects Agency. *SIAF Models and Data Support, Final Report*. Appendix C: Date, vol. 4.

Assistant Chief of Staff, G-2, HQMC. *Memo* to Assistant Deputy Chief of Staff, Programs. Subject: Concept for the Marine Corps of the 1970s, 18 March 1969.

Bearce, Larned V. *Mission of the Force Reconnaissance Com-*

---

*All of the listed documents are on file at the USMC History and Museums Division in Washington, D.C.

    pany, Individual Study Project, Marine Corps Staff Col-
    lege, Quantico, 2 February 1970.
Carr, Capt W. D. *Tactical Employment of the A-6A/RABFAC
    Beacon*. AWS Quantico Staff Study, 28 May 1971.
Chapman, Brig Gen L. F., Jr. *Memo* to General Shoup. Subject:
    Pathfinders; personal opinions on, 4 August 1961.
Chilson, LtCol Virgal R. *Aerodynamics of Premeditated Free-
    Fall Parachute Jumping*, 14th Aeromedical Panel Meet-
    ing, NATO, Athens, Greece, 11–15 May 1959.
CMC. *Letter*. Subject: First Force Reconnaissance Company ac-
    tivation, 13 May 1957.
CMC. *Letter*. Subject: Authorizing all levels of maintenance for
    parachutes, 22 February 1960.
CMC. *Letter*. Subject: Ground Reconnaissance Units, 26 June
    1963.
Commander, Amphibious Force, US Atlantic Fleet. *Report of
    Phase II, Exercise LANTFLEX-52*, 2 June 1952.
Commander, Amphibious Force, US Pacific Fleet. *Letter*.
    Subject: Operations in Amphibious Reconnaissance and
    Raiding Exercises 8 October–3 November 1951, 29 March
    1952.
Commander, Amphibious Group One. Operations Order 301-62,
    SEATO Exercise TULUNGUN.
Commander, Amphibious Group One and Commander, Am-
    phibious Group, US 7th Fleet. Post Exercise Report of
    Exercise BACKPACK, 25 July 1964.
Commander, 7th Fleet and CG, Philippine Army. Letter of In-
    struction for SEATO Amphibious Exercise TULUNGUN,
    13 December 1961.
Commander, Amphibious Training Command, US Pacific
    Fleet. Presentation to the Naval War College, "The Na-
    vy's Role in the Amphibious Assault," 2–3 November
    1955.
CG, Combined Landing Force (TF 262). *Letter*. Subject: Exer-
    cise Report of SEATO Amphibious Exercise TULUNGUN,
    26 May 1962.
——. OPLAN 302-62.
CG, V MAC. Amphibious Reconnaissance Battalion, Ready Re-
    ports, April and June, 1944.
——. Amphibious Reconnaissance Company Ready Report,
    March 1944.

CG, Fifth Amphibious Force, US Pacific Fleet. *Letter*. Subject: Underwater Demolition Teams, 2 March 1944.

CG, 1st Marine Division. *Letter*. Subject: Report of Force Reconnaissance Company, 14 December 1957.

CG, FMFLant. LANTFLEX-52 Report, 22 December 1951.

——. *Letter*. Subject: A Concept for the Marine Corps in the 1970s, 4 April 1969.

——. *Letter*. Subject: Organization of Radio Intelligence Platoon, 14 June 1950.

——. Task Force Organization, 1 July 1948 to 30 September 1951.

CG, FMFPAC. *Force Troops* (a yearbook) 1953.

——. Quarterly Combat Readiness Reports, 1961–65.

——. *Letter*. Subject: First Force Reconnaissance Company Activation, 10 June 1957.

——. Report of CINCPACFLT Amphibious Operations Conference, 12 March 1966.

——. Command Chronologies, 1965–70.

CG, Force Troops, FMFLANT. *Letter*. Subject: Mission, organization, and concept of employment of the Pathfinder Platoon, 27 March 1961.

CG, Marine Corps Development and Education Command, Quantico. Report on Steerable Parachutes, Project Directive 20-69-10, 2 February 1970.

CG, VII Marine Expeditionary Force. Final Report, Exercise BACKPACK, 27 March 1964.

CG, Task Force DELTA. Combat After Action Report, Operation HASTINGS, 15 July to 3 August 1966.

CG, III MAF. *Letter*. Subject: Policy Guidance for Long Range Reconnaissance Patrols, 17 June 1967.

——. *Staff Study*. Subject: Deep Surveillance and Reconnaissance, 22 September 1969.

——. Command Chronologies, May 1965 to January 1970.

——. Message files, including incoming and outgoing ranging from Confidential to SPECAT Exclusive and Top Secret, 1965–70.

CG, 3rd MarDiv. TRIAD, November 1960 to June 1965.

——. Report of Operation RECONNEX 55I, 1 June 1955.

——. *Letter*. Subject: Scuba Qualified Personnel, 11 January 1965.

——. ACofS Staff Study. Subject: Special Intelligence Study, 16-67, A Shau Valley, 29 June 1967.

CG, Troop Training Unit, US Atlantic Fleet. *Letter*. Subject: Landing Force Umpire Control Director Report, 5 December 1951.

CO, Fifth Force Reconnaissance Company. Command Chronologies, 31 January 1967 to 15 October 1969.

CO, First Force Reconnaissance Company. Command Chronologies, 1965–74.

———. Individual Award Recommendations, 1969–70.

———. *Letter*. Subject: Intelligence Symposium Presentations, 20 May 1960.

———. *Letter*. Subject: PHIBLEX RECOMMEX (Puget Sound), 9 December 1963.

———. *Letter*. Subject: Review of Requirements for scuba, 24 February 1965.

———. *Letter*. Subject: Unusual Incident During Parachute Training, 8 May 1962.

———. *Letter*. Subject: Exercise AUMEE, 24 July 1962.

———. *Letter*. Subject: Acquisition of Free-fall Parachutes Currently in Use by Both Army and Navy, 15 May 1963.

———. *Letter*. Subject: SEATO Exercise TULUNGUN, 30 April 1962.

———. *Letter*. Subject: In Flight Recovery of Reconnaissance Personnel, 11 June 1962.

———. *Report*. Subject: FMF Organizations Test Program, 10 February 1961.

———. *Report*. Subject: Blank-gore Parachute Evaluation and Stabilized Free-fall Parachuting Instruction, 1 April 1958.

CO, First Reconnaissance Battalion. Command Chronologies and Patrol Reports, 1965–67.

———. *Report* Subject: FMF Organization Test Program, 14 February 1961.

CO, Marine Corps Test Unit #1. Files, 1956–57.

CO, Second Force Reconnaissance Company. Command Chronologies, 1966–74.

CO, Third Force Reconnaissance Company. Command Chronologies, 1969–70.

CO, Third Reconnaissance Battalion. Command Chronologies, 1966–69.

Davis, LtGen Raymond G. "Military Operations in Counterinsurgency," presentation to CIRADS-4, Fort Bliss, Texas, 15–17 September 1970.

DeHority, LtCol C. M. "Amphibious Intelligence," presentation to Naval War College, 31 August 1948.

Gray, LtCol A. M., and Maj T. J. Geraghty. "Marine Corps Intelligence in Counter-insurgency, I Corps Tactical Zone/III MAF Area," presentation to CIRADS-4, Fort Bliss, Texas, 15–17 September 1970.

HQ, V Amphibious Corps. Corps Training Memo No. 25-44, "Reconnaissance Patrols Landing on Hostile Shores," 28 March 1944.

HQMC. Tables of Organization: D-817, 15 December 1942; E-333, E-334, E-335, 28 April 1944; Prov-4623, 22 May 1957, K-4623, P-4623, 16 September 1968.

——. G-3 Division Point Papers, WestPac, 1966–70.

——. Historical Division, Miscellaneous Files, 1950–63.

——. Historical Division, Oral History Tapes:

#42, Capt Patrick G. Collins

#44, Sgt Richard A. Vandeusen

#81, Capt David Whittingham

#101, Cpl John W. Easterling

#144, LtCol Roy Van Cleve

#222, Capt Jerome T. Paull

#307, GySgt Maurice J. Jacques, Sgt J. Haferkamp, Maj Duane Colby

#339, Capt J. J. Compton

#416, Cpl George P. Solovskoy

#603, SSgt David L. Arnold

#621, 1stSgt Clovis C. Coffmann, Jr.

#643, GySgt Gus A. Koch

#701, Sgt Gerry L. Arnold

#827, 2ndLt Andrew R. Finlayson

#1053, Sgt D. W. Carson, Cpl Daniel Costa, LCpl Nicholas F. Novatney

#1243, 2ndLt Andrew R. Finlayson

#1281, GySgt Billy M. Donaldson

#1334–35, 1stLt Robert F. Drake, LCpl Gary M. Aushback

#1444–45, Sgt George Woodcock, Jr., LCpl Edward J. Unkle

#1467, 2ndLt Andrew R. Finlayson

#1508, 2ndLt Joseph K. Taussig

#1509, 1stLt Robert E. Drake, LCpl Johnny D. Mallard, LCpl David Mathis

#1510, 2ndLt Andrew R. Finlayson

#1539, Col T. M. Horne

#1591, SSgt George Woodcock

#1598, GySgt Walter M. Webb, Jr., Sgt Thomas G. Vallario, Sgt James W. Hager, LCpl John Slowick

#1712, Cpl J. T. Morrissey

#1733, Cpl J. T. Morrissey, LCpl Gary R. Guerman, LCpl William P. Kress

#1833, 1stLt James R. Rhodes

#1877, 2ndLt Andrew R. Finlayson, Sgt James F. Hawkhurst, Cpl William F. Kelley, LCpl Ringer Gardner

#1914, Sgt Donald M. Woo, Cpl Charles D. Wilkins, Cpl Donald S. Cruz

#2425, Capt Philip F. Reynolds, 1stLt Donald W. Blair, 2ndLt Willis M. Gregory, Cpl Arthur W. Wheat, Cpl Olaf L. Janis, Sgt Danny M. Slocum, Sgt David E. Metz, Sgt William P. Kress, Cpl Billy P. Babin, Cpl Harlan E. Holmes, Sgt Robert L. Mixton, HM3 David L. Thompson, Cpl Alston E. Lancaster

#2507, Cpl Donald A. Laidtke

#2515, Cpl R. E. Belinski

#2970, HM3 Harvey E. Messier

#3155, 1stLt P. F. Kelly, Cpl Don W. Stevens, Cpl Willis T. Kern, Cpl James O. Flynn

#3156, Cpl David A. Miller, LCpl Joseph M. Jennings, Cpl Douglas A. Birow, LCpl Kenneth C. Uphold, LCpl Frank L. Sherman, Cpl Ernest L. Wilkinson, Sgt William P. Kress

#3738, 1stLt F. R. Leenerts

#3761, Sgt D. M. Slocum

#3846, Maj R. E. Simmons, 1stLt Andrew R. Finlayson, PFC Richard A. Flemming, PFC Robert H. Grant, PFC Glenn E. Greggs, Sgt David B. Thompson, LCpl Gregg A. Davis, Cpl Sam D. Carver, Cpl Theodore A. Ott, PFC Elvis L. Thurmon, HM3 Gustin A. Welch, PFC Jack L. Cox, PFC Jean P. Green, PFC Robert A. Meyer, SSgt Roger A. Cobb, Cpl Michael G. Finkle, PFC Cross Thurmond, Sgt John McDonald, CPL Richard E. Spangler, PFC Charles T. Heinemeier, Cpl William T. Twiler, Cpl Robert L. Williamson, Cpl George H. Hopkins, SSgt Albert L. Shark

#4015, Sgt Ronald W. Peters, Cpl Ronald L. Williamson

#4074, Sgt Joseph R. Crockett, Sgt Robert C. Flagher, 1stLt Wayne E. Rollings, 1stLt Richard E. Miller

#4383, Maj R. E. Simmons, Sgt Theodore A. Ott, LtCol R. D. Mickelson, LtCol John E. Quigley, Maj Bryon A. Norberg, LtCol Charles S. Morris, Maj James John, Cpl Richard C. Koch, Maj Van S. Reed

#4387, Sgt Kenneth L. Smith

#4425, 1stLt Russell L. Johnson

#4688, 1stLt Wayne E. Rollings

#4921, Sgt J. T. Keysacker

HQ, 1st Marine Amphibious Corps. "Patrol Report on Choiseul Bay Area, Solomon Islands," 4 October 1943.

———. "Reconnaissance Report of Empress Augusta Bay Area, 23–26 September 1943.

Hughes, R. D., et al. Final SIAF Report No. 8, Characteristics of SIAF-type Operations in Vietnam, 23 December 1969.

———. Final SIAF Report No. 16, vol. 1, Characteristics of SIAF-type Operations in Vietnam, 30 October 1970.

OIC, Sub Unit #1, First Force Reconnaissance Company. *Letter*. Subject: Activities of Sub Unit, 10 March 1965.

Rosenau, Capt Robert C. Staff Study, "Emerson Closed Circuit System," Quantico, 28 May 1971.

Ryan, Capt Patrick J. *Letter*. Subject: Report of MCLFDC Project, 13 March 1963.

Shulimson, Jack. U.S. Marine Corps Operations in the Republic of Vietnam, July–December 1965.

Walker, Capt E. H. IV. *Memo*. Subject: Parachuting from High Performance Aircraft, 16 January 1962.

Personal Papers*

Maj L. V. Bearce
LtCol Patrick G. Collins
LtCol Ernest L. DeFazio
WO2 James Doner
Maj Thomas Gibson
1stSgt Donald N. Hamblen
SgtMaj Maurice Jacques
Maj James L. Jones
SgtMaj Neal D. King

Maj James S. McAlister
Col Bruce F. Myers
2ndLt Bruce H. Norton
Mr. David Robin
Capt Robert Rosenau
LtCol Patrick J. Ryan
Maj James Steele
Col Gerald Turley
Maj David Whittingham

*Diaries, copies of official letters and reports, orders, commendations, clippings, photographs, and personnel rosters.

Personal Interviews

HM1 Eugene Bliss—9 September 1974, 21 October 1974, 12 April 1976.

Maj L. V. Bearce—16 October 1974, 30 November 1974.

GySgt Lawrence Bell—4 November 1974.

GySgt Robert Boland—18 March 1975.

Capt Clovis C. Coffman—22 August 1975.

Capt Danny L. Cook—22 October 1974.

Col John D. Counselman—19 April 1975.

LtCol Patrick G. Collins—16 June 1975.

WO2 James Doner—17 December 1974, 27 June 1974, 16 September 1974, 22 August 1975.

Capt Andrew R. Finlayson—8 January 1975.

Sgt David Foster—7, 14, 19 November 1974.

Capt John P. Freitas—16 March 1975.

LtCol Ernest L. DeFazio—12 September 1974, 28 April 1975.

LtCol W. C. Floyd—18 September 75 (taped interview from Okinawa).

Gen Regin Fuller—29 September 1975.

Maj Thomas Gibson—25 October 1974.

Sgt Robert Gonzales—6 November 1974.

1stLt W. C. Grubbs—4 November 1974.

Capt Johannes Haferkamp—1 March 1975.

Maj Frank Gould—16 October 1974.

SgtMaj Dionicio Garcia—1 October 1974.

1stSgt Donald N. Hamblen—25 October 1974.

1stLt James Holzman—29 October 1974, 14 November 1974.

GySgt Duke Hamilton—7, 14 November 1974.

MajGen Kenneth Houghton—18 November 1975.

SgtMaj Maurice Jacques—19 August 1975.

GySgt Clarence Johnson—1 October 1974.

Maj James L. Jones—8 June 1975.

GySgt Lawrence Keen—4 December 1975.

LtGen Victor Krulak—11 November 1974.

Capt Lawrence Livingston—15 December 1974.

SgtMaj Neal D. King—19 May 1975.

Col Francis Kraince—10 June 1975.

Brig Gen Paul X. Kelley—6 November 1974.

LtCol Alex Lee—19 August 1975.

Col Richard D. Mickelson—18 November 1975.

1stLt James Moore—27 November 1974.

Capt Wayne Morris—2 September 1975.

Maj James McAlister—21 November 1974, 8 December 1974.
Capt Alfons Mednis—28 April 1975.
MGySgt Mike Merrit—14 September 1974.
WO2 Edwin Miller—12 March 1975.
Col Bruce F. Meyers—21 April 1975, 4 June 1975.
2ndLt Bruce H. Norton—11, 13, 22 August 1975.
Mr. Bobby J. Patterson—11 September 1974, 26, 30 April 1975.
SgtMaj William Purdy—21 October 1974.
Maj James E. Reilly—11 October 1974.
Mr. David Robin—28 September 1975.
Capt Robert Rosenau—14 September 1974.
SSgt Frank Schemmel—20 August 1975.
MSgt James B. Schmidt—12 April 1976.
GySgt Donald Servantes—24 June 1975.
Maj William Snyder—20 August 1975.
Maj James Steele—15 October 1974, 8 May 1975, 20 February
     1988.
GySgt Jerry Tierheimer—15 August 1975.
GySgt Bruce D. Trevathan—18, 19 November 1974, 3 December
     1974, 14 March 1975.
Col D. M. Twohmey—18 November 1975.
Mr. Joseph Z. Taylor—22 May 1975.
LtCol Gerald Turley—16 May 1975.
BrigGen William Weise—20 February 1988.
SgtMaj Jess M. Wise, Jr.—1 October 1974.
Maj David Whittingham—21 October 1974, 24 December 1974.
CWO3 D. R. Zoerb—26 March 1975, 17 April 1975.

Letters
Capt Andrew Finlayson—21 January 1975.
LtGen William K. Jones—15 November 1974, 4 December 1974.
Capt Charles Nelson—23 August 1975.
LtCol Patrick J. Ryan—12 November 1974, 21 November 1974.
Col William Weise—11 April 1975.

INDEX

◇◇◇◇

About the Authors

MICHAEL LEE LANNING recently retired from the United States Army as a lieutenant colonel after over 20 years of active duty. He served in infantry, airborne, ranger, armor, and public affairs assignments in Europe, Southeast Asia, and throughout the United States. Born and educated in Texas, Lanning now divides his time between Eastsound on Orcas Island in the state of Washington, and Tempe, Arizona. His previous books include *The Only War We Had: A Platoon Leader's Journal of Vietnam, Vietnam 1969–1970: A Company Commander's Journal, Inside the LRRPS, Rangers in Vietnam,* and *The Battles of Peace.*

RAY WILLIAM STUBBE enlisted in the Navy in 1955 and served aboard destroyers and with Naval Intelligence before his discharge. Following college, seminary, and Ph.D.-level education, he was ordained a Lutheran minister in 1965 and organized a mission congregation. Stubbe reentered the Navy in 1967. Following a tour in Vietnam, he served primarily with Marine units and on amphibious ships with a brief interlude—upon suggestions from Navy SEALs—to complete the U.S. Army Airborne training. Stubbe is listed in the 3rd edition of *Who's Who in Religion* and has written numerous professional theological and psychological monographs, articles, and books. These include a treatment of C. G. Jung's Psychological Typology, a religious treatise on the "wounded healer" motif, an extensive bibliography on Post Traumatic Stress Disorder in Dr. William E. Kelley's *POST Traumatic Stress Disorder and the War Veteran Patient* (Brunner/Mazel Publishers), and the monograph *Khe Sanh Bibliography,* published by the U.S. Marine Corps. Pastor Stubbe currently resides and ministers in Milwaukee, Wisconsin, and is working on a definitive history of the Khe Sanh 1962–1968.